Jacques Jomier

How to Understand ISLAM

SCM PRESS LTD

Translated by John Bowden from the French
Pour connaître L'Islam
published 1988 by Les Editions du Cerf,
29 bd Latour-Maubourg, Paris

© Les Editions du Cerf 1988

with additional material by J. S. Nielson

Translation © John Bowden 1989

British Library Cataloguing in Publication Data

Jomier, Jacques
How to understand Islam
1. Islam
I. Title II. Pour connaitre Islam
English 297

ISBN 0–334–02070–0

First published in English 1989
by SCM Press Ltd, 26–30 Tottenham Road, London N1 4BZ
Second impression 1993

Typeset at The Spartan Press Ltd
Lymington, Hants
and printed in Great Britain by
Butler & Tanner Ltd, Frome and London

Contents

Introduction

Islam emerged in the seventeenth century of our era in Arabia or, to put it another way, in a region where Asia and Africa meet, half-way between the Mediterranean Sea and the Indian Ocean. Its name is inseparable from that of Muhammad, the prophet who preached it. At that time the neighbouring great powers, the Byzantines and the Persians, were weak and exhausted from half a century of wars which had set them at each other's throats. A political and religious movement, Islam very soon crossed the frontiers of Arabia, propagating itself both by preaching and by military activity. The first Muslim armies benefited from the political situation, as did so many other ethnic groups which invaded the two empires, now victims of their own decadence. But it very soon became evident that Islam did not fall into the same category as the other groups. While the ancient Graeco-Roman civilization was gradually to absorb the invaders who had come from the heart of Europe to the shores of the Mediterranean, by contrast it was Islam which assimilated the peoples it conquered, first imposing its own social and political order on them and then looking for conversions, which were not slow in coming.

Constantly expanding over fifteen centuries except in Spain, India and the Balkans, where its advance was followed by a degree of withdrawal, Islam has not ceased to make its mark on the political, cultural and religious history of the world. Today it embraces between a sixth and a fifth of the human race, if we calculate that there are almost 900 million Muslims in a total world population of over five billion. That is a force to be reckoned with.

Many people believed that the colonial period would strike a very heavy blow with the occupation of almost all the Muslim countries. The eighteenth, nineteenth and first half of the twentieth centuries passed; during them the Muslim community turned in on itself and weathered the storm, taking care to maintain a degree of internal cohesion and jealously preserving its heritage, becoming open to modern technology to the degree that this proved necessary for the community to catch up on its backwardness and skilfully exploiting the rivalries which divided the Westerners. Paradoxically, it grew considerably during these years, benefiting from a new type of peace which facilitated proselytism, while the dismantling of many traditional societies brought in numerous converts, particularly in Africa, who had been disorientated by the upheavals. Today, now that they have regained their political independence, the Muslim countries are going into the future in the midst of difficulties, but holding some important trump cards.

If we are to understand the many faces of Islam, we must first be clear about our own standpoint. Historians see the political and cultural aspects: they examine the empires, the kingdoms which Islam has created and ponder the vicissitudes which led to the formation of this immense world extending from Dakar to Indonesia, and in the other direction from the Balkans and western China to the Indian Ocean and the coast of East Africa. They study the type of civilization which Islam has inspired, with the movement of crowds and scholars attracted by the annual pilgrimage to Mecca, the development of trade and economies, of study and culture, and the creation of mosques, palaces and colleges, some of which are among the masterpieces of Muslim architecture. They are interested in techniques and especially agricultural methods which have been transmitted from one country to another, in the plants which travellers brought, in scientific discoveries, in the heritage which has been preserved and augmented in this sphere. Historians of literature and ideas also study the role played by Muslim authors and thinkers in the intellectual life of the Middle Ages and the place that non-Muslims have occupied in this cultural activity. The methods of the humanities are beginning to be applied to all these investigations.

Without falling into the excesses of the pre-Islamic Arabian poets, each of whom wanted to exalt his own tribe and deprecate that of his rivals, it should be enough to say that Muslim history and civilization fully bear comparison with other histories and civilizations. And even if today the West has a considerable lead in the sphere of science and technology, that should not make us forget either the glories of the Muslim past nor its profoundly human values, which are largely put into practice today in societies that are still in many respects traditional. These are values of which industrial civilization seriously risks losing its awareness.

By contrast, the religious study of Islam is a more delicate matter. The religion has a special dimension, personal and hidden, that of the relationships between men and women and their creator. Its legitimacy and its limits have been the subject of passionate discussion over recent centuries. In this area the *a priori* ideologists often get in the way of a faithful observation of the facts, or offer a very biased interpretation. I shall try to avoid this danger. So we shall be looking at the religious experience of Muslims through the practices required by the Law or engaged in out of devotion, everyday piety and mystical literature. This has a positive value which any honest person must recognize; and if Christians are still held back by scruples, they should re-read the lines which the declarations of the Second Vatican Council devoted to this question.

Islam is the framework in which Muslims express themselves when they turn to God, the Creator, the Master of the Universe, who gives men special guidance by sending them prophets. However, as in any religion, deep human forces play a part, so that it is impossible to draw a dividing line between what is characteristic of a person as a human being, what is characteristic of a believer as the adherent of a particular religion, and what is characteristic of a believer as the beneficiary of a specific grace of God which rests on him or her.

However, this dimension is by no means the only one. On this earth on which human beings struggle and seek, there are numerous religious faiths. Unless one is indifferent to all of them, one day or another questions of the truth of the rival religions will emerge; and relationships between the religious groups are not easy. Some people, abandoning that quest for truth, will be ready to put them all on the same level, in a kind of egalitarian syncretism. This is an illusory solution, which owes more to resignation than to broad-mindedness. The best approach is to consider each religion, to try to understand it, to try patiently to explain it to oneself, avoiding useless attacks, in the awareness that God has ways which are not ours.

Rivalry between religious groups is fatal. Even if many pages of the past were far from being ideal, and some of them were regrettable (but is there any group of human beings which is beyond criticism?), it is time to be open to the future and to join together in discovering rules of conduct which both take account of the right to truth and respect the opinions of others. In this sphere some deontological principles would be a welcome aid towards ordering relationships between religious groups and specifying on the one hand what type of proselytism is normal and on the other what pressures or compulsions are unjustifiable. For the moment there is the United Nations Declaration of Human Rights.

We cannot study Islam without coming up against problems at one time or another. Today Muslims complain about Christian mission just as they used to complain about Western imperialism. Western Christians still remember stories of the time, not so long ago, when Muslim armies invaded their countries and forbade anyone who had gone over to Islam in a moment of weakness or discouragement to return to his original faith. There are also problems for Christians living in Muslim countries. I shall not be stressing these negative aspects, but bringing out positive ones; however, we must keep the negative aspects in mind from time to time so that we have the full picture. What we should hope for, in the light of Vatican II, is that with an eye to the future Christians and Muslims should together define a kind of relationship which embraces the recognition of positive values, the acceptance of differences, and the sensitivity to know how and when these differences may be talked about without sacrificing any essential aspect of faith.

When an African bishop was asked about Muslim-Christian dialogue and what advice he would give to Christians called to engage in it, he stressed three points:

– those involved in the dialogue should be well aware of the differences between Islam and Christianity;

– they should deepen their Christian faith;

– then they should engage in dialogue in a spirit of reconciliation between believers.

I personally would add in conclusion that dialogue is at the opposite pole from syncretism. While being aware that there are important questions on which we differ, we should first try to deepen that which is common to us. God will illuminate those on either side who believe in him and desire to serve him unreservedly.

This book is meant to set up the first markers along this way.

1

The Emergence of Islam

The geographical and human setting

Islam, then, appeared in Arabia, at the beginning of the seventh century of the Christian era, in a pagan Arab environment in contact with small enclaves of Judaism and Christianity. The Arab population lived, as it still does, in vast stretches of desert. The dryness prevents the growth of any vegetation. Everything is arid; the heights are utterly bare and nothing covers the rocks, the cliffs, the boulders, Only the river beds, which the very rare rains fill for a day or two when they come, preserve subterranean traces of moisture that allow the occasional tuft of grass to shoot up here and there. Sometimes a few trees succeed in gaining a hold, and their spiny branches provide food for goats. By contrast, where there are springs, normal vegetation appears, with palm trees, vines and cereal crops. These are the oases, the shade and freshness of which seem like paradise to the nomad after days in the desert. Flocks can exist wherever there is a little greenness; the shepherds have the art of discovering pastures.

The names of the two cities, Medina and Mecca, are constantly mentioned in the history of Islam. Mecca is less than sixty miles from the Red Sea, half-way between Aden on the Indian Ocean and Gaza on the Mediterranean. Medina, more than 250 miles north of Mecca, is further from the sea. Between it and Syria the traveller would have come across a girdle of other oases containing, as it did, a substantial Jewish population (or more precisely Judaized Arabs, converts to Judaism); they were very well organized, with rabbis and schools. The Jewish colonies in southern Arabia are well known. Similarly, when Islam emerged there were Christian centres in Arabia, as in the oasis of Najran, around 500 miles south-east of Mecca, or in certain southern cities which had churches.

In Mecca itself there were sometimes Christian slaves, Christian merchants and even itinerant monks who came to preach at the fairs. Muslim texts indicate that there were Christians among Muhammad's followers. One of them, who

traveling from place to place

5

could read Hebrew (and probably Aramaean) and who knew the scriptures, is said to have been the first cousin of Muhammad's wife Khadija, and several relatives of this man, whose name was Waraqa bin Nawfal, were also Christians. The texts also know of a first cousin of Muhammad who, after first having been converted to Islam, became a Christian when a large number of Muslims emigrated to Ethiopia. Many biblical or rabbinic stories related in the Qur'an were known at Mecca and Muhammad's opponents said of them, 'These are stories of the men of old.' They spoke of them as being in circulation then.

What sect or trend did these Christians belong to? We do not know exactly. It seems that they were members of movements marginal to the mainstream Christianity of the time; the doctrine of the Qur'an is in fact more like a Judaism with some Christian elements than the Christianity of the Gospels or the great church. And to begin with, Islam was said to be in complete accord with these Christians of Mecca. If it is true that the Christians were expecting a prophet, as Muslim tradition reports, that would bring us close to groups like the Elkesaites mentioned by the heresiologists. We should not forget that in the Near East the deserts have always been a place of refuge or exile for all kinds of non-conformists whose faith was not accepted by the authorities of the great powers like Egypt and Byzantium. There must have been many different trends among these Christians or Jewish-Christians.

Mecca was neither a city of shepherds nor a cultivated oasis but very much a centre of trade and pilgrimage, a real Arab centre. Each year, in winter, a caravan for Mecca would go to Aden on the Indian Ocean in search of merchandise brought by sea from India (thanks to the winds which regularly blow in the same direction at particular times of the year and which are known as the trade winds); the merchandise was brought to Mecca and from there taken the following summer by another great caravan to Syria or Egypt. From there, in turn, other merchandise was brought southwards. And so on.

The city of Mecca, situated in the midst of small, barren hills in the desert, had its temple, the Ka'ba; this is an almost 'cubic' building, hence its name, which in Arabic means cube. The building is about seventy-five feet high, thirty feet long and forty feet wide. A black stone, an object of veneration, was and is set in the eastern corner of the Ka'ba, on the outside, at about chest height. There are many stories about its origin, but despite everything that still remains obscure. The edifice formed a pantheon in which all sorts of statues and sacred stones had been placed. Some texts say that there was even an icon of Jesus and Mary. This temple was the centre of a pagan cult, with the worship of sacred stones, astral deities, and so on. But a supreme God, Allah in Arabic, the Creator God, dominated the other gods. Every year a great pilgrimage brought thousands of Arabs together at a particular time; however, all through the year it was possible to perform less solemn devotions at Mecca, especially the lesser pilgrimage, or 'Umra. Similar gatherings took place at other points in the region: fairs for trade here and there, and pilgrimages; we often hear of literary contests at the fair. The Arabs were fond of eloquence and poetry; they were ready to enjoy the literary qualities of the Qur'an.

However, the situation at Mecca was not really stable. The tribal equilibrium of the desert, where the poor in each encampment were looked after by the group, had broken down in the city, where commerce and money reigned supreme. A new time of unity had to be found by society. Historians have noted a certain number of factors of imbalance which favoured emergent Islam. Marxist historians in particular would look to economic causes as an explanation for the origins of Islam. In fact the question is not as simple as that.

First, it is certain that the economic situation at Mecca depended on the state of trade and competition. Competition arose when mer-

The Ka'ba covered with black hangings and brocade. The court of the mosque is surrounded with arcades the lower parts of which are ancient; the vast upper extensions were added in 1960–65.

chants from the Byzantine empire began to use the Nile and the deserts west of the Red Sea as trade routes with India. By this route they arrived at the port of 'Aydhab, in the middle of the Red Sea, where the winds begin to be favourable to navigation. It is equally certain that during the fifty years preceding the emergence of Islam, the wars between Persia and Byzantium made certain routes impracticable for commerce. But to what degree did these different factors come into play? It is hard to say.

Secondly, the egotism of the rich families of Mecca contrasted with Islam's message of brotherhood. Some historians have sought to see Islam above all as a social movement. This would be gravely to neglect the religious aspect; but there is no doubt that one of the reasons for the success of Islam was that it brought a new type of brotherhood, wider than that of the tribes, with care for orphans, the poor and the weaker members of society, looking to better days when success in war became the source of plunder and immense riches. For the moment it was necessary to live through years of what was sometimes very harsh poverty. The support and generosity of the more fortunate Muslims who shared all their possessions made it possible to survive the crises without damage.

Finally, Arabia was looked down on by the great neighbouring empires, Byzantium and Persia, though the nomads, whose incursions were feared by those living in settled conditions, were respected on the frontiers of the cultivated areas, which were guarded by bodies of auxiliaries. With Islam the Arabs became the equals and then the masters of those who scorned them. They had their own religion, their own Prophet and their own sacred book. The Qur'an itself echoes this triumph. So it is written that God revealed the Qur'an (sc. to the Muslim Arabs) so that they should not say: 'The scriptures were revealed only to two sects before us' (Qur'an 6, 156). Commentators explain that this means the Jews and the Christians. In the line of the biblical religions, Islam appeared as an Arab religion for the Arabs before being proclaimed as the only religion willed by God for all humankind, which would remain valid until the last days of the history of the world.

Later, when Islam spread among non-Arab populations, other factors came into force; we shall have to examine these, but we must never neglect the strictly religious factors.

The life and work of Muhammad

Muhammad was born in Mecca around 570. He never knew his father, 'Abd Allah, who died before he was born. He lost his mother when he was six years old and his grandfather, who had then taken care of him, died when he was eight. An orphan, he was brought up by his uncle Abu Talib, the father of Ali, with whom he struck up a deep friendship. His family was a family of nobles in the city, but it had lost some of its influence. When he was grown up, Muhammad became involved in trade, which led him to travel; twice he went to Syria. Some traditions refer to incidents which took place during his travels, like his meeting with the Christian monk Bahira (this meeting gave rise to utterly contradictory traditions among Muslims and Christians). When he was about twenty-five, he married a rich widow called Khadija, aged about forty, for whom he had been working as a trusted agent. While his uncle Abu Talib and his wife Khadija were alive, they were both his loyal and valued supporters.

It is difficult to see from the traditions which speak of the life of Muhammad at this time what his relation was with already existing groups, especially with the peripheral trends in Judaism and Christianity. And when the texts describe his first vision in the desert during a retreat into solitude, we do not know what the influences were which led him to adopt these practices of asceticism and devotion. They merely stress the sincerely religious side of his character.

Around 610 he went on a long retreat in a cave on Mount Hira, some miles from Mecca, right in the desert. There he had a dream. Other traditions speak of a vision during a vigil. He saw a superhuman being who ordered him to recite a text and called him the 'Messenger of God' (*rasul Allah*). This text consisted in what now form the first five verses of chapter 96 of the Qur'an. Here they are:

> In the name of God, the Compassionate, the Merciful
> Recite in the Name of your Lord who created, created man from clots of blood!
> Recite! Your Lord is the Most Bountiful One, who by the pen taught man what he did not know.

In fright, Muhammad hastily returned home. His wife Khadija understood; soon she encouraged him and took him (or according to another version went by herself) to her first cousin, Waraqa bin Nawfal, whom I mentioned earlier. He affirmed that the vision was that of an angel sent by God.

During a period estimated at between two and three years, nothing came of this. These events were to be the object of numerous commentaries in the small circle of those who knew about them, and this was to be the occasion for sharing ideas and stories about earlier prophetic messages.

Around 612 the phenomena began again. The texts which speak of them are more numerous, and it is almost impossible after an interval of fourteen centuries to recreate all the precise details of the situation. Two passages in the Qur'an describe a heavenly vision. Furthermore, traditions indicate that at these moments Muhammad was in a state of physiological trouble. He heard indistinct noises and little by little the meaning of the message became clear. But he had been recommended not to rush things nor to be hasty about expressing what he had to say (cf. Qur'an 75, 16–19). Muslims regard the texts thus proclaimed as messages coming from God through the ministry of the angel Gabriel. Committed to memory to begin with, and partially fixed in writing, they were finally brought together some years after the death of Muhammad and form the Qur'an, the holy book of the Muslims.

Some people in Muhammad's immediate entourage were quickly converted to the new faith: his wife Khadija, his cousin Ali, and Abu Bakr, who was to be the first caliph, were among the first believers. The new religion took its stand in the line of the biblical religions. The Qur'an affirmed that Muhammad was the Messenger of God, sent to the Arabs as Moses had been sent to Pharaoh (Qur'an 73, 15). From then on the adherents to the new faith, who became increasingly numerous, began to group themselves around their spiritual leader, praying either with him or according to his instructions, ceaselessly repeating parts of the Qur'an. The Qur'an was the most original element in their life. It was to it that they all referred, and its authority was absolute. The Muslims formed a community cemented by the Qur'an. Later, when their number had grown considerably, they could rightly be called the people of the Qur'an.

The message of the Qur'an

The message of the Qur'an was very simple: the announcement of the Last Judgment and threats against those who deserved eternal fire on that day, along with happiness for the elect. The earliest declarations stress social justice; it is the wicked rich who are condemned most vigorously. Little by little the sphere of these condemnations extends to those who reject the oneness of God or say that Muhammad was a liar and that the Qur'an was an utter forgery. When the corpus of the messages of the Qur'an began to be formed, it contained the essentials of any monotheistic faith, with a moral code like the Decalogue and deep concern for mutual aid. Many people could believe that this was simply a new brotherhood of the poor of Yahweh.

The role of earlier biblical prophets was stressed, especially that of Moses. The Qur'an specifically reports the fact that several people who were opposed to the prophets whom God sent them were mercilessly chastized. The flood had drowned those who had refused to listen to Noah. The people of the city in which Lot lived had been annihilated. Pharaoh, who had opposed Moses, had been drowned with his soldiers while crossing the Red Sea. Generalizing from these examples, the Qur'an sees this form of divine punishment as the great law of the religious history of the world, the immutable 'custom of God'. Anyone who opposes God's messengers is annihilated. These stories, and the affirmation of this law, constitute a direct threat to opponents who refused to accept the prophetic character of Muhammad.

The figure of Moses is put in a good light from the earliest pages of the Qur'an, with his twofold aspect as the recipient of revelation and leader of his people. In some respects Muhammad then appears as a new Moses, the Moses of the Arabs. The Qur'an does not stress any opposition at this period between the new religion and the religion of contemporaries who follow Moses or Jesus. On the contrary, at this point it cites these latter to confirm its own authority: 'If you doubt what We have revealed to you, ask those who have read the scriptures before you' (Qur'an 10, 94). Islam always appeared as the Arab form of the eternal biblical religion. God is worshipped as Omnipotent Creator, Master of the Universe, infinitely merciful. It was only later, at Medina, that the problem of a possible disagreement between Judaism and Christianity began to arise.

We should note, finally, that the stylistic quality of the Qur'an impressed contemporaries from the beginning. 'Umar, who was to be a caliph, is said to have been converted after hearing a Qur'anic text which bowled him over. This outcome is also attributed to the prayer of Muhammad who, desiring the conversion of a strong man who would become the champion of rising Islam, asked God to attract either 'Umar or another: it was 'Umar who was attracted.

Aware of this literary beauty, but refusing to commit themselves to his enterprise, some pagan inhabitants of Mecca accused Muhammad of being a soothsayer, a man possessed by a jinn or under a spell. The Qur'an protests vigorously against such insinuations.

Muhammad is called to follow the same direction as the prophets of the Bible

84. We gave him [Abraham] Isaac and Jacob and guided them as We guided Noah before them. Among his descendants were David and Solomon, Job and Joseph and Moses and Aaron (thus are the righteous rewarded);
85. Zacharias and John, Jesus and Elias (all were upright men);
86. Ismail, Elisha, Jonah and Lot. All these We exalted above Our creatures, as We exalted some
87. of their fathers, their children, and their brothers. We chose them and guided them to a straight path.

88. Such is God's guidance; He bestows it on whom He pleases of His servants. Had they served other gods besides Him, their labours would have been vain indeed.
89. On those men we bestowed the Scriptures, wisdom and prophethood. If this generation denies these, We will entrust them to others who truly believe in them.
90. Those were the men whom God guided. Follow[1] then their guidance and say: 'I demand of you no recompense for this. It is an admonition to all mankind.'

1. The order is addressed to Muhammad.

Qur'an 6, 84–90

The opposition of the people of Mecca to the new religion

The number of disciples slowly grew amidst an opposition which, if not savage, was at least bitter and persistent. Four years later, around 616, the disciples were numerous enough for about eighty of them to be sent to Abyssinia to escape the vexations and brutality which had led to the death of one or more Muslims. A man called Yasir is generally regarded as the first martyr of Islam. His wife was also killed, and their son turned apostate under torture. Those of little account, slaves or freemen who had no direct protectors, were the first victims of these acts of violence. They included the African Bilal, a convert to Islam, on whom his pagan master inflicted terrible suffering: he put him in iron armour and exposed him, prostrate and unable to move, to the burning rays of the Arabian mid-day sun. The passion of Bilal, who refused

to deny his faith, inspired the pity and the anger of Abu Bakr as he passed by; he ransomed him and freed him. Bilal was to become the first muezzin of Islam.

Muhammad did not leave Mecca. The opposition ordered that new believers were to be boycotted. It was forbidden to trade with them or marry them. Then the hostility seemed to die down. However, the Qur'an itself began to counter the attacks of the opponents. These called for miracles to prove the authenticity of Muhammad's mission. The only response was that the Qur'an was itself the miracle. Impossible for any creature to imitate, it suggested that it could only come from God. Then little by little the opponents were called on to produce texts comparable to those of the Qur'an. They could even enlist the aid of humans or jinns to do so.

The year 619 was very hard for Muhammad, because in it he lost his two main supporters. Khadija and Abu Talib died within a few months of each other. The latter remained a pagan to his last breath (when according to some sources he was converted at his dying breath). The rest of Muhammad's family was not particularly well-disposed towards him, and after the death of Abu Talib another uncle who could have protected him came to be violently opposed to him. This uncle, whose memory has been castigated by all the tradition, has been given the surname Abu Lahab, the father of the flame (i.e. destined for the fires of hell). When he was interrogated by Abu Lahab about the eternal fate of one of their ancestors who had died a pagan, Muhammad retorted that he was in hell. Hence the break.

Rejected by his clan, Muhammad had to find new protectors at any price; otherwise, according to the law of the desert, the firstcomer could assassinate him without fear of reprisals. He looked first in at-Ta'if, the summer resort of the rich of Mecca, up in the hills. He then pursued his quest among the nomads, but in neither case was he successful. Finally he came to an agreement with the pagan Arabs of Medina, who were ripe for conversion. It is at this period that tradition places a famous journey by Muhammad, destined to give him courage: the angel Gabriel is said to have taken him to Jerusalem and then to the seventh heaven, before the throne of God. It was there that he received the order to pray ritually five times a day.

Medina, the pre-Islamic name for which was Yathreb, was a city in the middle of an oasis. Its existence goes back to the dawn of time. It is already mentioned on a stele of Nabonidus king of Babylonia in the sixth century BCE. With a population which was half Jewish and half Arab it was then to take the name Medina, i.e. in Arabic 'the city', to signify that it had become the city of the Prophet.

Once accepted by the pagan half of the oasis, who were converted, Muhammad decided on the emigration of his supporters in Mecca. This operation took place by stages during the summer of 622. This year (the lunar year) is now considered to be the first year of the Muslim era and each year on the first day of the first lunar month of the year Muslims celebrate the memory of the exodus – Hijra, to use the Arab term.

During the last years in Mecca there may have been around two hundred Muslims there. The rallying of the people of Medina *en masse* was completely to transform the situation.

Muhammad at Medina (622–632)

According to the laws of the desert, the party which is forced to flee its home declares war on its old fellow-citizens by the very act of its flight. So from that moment on, the Muslims regarded themselves as being in a state of war with the people of Mecca.

The situation changed completely at Medina. From being a small sect attractive to the poor of Yahweh, Islam became a political power, a state. Moreover, little by little it affirmed itself as the only form of religion which had remained faithful to the biblical ideal. After appearing as the

> *You are the noblest nation that has ever been raised up for mankind. You enjoin justice and forbid evil. You believe in God.*
>
> Qur'an 3, 110
> *addressed to the Muslim community*

Arab form of the eternal and immutable biblical religion, Islam became a universal religion, destined to supplant all the others. The beginnings of Muslim political organization date from 622.

In accordance with the laws of the desert, the man who asks for refuge from another tribe enjoys the status of a guest. In this instance Muhammad placed himself above the law. He was not the guest but the ruler of Medina. So he attracted the implacable, if underhand, hostility of the man who had been forced out of first place by his coming. While going through the motions of coming over to Muhammad, this man surreptitiously became the leader of the opposition: in the Qur'an and in history, these opponents go under the name of hypocrites (the *munafiqun*). At Medina, many of the texts which continued to be handed down by Muhammad touched on questions of law. They deal with the difficulties encountered by believers (laws of war, marriage, inheritance, contracts, loans, retribution, the penalties to be inflicted for certain crimes, liturgy, religious obligations, political orientation, solutions of specific difficulties of the community and even of the Prophet's wives and family, etc.).

To begin with, relations with the Jews whose three tribes made up half the population of the oasis were peaceful. They were offered a treaty of protection and could not refuse it. Free to organize themselves within their community, they had to hand over to the Muslims all external politics, initiatives in war, and so on. These restrictions on their freedom and the secondary place with which they were left did not please them, and they sought to regain their former position. Hence their quiet manoeuvres which the Muslims did not tolerate, and repressed with an iron hand.

As for the Muslims themselves, a policy of fusion united the emigrants from Mecca and the people of Medina who had been won over. Each former inhabitant of Mecca was personally bound by a pact of brotherhood to an inhabitant of Medina. The effect of these measures was to cement the young community.

Shortly after their arrival in Medina, the Muslims with Muhammad at their head became masons and built what was to become the mosque of Medina, the command post of growing Islam and the place where Muhammad and his wives lived. The complex was made up of a large courtyard, part of which was protected against the sun by a scanty roof and as many rooms opening on the courtyard as Muhammad had wives. It was there that he was to be buried in 632, and it is there that hundreds of thousands of pilgrims come each year to pray at his tomb. This sharing of the work of building the most famous sanctuary of Islam after the Ka'ba has remained an example among Muslims, who talk of it even now.

Initially ritual prayer was offered in the direction of Jerusalem, in conformity with Jewish custom. A fast of one day a year, that of the 'Ashura (the tenth day of the first month of the lunar year), had also been instituted in accordance with Jewish custom.

Muhammad wanted the Jews of the oasis to be converted and to join him. After several months and many exhortations which are echoed in the Qur'an, it emerged that the Jews begrudged the alliance imposed on them, and above all that they had no intention of coming over to Islam. At this point two decisions show the break between the Muslims and the Jews. The direction of prayer was changed, and from then on they prayed towards the Ka'ba in Mecca; and the fast of the month of Ramadan replaced that of the 'Ashura.

13

The Qur'an clearly affirms that Islam is a return to the purity of the religion of Abraham, who was neither Jew nor Christian. The texts speak of Abraham who built the Ka'ba with the aid of his son Ismail (other stories from outside the Qur'an locate at Mecca or in its neighbourhood both the fight of Hagar, maddened at the prospect of dying of thirst – see Genesis 21.14–19, and Abraham's sacrifice – this sacrifice is mentioned in Qur'an 37, 102–109, though without giving the name of Abraham's son). According to the Qur'an Abraham also received the order to call men to make a pilgrimage to Mecca. He prayed God to feed the inhabitants of this place and to send a prophet to the Arabs. So the mission of Muhammad is directly connected with this prayer of Abraham.

At Medina the Muslims were on their guard against the pagans of Mecca. They made several raids on the caravans from Mecca. When the leader of one of these raids violated the prohibitions of a sacred month, a revelation took place shortly afterwards to demonstrate his innocence (Qur'an 2, 216–217). In March 624 their first major encounter brought victory to the Muslims at Badr (a valley between Medina and the Red Sea). There three hundred Muslims defeated a thousand men from Mecca who had massed to protect one of their great trading caravans which was in danger of being pillaged. This victory, which caused a great stir, is celebrated each year on 17 Ramadan, the date of the lunar calendar on which it took place. Two other major encounters later brought the two adversaries face to face: a defeat of the Muslims, who were forced into a corner at Uhud, at the foot of the mountain of the same name a few miles from Medina (in 625), and the failure of an attack by the men of Mecca supported by a mass of allies who were disturbed at the rise of Islam. This attack, aimed at laying siege to Medina, was neutralized by the ditch which the Muslims dug to protect the city and break the force of the cavalry charges. It is called the campaign of the Ditch (627).

Each of these operations was the occasion for liquidating, one after the other, the three Jewish tribes of Medina, since the Jews proved to be concerned with achieving an understanding more with the people of Mecca than with the Muslims. The last liquidation, the only bloody one, ended in the massacre of between 600 and 900 Jewish warriors who had resisted and were finally forced to surrender; they were executed in a way which recalls certain episodes in the Hebrew Bible. The women and children were reduced to slavery and sold. The warriors could live if they were converted to Islam. Only two (or, four, according to other sources) chose this course. The others died martyrs for their faith.

In 628 the Muslims went to Mecca as pilgrims seeking to go on pilgrimage. Their arrival disturbed Mecca and negotiations began. A truce was signed between the two parties. For the first time, the Muslims gained official recognition. It was a great success, a 'manifest victory', as the beginning of one of the surahs (chapters) of the Qur'an puts it (Qur'an 48, 1–2). As often happens when a movement of rebellion triumphs, yesterday's rebel is now considered an equal. Whatever the concessions required of him, his existence is at last recognized, and that is an enormous gain. The truce was signed at Hudaybiya.

Their hands freed in this direction, the Muslims multiplied their raids elsewhere. They went further and further into Arabia, particularly northwards, gathering plunder and provoking conversions to Islam. By virtue of the truce of Hudaybiya they were even allowed to return to Mecca for several days in 629 to perform the lesser pilgrimage. In 630 they returned to take Mecca, without striking a blow, following an incident provoked by the allies of the people of Mecca which the Muslims hastened to consider as a violation of the truce. The victorious Muhammad granted what amounted to a general amnesty to his compatriots. He pardoned them after the victory, though as we shall

The great boundary stone marking the beginning of the sacred territory of Mecca, prohibited to those who are not Muslims.

see shortly, he resorted to much rougher procedures during the struggle. This political broad-mindedness prepared for a general rallying of the people of Mecca. Paganism did not arouse much enthusiasm, and unlike the Jews, the pagans preferred conversion to martyrdom. The Ka'ba was 'purified' of all its idols. It is said that the icon of Mary and Jesus stood alongside other statues. Was it suppressed at the same time as the others? Or was it only taken away later? At all events, it had to go. From then on Mecca became the Holy City of Islam, the citadel of Muslim monotheism, as it has remained to this day.

The reversal of the situation, the victory and the numerous raids in various directions in Arabia, led to mass conversions. The year 631 was one of delegations coming to submit and to embrace Islam. That year, on the official pilgrimage presided over by Abu Bakr in the absence of Muhammad, it was announced that the territory of Mecca would be closed to non-Muslims for pilgrimages from the next year onwards. The pilgrimage of 632, traditionally called the 'farewell pilgrimage' (because it was led by Muhammad himself a few months before his death), consisted only of Muslims. This measure also amounted to a ban on non-Muslims engaging in the trading which took place on this occasion. That was a risk to be run; in fact, here again the Muslims succeeded in imposing their will.

As the years passed, the tone of the Qur'an became more and more assured when it was concerned with the person of Muhammad. God 'leans over him' (literally, prays for him, a word which Muslims understand as 'blesses him': the root 'pray' comes from the Syriac and also denotes prostrations), and the faithful are called upon to recite words of salutation over him. Similarly, it appears increasingly clearly that the only great sin is sin against belief in the oneness of God: the Qur'an states that this is the only sin which cannot be forgiven.

It is impossible in a few pages to do more than outline the major features of this history.

Thousands of traditions have provided us with a great many details. The private life of the Prophet was so public that the Qur'an even had to ask the faithful to show some discretion about it, as about the life of his wives. The number of these had grown. Though monogamous for most of his life, Muhammad had remarried after the death of Khadija. It was only at Medina that he began to have several wives at the same time. First there was 'A'isha, daughter of his friend Abu Bakr, whom he took in addition to his first wife and who became his favourite. She was only eleven when he married her (other traditions say nine). He then married several more times and finally had nine wives simultaneously. By some of them he had several daughters who died young, or who produced no offspring. The only exception was Fatima, married to Ali, who gave him two grandsons, Hassan and Husayn. An Egyptian woman, a secondary wife, Mary the Copt, had a son by him who died very young. The customs of the time and the alliances between families which were sealed by marriage justified this conduct; this was the way in which Arabian chiefs acted. Only in one case did Muhammad's action offend against customary morality, when his adopted son repudiated his wife Zaynab so that he could offer her for the Prophet to marry. But immediately afterwards a revelation of the Qur'an affirmed the legitimacy of the marriage by abolishing all ties of affinity through adoption.

Moreover, the simplicity of life at Medina as compared with the luxury of the courts of Byzantium and Persia one day reduced 'Umar, the future caliph, to tears. Between 622 and 628, before victories and plunder had made life easier, as 'A'isha was to report later, the Muslims hardly ever had enough to eat.

In 632 Muhammad died at Medina, either from an illness or, as certain sources say, from the after-effects of a Jewish attempt to poison him some years earlier. His eventful life was to give a new direction to the history of the world. He was buried where he died.

Despite so much apparent success, the situation was still precarious. Muhammad's death was the signal to the allied tribes for a general revolt in Arabia which took many months to put down. However, this was finally achieved. There was a risk that the Muslim community of Medina might divide over the choice of a successor. A small group, made up of Muhammad's most prominent companions, nominated Abu Bakr as caliph, i.e. to succeed the dead Prophet as head of the community. The community immediately ratified the choice. In the end the transition took place without conflict, thanks to the strong personality of many of the Prophet's companions.

Whereas at Mecca the Muslims had presented themselves as being in line with the former biblical religions, at Medina the break had become complete. It began with the Jews of Medina, who remained deaf to the call to conversion. Little by little the Qur'an accused them of manipulating the holy Books, and the commentaries on the Qur'an above all interpret this accusation as a charge of concealing the predictions of the coming of Muhammad which according to the Qur'an should have been found in the Torah and in the Gospel. It is no longer a matter of consulting those who know the Jewish and Christian scriptures, as the Qur'an was still saying at Mecca, probably with the group around Waraqa bin Nawfal in view. Suspicion is cast on all that these latter can say.

However, on the one hand some Christians are still praised; as is shown by the verse which comes after the one that I shall now quote, these are people with a leaning towards Islam:

> You will find that the nearest in affection to them [the faithful] are those who say 'We are Christians'. That is because there are priests and monks among them; and because they are free from pride' (Qur'an 5, 85).

But in fact Islam increasingly claimed to be the reformer of Judaism and Christianity, the primitive purity of which had been lost by Jews and Christians.

As Arnold Toynbee wrote:

> Islam, like Communism, succeeded to the degree that it claimed to be reforming the abuses which had crept into the Christianity of the time. And the success of Islam from the beginning shows the power that a heresy can have when it claims to be reforming an orthodoxy which does not seem inclined to reform itself (*The World and the West*, Oxford University Press 1953).

Allah (God)

2

The Expansion of Islam

Now, at the end of the twentieth century, the newspapers, the radio and the television often report on Muslim leaders: they mention what goes on in countries which are wholly or partially Muslim, especially since the oil crisis after 1973, the events in Iran in 1979 and the political role played by the imam Khomeini with its international repercussions, particularly in Iraq and Lebanon. They recall the differences between Shi'ites and Sunnites, and quote the statements by Colonel Qadhafi in Libya along with discussing many other issues. If we are to find our bearings in all this news, a quick look at the history of the expansion of Islam may prove useful. In fact there are a certain number of proper names among the pioneer figures of Islam which are still used today and which are borne to perpetuate the memory of the great men or saints of the past. Similarly, it is good to know roughly at what periods the various regions of the Muslim world went over to Islam and what trends of Islam they follow. There are historical atlases in which a series of maps with arrows and dates indicate the main thrusts of Muslim expansion, some military and others peaceful, led by proselytism through traders, teachers or preachers often belonging to brotherhoods. This chapter sets out to give the same kind of information, but in a more summary fashion.

We shall pay particular attention to the Islamization of Africa, keeping for the end of the book some reflections on the factors which have been relevant in these areas, and still are.

The conquests under the first four caliphs (632–661)

The military force which the growing community had mustered was not demobilized on the death of Muhammad in 632. It comprised not only that original faithful but also the military leaders from the pagan part of Mecca who had joined it after their late rally. Several of the latter

Some dates between 550 and 650

Western Europe	Near and Middle East	Islam
The Visigoths at Toulouse, in Aquitaine and Spain.		
End of sixth century, the Lombards in Northern Italy.	570, conquest of Yemen by the Persians. End of sixth century, attacks by the Avars against the Byzantines.	c.570, birth of Muhammad.
590–604, in Rome, St Gregory the Great, pope.		
594, death of St Gregory of Tours, bishop and writer.		
	610–641, Heraclius, emperor of Byzantium.	610, Muhammad in the cave of Mount Hira; his first visions, beginning of his prophetic activity.
	611, beginning of the Persian invasion of the Byzantine empire.	
	613, the Persians in Palestine.	
	614, Jerusalem captured by the Persians.	612–622, the first Muslim community in Mecca.
	617–618, the Persians in Egypt.	
	622, Byzantine counter-offensive towards Armenia and Iraq.	622, the Hijra.
		622–632, the first Muslim community in Medina; raids and battles within Arabia.
629, Dagobert I, king of the Franks.	628–629, victorious peace of Byzantium; the Persians leave Palestine.	
	630, Heraclius brings the relic of the true cross to Jerusalem.	630, Mecca falls to the Muslims.
		632, death of Muhammad, caliphate of Abu Bakr.
	634–638, Byzantine Syria and Persian Iraq begin to fall under Muslim attack.	634, death of caliph Abu Bakr, caliphate of Umar b. al-Khattab.
	638, Jerusalem captured by Muslims.	
	639–42, Egypt captured by the Muslims.	
	642, battle of Nihawand completes the collapse of Persia to the Muslims.	
	643, capture of Cyrenaica by the Muslims.	
		644, death of caliph Umar, caliphate of Uthman b. al-Affan.
The Greeks have been defeated in a neighbouring land. But in a few years they shall themselves gain victory; such being the will of God before and after.		647, first Muslim raid on Tunisia.
On that day the believers shall rejoice in God's help. He gives victory to whom he will. He is the Mighty One, the Merciful.		650–656, promulgationn of the official text of the Qur'an under the aegis of caliph Uthman.
Qur'an 30, 2–4; surah of c.618–620		

distinguished themselves in later campaigns: among them Khalid ibn al-Walid, converted only shortly after the capture of Mecca, who played a decisive role in putting down the general uprising in Arabia after Muhammad's death and then took an active part in the conquest of Syria.

The first caliph was Abu Bakr (a name which has become Boubaker in some African languages); he reigned for two years before he died (632–634). During the difficult years he had put his fortune at the service of the community. His daughter 'A'isha had married the Prophet. He was the only one to have been chosen to accompany Muhammad on the Hijra, during the move from Mecca to Medina. Later he had been entrusted by Muhammad with presiding over the pilgrimage of 631, and the following year with presiding over the prayers at Medina in Muhammad's place when he himself was too weak to do so.

The first task of the caliphate was to pacify Arabia, which at that time was in utter revolt. The operations which lasted up until 633 were severe, and a large number of companions who knew whole passages of the Qur'an by heart died in them. It was at that time, following these events and on the advice of 'Umar, that Abu Bakr set in motion the first written version of the whole Qur'an with the aim of preserving its text.

'Umar ibn al-Khattab, the second caliph, was assassinated after a reign of ten years (634–644). During this time the conquests extended beyond the frontiers of Arabia. On the death of 'Umar, the Byzantine empire had lost its two finest provinces: Syria (occupied by the Muslims between 634 and 640; Jerusalem had fallen in 638 after a long siege) and Egypt (from the end of 639 to 642). Iraq had been conquered between 636 and 646 from Persia and the latter had found itself at the mercy of the Arab armies after the battle of Nihawand, which the Persians lost in 642. In the north, the Muslims reached Armenia.

'Umar was a very great politician. It has been possible to compare his role in Islam with that of St Paul in Christianity. In particular he had the wisdom to understand that the administration of a great empire was a complicated matter, for which the Arabs were not prepared. So for the moment he left the local administrative organizations in place, with their own officials and their own language, and only implemented Arabization little by little. However, he did create several offices for Muslim administration, for example one for pensions with a large register to indicate what was due to Muslims in their old age and after their services.

During Muhammad's lifetime, the war against Mecca had been waged to recover property of which the Muslims had been dispossessed simply by virtue of their exodus and the hostility of other pagans. Some very clear verses in the Qur'an legitimate this kind of war. Subsequent wars were also legitimated, but after the event. At the time, it seems that the old atavism of the nomads attracted by the riches of sedentary culture were allied to the desire to propagate Islam. Later the doctors of the Law found religious justifications for these expeditions, while certain Muslims (more rarely) simply saw them as a profane phenomenon, characteristic of the Arabs as a people.

The movement had been launched: it was not to stop so soon. A whole Arab empire was in process of formation which was to last for two centuries.

As R. Mantran has pointed out in his article on Islam in *Encyclopedia Universalis*, Paris, the religious aspect is usually combined with a political, offensive and imperialistic aspect down to the beginnings of modern times, and from the end of the nineteenth century with a defensive and anti-imperialistic attitude to the Western world.

Under the reign of the third caliph, 'Uthman ibn Affan (644–656), the conquests continued eastwards. Towards the west a raid penetrated as far as Tunisia and then withdrew. As a person, 'Uthman is very controversial even among Muslims; siege was finally laid to him in his own house in Medina. One of the charges laid against him was that of favouritism towards his own kin. He died at the hands of Muslim assassins. His name remained attached to the edition of the Qur'an which bears it. He appointed a committee to fix the official text, and a copy of this text was then sent to each of the garrison cities founded by the Arabs in conquered countries.

The fourth caliph, Ali ibn Abi Talib (656–61), was the son-in-law and the cousin of Muhammad, whose daughter Fatima he had married. In his reign the internal tensions which had long divided the community burst into the open. On the one hand, the influx of riches from immense plunder seemed normal to some while others, remembering the simplicity of life in the earliest days, favoured a more ascetic orientation. Moreover, personal rivalries became more bitter, ending in a kind of civil war: Ali and his supporters were opposed by a group in which 'A'isha occupied a predominant place. This resulted in violent clashes and even an armed confrontation. Ali was victorious at the 'Battle of the Camel' (656), but a rival with different skills was waiting for him: Mu'awiya, the govenor of Syria, a very strong personality, often decried since then, who was wholly bent on seeking the expansion of Islam and extending the frontiers of his own power. He was the son of Abu Sufyan, the man who, forty years earlier at Mecca, had done everything possible to wipe out emergent Islam and had fought fiercely until the truce of Hudaybiya. Mu'awiya had kept out of the conflict between Ali and 'A'isha, but like 'A'isha he demanded the punishment of 'Uthman's assas-sins. The parties of Ali and Mu'awiya came to blows. The battle which followed at Siffin in 657 was indecisive. Ali, the intrepid warrior, the champion in single combat, did not have the diplomacy (or the guile) of his adversary, who was skilled enough to be able to profit from the situation. Arbitration was suggested and accepted by the two rivals. Ali came out worse; little by little his supporters left him, and in 661 he was assassinated, like the two previous caliphs.

Mu'awiya triumphed and then became caliph. Internal troubles led to a halt in the process of conquest. However, a Muslim fleet with Syrian ships had already begun to operate on the Mediterranean. As governor of Syria, Mu'awiya had understood the importance of the sea for the expansion of Islam.

The first four caliphs form a separate group from all others who were invested with this office. The Ottoman Turks wrote their names on great calligraphed banners in many of their mosques. Modern Reformist Muslims honour them as a group and some even add that after them Islam lost its original purity, which it has still not regained. So according to this Reformist tendency, the ideal would be to return to the sources, to the Islam of the Qur'an and the first companions of Muhammad.

Only the Shi'ites, the supporters of Ali, limit their esteem to those of the companions who were on his side. They are hard on those early Muslim men and women who were opposed to him.

The major divisions of the Muslim world

These events led to a number of schisms within the Muslim world. These schisms still exist today. They have nothing to do with questions of dogma, since in Islam dogma is very simple, and all are agreed on it. The schisms are political in origin and relate to the caliphate, or more precisely to the qualifications for a caliph, i.e. head of the Muslim community.

The main group is that of the Sunnites or people of the tradition which supported Mu'awiya and then the caliphs who succeeded him. For them, the caliph must normally be chosen from among the Quraysh Arabs. They now represent nine-tenths of all Muslims.

Those who do not admire the authority of Mu'awiya and seceded are the origins of two groups which in turn are sub-divided.

1. The Kharijites (now very few in number), whose descendants still live in the Algerian Sahara (the Mzabites of the seven towns around Ghardaia in the oasis), the island of Djerba in Tunisia and in 'Uman (Oman, south-east of Arabia) and in some other places. A number of Muslims in East Africa, Arab emigrants, belonged to this group at the end of the nineteenth century. The term Kharijite, denoting those who 'went out' by rebelling, has subsequently ceased to be used, and has been replaced by Ibadi. The original Kharijites did not accept either Ali or his rival as caliphs; they wanted the caliph to be chosen from among the most competent Muslims, regardless of whether or not they were Arabs and indeed whether or not they were free men.

2. The Shi'ites. Their name is derived from an Arab word meaning 'partisans'. They are the supporters of Ali and represent a minority in the Muslim world. For them, the caliph should automatically be chosen from among the direct descendants of Ali and Fatima. So they preserve the official list of those who should have governed the Muslim world; they venerate their memory and are careful to preserve their teaching. Not all the Shi'ites agree on the number of these 'imams', as they call them. For some there were twelve imams, for others seven. Then the last (the seventh or the twelfth, depending on the group) disappeared mysteriously, to remain hidden to the end of time. He will then reappear and become the head of the community.

The Shi'ites who recognize twelve imams are the most numerous. Though for a long time they

remained in opposition, on various occasions they did hold power, when Shi'ite dynasties became the heads of countries. So it is that Iran has been governed by the Shi'ites since the fifteenth century of our era.

The Shi'ite groups who recognize only seven imams are not so large. At present they include on the one hand the Bhoras and on the other the Ismailites under the Aga Khan. These two groups derive from a schism which came about among the ranks of the Ismailites in the eleventh century of our era for personal reasons: one branch of this sect supported the claims of al-Musta'li, canvassing for the succession of his father as Fatimid caliph of Egypt. Another branch supported Nizar, al-Musta'li's brother. Hence the names borne by these two branches, as can be seen in the table on p.23. Despite the modest numbers of their respective communities, the Bhoras and the Ismailites under the

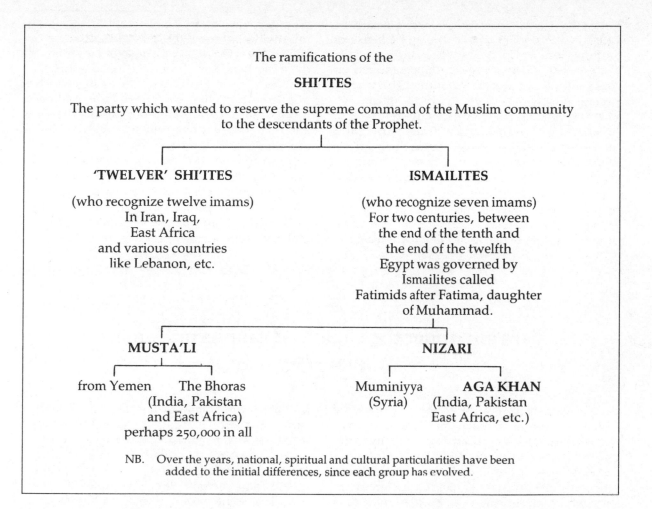

The ramifications of the

SHI'ITES

The party which wanted to reserve the supreme command of the Muslim community
to the descendants of the Prophet.

'TWELVER' SHI'ITES

(who recognize twelve imams)
In Iran, Iraq,
East Africa
and various countries
like Lebanon, etc.

ISMAILITES

(who recognize seven imams)
For two centuries, between
the end of the tenth and
the end of the twelfth
Egypt was governed by
Ismailites called
Fatimids after Fatima, daughter
of Muhammad.

MUSTA'LI

from Yemen   The Bhoras
(India, Pakistan
and East Africa)
perhaps 250,000 in all

NIZARI

Muminiyya   **AGA KHAN**
(Syria)   (India, Pakistan
East Africa, etc.)

NB.   Over the years, national, spiritual and cultural particularities have been
added to the initial differences, since each group has evolved.

Aga Khan show great vitality. For several centuries during the Middle Ages they were the inspiration for revolutionary movements before which the Muslim world trembled, but now they have settled down. Rich and powerful, they devote part of their resources to the education and welfare of their followers.

Until the return of the hidden imam who must reappear at the end of time, authority belongs to different religious leaders depending on the different branches: these branches are indicated in the box on the Shi'ites.

In fact, with time each of the different Shi'ite groups has taken on a distinctive personality. First, they all have a great devotion to the Prophet's family, Fatima, Ali and the different imams, whose tombs have become places of pilgrimage. The persecutions to which Ali's family fell victim, notably the assassination of his son Husayn at Karbala (in Iraq, at the beginning of the cultivated valley on the route which comes down from Medina) in 680, have left a profound mark on them. The suffering of Husayn, killed for his opposition to Mu'awiya's son Yazid, who succeeded his father as caliph, was a particular cause of the revival among them of a sense of suffering unknown to Sunnite Islam; each year the memory of this event is commemorated on the tenth day of the first month of the year in processions which often figure flagellants. In Iran the Shi'ites (the 'Twelvers') often have a tendency to stress notions of ritual purity, and for a long time those who observed them strictly were much more demanding than the Sunnites on this point, rejecting food prepared by non-Muslims and regarding the latter as impure beings, contact with whom defiled. They regard temporary marriages (unions formed for a few months or days) as legitimate, whereas the Sunnites reject them. They accept that the faithful should conceal their thoughts in some circumstances (the theory of *kitman*). However, on the other hand they have developed a theory of prophecy in connection with the imams which is not without interest. In general they tend more towards mysticism than other groups. Iranians add that Shi'ism is the form of Islam which most accords with the Iranian spirit.

In addition to their specific characteristics, in order to defend themselves, in the past the other Shi'ite groups have had to adopt a practice of silence in self-defence, and they keep part of their heritage to themselves, inaccessible to those who are not members of their group.

Expansion under the Umayyad caliphs of Damascus (661–750)

Each of the first four caliphs had been chosen by a small electoral body and the community had ratified the choice, giving an oath of loyalty to the one who had been chosen. From Mu'awiya onwards the caliphate became hereditary, remaining the property of a particular family. In fact, in his lifetime Mu'awiya had designated his son Yazid as his successor; he had succeeded in gaining recognition of Yazid as his heir first in Syria and then in the provinces. The caliphate was to remain in this family for little less than a century. This was the Umayyad caliphate, so called after Umayya, the ancestor whom this dynasty followed, one of the pre-Islamic Quraysh nobles at Mecca. It is also called the Damascus caliphate, since this city was chosen by the caliphs as a residence after their first four predecessors had lived in Medina.

When Mu'awiya came to power, the first wave of conquests paused before the deserts (east of Iran and Tripolitania) or the mountains (northeast of Iran, Armenia). After the end of the war, progress was resumed. Countries were often seized in several stages: a first wave advanced, fought or laid siege, and then withdrew; subsequently another wave finally occupied the territory. This sometimes took place centuries later, as was the case with Byzantium, capital of the Byzantine emperor. This was besieged in 668/9, then in 674–680, then in 716–718, and was finally captured only in 1453. Similarly, Tunisia was the object of a first raid in 647, but was not really conquered until 670; all of northern Africa was to be subjected, despite fierce·resistance, between 670 and 700. General Tariq disembarked on the coast of Spain in 711 and left his name in Gibraltar (in Arabic Jebel Tariq, the mountain of Tariq). A victorious campaign gave him the country. From there other Muslims were to invade the south of Gaul (now France) and a raid in 732 got as far as Poitiers, less than 200 miles from present-day Paris, where it was repulsed.

The advance continued in the east of the Muslim world. Kabul, the capital of present-day Afghanistan, was besieged at a very early stage by an army which still contained two first-generation Muslims who had been Muhammad's companions. It was abandoned and only later incorporated into the Islamic world. It was captured after 800 and its ruler was converted to Islam.

Western China had been reached by the end of the seventh century and a new victory in 750 consolidated the occupation.

In present-day Pakistan, the River Indus (in the region of present-day Sind) was reached around 711–712, and the city of Multan remained a Muslim outpost for several centuries.

The epoch of the 'Abbassid caliphs of Baghdad (750–1258)

So far all the power had been concentrated in the hands of the Arabs. Converts from other people were discontented under such a hegemony, which nothing in Islam could justify. Moreover, a revolt overthrew the Umayyads. The dynasty which replaced them consisted of caliphs descended in a direct line from an uncle of Muhammad called 'Abbas, hence the designation 'Abbassid given to this caliphate. The movement was supported by non-Arab Muslims. The caliphate is also called the caliphate of Baghdad, when this city was built to replace Damascus as the residence of the authorities.

The period of five centuries which now began was to see the end of the political unity of the Muslim world. The Arab empire was still at the height of its glory, with the prestigious reigns of certain caliphs like Harun al-Rashid (786–809) and al-Ma'mun (813–833), but one by one the various provinces of the empire had regained or were regaining their independence. The caliph soon only had an honorary sovereignty over the Sunnite world; this only manifested itself in the confirmation of local rulers, or with a high hand on the pilgrimage to Mecca. Political disintegration soon set in and the Shi'ites even gained political control of Baghdad and Iraq. Spain, which never went over to the 'Abbassids, still recognized the Umayyad caliphs, a descendant of whom established himself in Cordova in 756. Egypt became independent in 868 before passing under the domination of the Fatimid, i.e. Shi'ite, caliphs (from 969 to 1171) who were opposed to the Sunnite caliphs of Baghdad. As for the Turks, the conversion of some of them and their entry into Muslim politics, whether as soldiers in the caliph's bodyguard or as rulers of independent states in Afghanistan or in India, are certainly characteristic features of this period.

On the other hand, the ninth and tenth centuries were a real golden age of civilization, literature and art in Baghdad. The caliphs, like great patrons, protected scholars, artists and writers despite palace revolts and all the troubles which ensued.

Otherwise, the expansion of Islam continued, sometimes peacefully and sometimes through wars; however, at this time the wars were waged by individual princes or states situated on the frontiers and no longer by the caliph.

For example in Mauretania in the western Sahara the dynasties of the Almoravids conquered and won over the Ghana of that time, north of the river Niger, with the capture of the capital Awdaghast in 1054.

Similarly, Turkish dynasties penetrated northern India shortly after the year 1000 and installed the first Muslim sultanate of India there. Around 1200 a second wave of conquest led by another Turkish dynasty extended the power of Islam all over the north and north-east of India. The rest of this sub-continent was the object of victorious campaigns in the thirteenth and fourteenth centuries and then was lost again, except for several Muslim enclaves which still remain today.

Around Byzantium the wars continued. Then came the age of the crusades. However, for Islam the crusades were only a local danger which could easily be removed; the peril came from the invasions led by the Mongols from central Asia, which caused unimaginable destruction. The Mongols were stopped in Syria-Palestine in the middle of the thirteenth century. Some decades later, they were converted to Islam.

This was also the period during which the influence of science and thought from the intellectual centres of the Muslim world spread over Western Europe, where it played a decisive role in the intellectual renaissance of the twelfth and thirteenth centuries.

The 'Abbassid caliphs of Cairo (1260–1517)

The last caliph of Baghdad was killed in the terrible Mongol invasions which reached as far as Baghdad and Syria. Egypt then attracted a survivor of his family and made him a caliph resident in Cairo. From then on there was a series of caliphs in Cairo, without any real authority, playthings in the hands of the Mamluk sultans of the city. Despite these troubles, Muslim expansion continued, still led by the Muslims on the frontiers.

By the end of the thirteenth century Islam had reached the north-west point of Sumatra (Indonesia), and from there penetrated to Java. Java went over to Islam with the conversion of local rulers first in the east of the island and then in the west; the centre was last to be affected. In itself Indonesia today has more than 130 million Muslims. It and the whole of the Indian sub-continent (Pakistan, India, Bangladesh) are the two most numerous Muslim areas in the world.

The thrust of the Ottoman Turks towards Europe was also one of the main events of this period. Having seized all (or almost all) Anatolia, established bridgeheads in south-east Europe and approached Byzantium from behind, the Ottoman Turks captured the city in 1453. Byzantium, also known under the name Constantinople, was to be renamed Istanbul by the Turks. It was from there that their armies were to advance into Europe, where they had strongholds for four centuries.

By contrast, the Muslims were gradually driven out of Spain, where the last Muslim kingdom, that of Granada, fell in 1492. The reconquest had taken 800 years.

The time of Turkish-Ottoman supremacy (1515–1919)

Apart from Africa, which will be the subject of the next chapter, Islam reinforced itself locally while beginning to be subject to the consequences of technological developments in Europe. Before steam navigation, new types of sailing ships ploughed the seas, creating European trading establishments. At first simple trading centres, these soon became military and political strongholds, posing threats to local independence; they were Dutch in Indonesia, English and India. If many factors thwarted the inventive and creative spirit in Arab countries, artistic and intellectual activity was to develop in Iran and in the India of the Great Moguls.

The Ottoman Turks were at the height of their power. They advanced on Europe, twice laying siege to Vienna, the capital of Austria, though they did not succeed in taking it (1529 and 1683). Driven out of Poland, where they had occupied a whole province (in the seventeenth century) and then Greece, they were finally to leave the Balkans (in the nineteenth and the beginning of the twentieth centuries), where the growing nationalist movements fought to recover their independence.

The nineteenth century and the beginning of the twentieth saw the intensification of the phenomenon of colonialism; the considerable technological advance in the West allowed foreign minorities to dominate numerous countries in which they found both raw material and markets for their manufactured products.

What had become of the caliphate during this time? After the conquest of Egypt in 1517, the Ottoman sultans of Istanbul (Constantinople) had taken over the title of caliph. But the Turkish revolution which was to break out after the 1914–1918 war was to do away first of all with the empire, which was replaced by a nationalist Turkish republic, and then in 1924 with the caliphate. So it is sixty-five years since the Muslim world had caliphs.

In the twentieth century the great problem of the Muslim world was how to free itself from the colonialism which had deprived it of almost all its territories. This liberation was finally achieved either by arms or by negotiations, and around 1965 very few Muslim countries were under non-Muslim rule. The latter amounted only to Israel and certain regions of central Asia. To establish their political independence and obtain a degree of economic and technological power as soon as possible, the Muslim countries have developed universities and specialist institutes, seeking to create an industrial substructure. With the aim of co-ordinating their efforts, several organizations bringing together representatives of different Muslim countries have been created, like the Muslim World League (*al-rabita l-islamiyya*) or the Islamic Conference. The oil weapon used by the petroleum-producing Muslim countries after the October 1973 war between Israel and the Arab countries and the subsequent influx of petrodollars had profound repercussions, not all of which are yet visible, leading to the creation of an Islamic bank and so on. In the absence of a caliph, the Muslim world is orientated on a kind of League of Muslim Nations. Only its internal divisions hamper its movement.

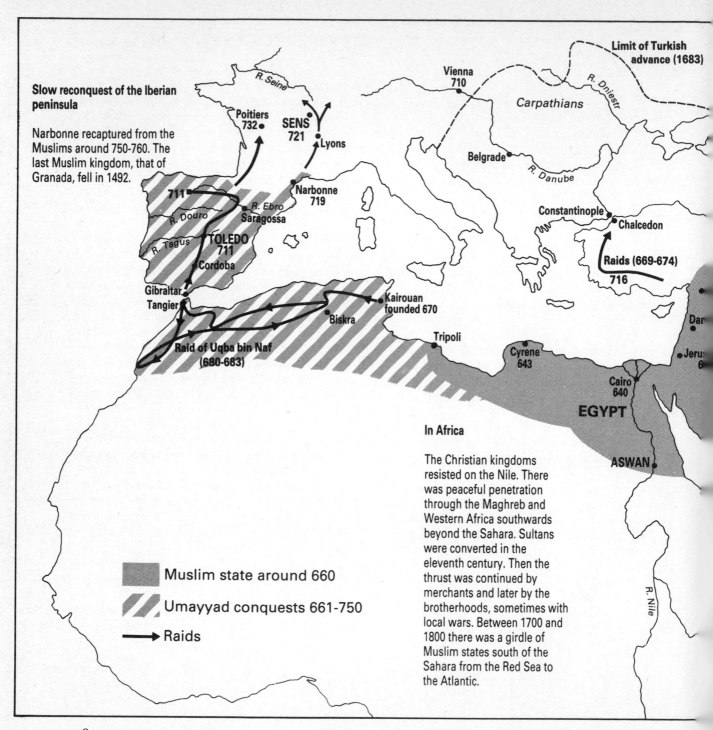

Slow reconquest of the Iberian peninsula

Narbonne recaptured from the Muslims around 750-760. The last Muslim kingdom, that of Granada, fell in 1492.

R. Seine

Vienna
710

Carpathians

R. Dniestr

Limit of Turkish advance (1683)

Poitiers
732

SENS
721

Lyons

Belgrade

R. Danube

Narbonne
719

R. Ebro

711

R. Douro

Saragossa

Constantinople

Chalcedon

R. Tagus

TOLEDO
711

Raids (669-674)
716

Cordoba

Gibraltar
Tangier

Kairouan
founded 670

Biskra

Dar

**Raid of Uqba bin Naf
(680-683)**

Tripoli

Jeru:
6

Cyrene
643

Cairo
640

EGYPT

ASWAN

In Africa

The Christian kingdoms resisted on the Nile. There was peaceful penetration through the Maghreb and Western Africa southwards beyond the Sahara. Sultans were converted in the eleventh century. Then the thrust was continued by merchants and later by the brotherhoods, sometimes with local wars. Between 1700 and 1800 there was a girdle of Muslim states south of the Sahara from the Red Sea to the Atlantic.

R. Nile

Muslim state around 660

Umayyad conquests 661-750

Raids

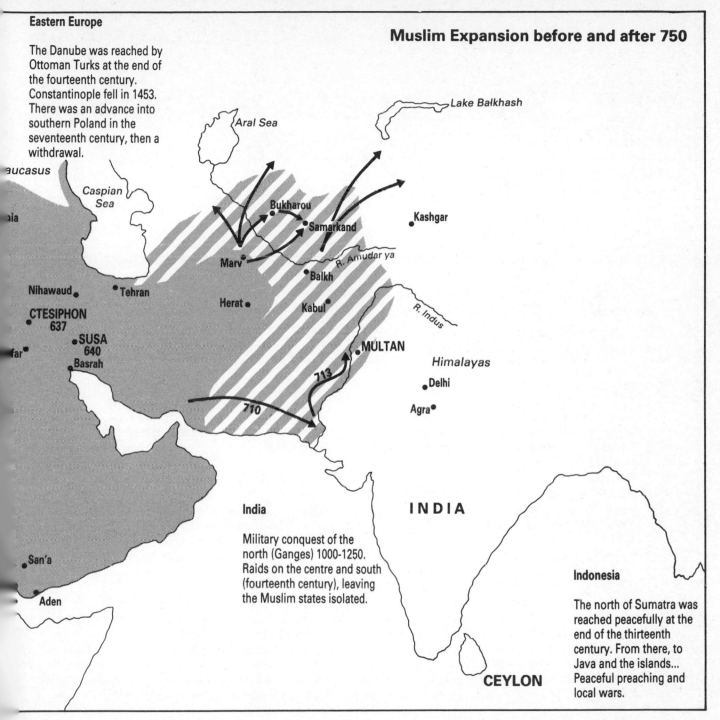

Muslim Expansion before and after 750

Eastern Europe

The Danube was reached by Ottoman Turks at the end of the fourteenth century. Constantinople fell in 1453. There was an advance into southern Poland in the seventeenth century, then a withdrawal.

Aral Sea

Lake Bałkhash

Caucasus

Caspian Sea

ia

Bukharou

Samarkand

Kashgar

Marv

R. Amudar ya

Balkh

Nihawaud

Tehran

Herat

Kabul

R. Indus

CTESIPHON
637

SUSA
640

Basrah

713

MULTAN

Himalayas

Delhi

far

710

Agra

India

Military conquest of the north (Ganges) 1000-1250. Raids on the centre and south (fourteenth century), leaving the Muslim states isolated.

INDIA

San'a

Aden

Indonesia

The north of Sumatra was reached peacefully at the end of the thirteenth century. From there, to Java and the islands... Peaceful preaching and local wars.

CEYLON

29

3

The Penetration of Islam into Africa South of the Sahara

Africa occupies a special place in the history of Islam. It comes directly after Asia in terms of the number of Muslims living there. Ethiopia served as a place of refuge for the first Muslims who were persecuted, as early as the lifetime of Muhammad. Egypt was conquered less than ten years after his death, and all the southern shores of the Mediterranean were occupied by the year 700.

South of Egypt, the Muslims had been stopped in their progress by the Christian kingdoms of Nubia, at the level of Aswan, along the Nile. A trade agreement had been made between the Muslims and these kingdoms after the Muslims had been forced to respect their independence. The penetration of Islam by this axis was also very slow. It only really revived after the fall of the Christian kingdoms of Dongola (fourteenth century) and Soba, near Khartoum (beginning of the sixteenth century). Blocked on this side, Muslim progress took other routes.

The Sahara desert formed a vast, sparsely populated tract; but the deserts, like the oceans, are there to be crossed, and caravans traverse them ceaselessly. After the failure of military attempts, it was the Muslim traders who opened up ways for Islam south of the Sahara.

Penetration was achieved through three areas:
– the most important movement began from North Africa and went through the Sahara towards the south;
– another current linked the ports of southern Arabia (and sometimes those of Persia) with the coasts of East Africa on the Indian Ocean.
– finally, there was a thrust from Arabia towards Africa through a short sound, via Somalia and southern Ethiopia. Later, the Red Sea crossing was immediately opposite the Sudan.

The penetration from North Africa

The establishment of Islam took place progressively. A series of Arabic texts, local chronicles, geographical works and accounts by great travellers, allow us to reconstruct the main stages of this penetration. The traders came first: the existence of areas which they occupied is attested very early in the towns of Gana at that time. A second stage was that of the conversion of kings and sultans, whose peaceful or warlike action resulted in the conversion of the nobility. In this context Islam was above all an Islam of finance, of men of letters, of warriors, of traders. The role played at a very early stage by the pilgrimage of rulers to Mecca and the existence of schools in which Arabic was taught should be noted. In fact, Arabic script was adopted and cultural links were established with Muslim centres in North Africa, Mecca and Cairo.

It took a long time for the mass of the people to be affected. It seems that it was the brotherhoods on the one hand and the holy wars waged by the Fulani kingdoms in the eighteenth and nineteenth centuries on the other which allowed penetration into the bush and the countryside. So we should look into these points in more detail.

First, the conversion of the rulers of kingdoms. This began south of the Sahara after the year 1000. So the Sanhaja Berbers of Mauretania (among whom a religious and political movement, that of the Almoravids, came into being) saw their chief Tarsina (who ruled from 1020 to 1023) embrace Islam. The warlike expeditions of the Almoravids (spurred on by Ibn Yasin) reached Gana, where it seemed inevitable that Islam should triumph; however, Gana became pagan again for a time.

Among the Songhay, at Gao on the Niger, the first Muslim king was za Kosoy, who ascended the throne in 1009.

Near Lake Chad, one of the rulers of the kingdom of Kanem, which had been reached by Islam from Kufra in the eighth century, was converted to Islam in the second half of the eleventh century.

In Senegal, a local ruler made the same move around this time.

Mali was only to be affected later. Its rulers became Muslims in the thirteenth century. The case of one of them, Sun Dyata, is not clear. But the pilgrimage of another, who became a Muslim in the last third of the same century, is attested. And the famous pilgrimage which King Kanku Musa made in 1324 was a talking point for all the Arab chronicles.

The dates of the penetration of Islam to the Hausa are a matter of discussion. In the fifteenth century, the towns of Katsina and Kano had Muslim princes. But things go further back than that. The *Chronicle of Kano*, a history of the city written in Arabic, gives us some idea of this first process of Islamicization. In the second half of the fourteenth century, Muslims arrived at Kano. They invited the ruler to embrace Islam, preached to the people, nominated a muezzin to call them to prayer, an imam to preside over them and a butcher to be sure that the animals whose meat the Muslims were to eat should be killed legally, and chose a place for prayer under a tree. The Muslims fell foul of the adherents of traditional religions; someone even defiled the place of prayer. The Muslims took steps to protect themselves and finally there was a flare-up.

It would happen that certain rulers left Islam to return to the faith of their ancestors. That happened among the Songhay and elsewhere. Finally, however, Islam was adopted again. Certain countries even went into eclipse or disappeared from the political scene and others replaced them. This was true of the Bornu, who succeeded the Kanem as the Muslim centre in the region of Lake Chad.

Since it came from North Africa, Islam propagated knowledge of Arabic, either in an elementary way, so that the faithful could say their prayers in that language, or more deeply. Funerary pillars with inscriptions in Arabic can still be seen at Gao on the Niger. They bear witness to the prestige that Arabic enjoyed in the eyes of the nobility of the country in the twelfth and thirteenth centuries, when they were inscribed. At that time there were centres of study in which the teachers of the country were assisted by scholars from the Maghreb: Kanem, Mali and Gana each had their own. Timbuktu was one of them (this city was then taken by Moroccans in 1590); Jenne also had its scholars.

Exchanges took place between these points of Arabic culture and other centres abroad. People coming from long distances stayed there, like Ibn Battuta, who in his famous travel accounts describes his stay in the Sudan (fourteenth century). Similarly, scholars from Sudan went to study in Arab countries. In the thirteenth century a school was reserved at Cairo for students coming from Kanem. Later an Egyptian teacher at Cairo in the seventeenth century explained that he had composed a certain book at the request of scholars coming from West Africa.

Nowadays the collections of Arabic manuscripts which can be found in many libraries in West Africa attest the place which Arabic has long occupied in the cultural life of this zone. Culturally, Muslim West Africa gravitated into the Arab orbit.

The second feature which characterizes Islam in West Africa is the role played by the Muslim religious brotherhoods – a role which they still play today. With their arrival the presence of Islam took on a new aspect and the penetration of the people became more effective. A brotherhood called Qadiriyya appeared in the regions bordering on the southern Sahara around the end of the fifteenth century. This name derives from that of Abd al-Qadir al-Jilani, under whose patronage it had put itself; al-Jilani died in Baghdad in 1166. This brotherhood spread throughout the world, over both India and the Arab countries; it is one of the two or three main brotherhoods which have made a powerful contribution to the Islamicization of Africa.

Among its members two scholars are known to have exercised a quite special influence: a scholar from North Africa, Muhammad Abd al-Karim al-Maghili, who came from the Hausa country (Kano, Katsina) around 1500, and Sidi Mukhtar al-Kabir at the end of the eighteenth century.

We shall return to this subject later in connection with the brotherhoods.

The last striking feature in the history of Africa south of the Sahara is the action of the Fulain in the eighteenth and nineteenth century. These Fulain are thought to have originated in East Africa; they came to the West several millennia ago and at a late stage formed kingdoms. First in Guinea, at Futa Jalon and Futa Toro, they began to make war with a view to subjecting to Islam tribes that were still pagan (at Futa Jalon in 1825 and at Futa Toro in 1776).

At Sokoto, another group led by Shehu Uthman Dan Fodio (who died in 1817), his brother Abdullayeh (who died in 1829) and his son Muhammad Bello (who died in 1837) conquered a vast territory extending from the present Niger to the northern Cameroons (Adamawa). This holy war of Uthman Dan Fodio was directed against the Hausa Muslim emirs, who were accused of practising a perverted Islam and were attacked in the name of the purity of the faith that the warriors of Sokoto came to re-establish. Both Uthman and his brother Abdullaye were affiliated to the brotherhood of the Qadiriyya, while his son Muhammad Bello joined a new brotherhood founded at the end of the eighteenth century by an Algerian whose tomb is at Fez, in Morocco, that of the Tijaniyya.

In the buckle of the river Niger there was a Fulain empire known under the name of the Empire of Masina. The example and the encouragement of the Fulain of Sokoto drove the ruler Shehu Hamadu, who reigned from 1810 to 1844, to act. He brought the empire to the summit of its power and succeeded in converting to Islam almost all the Fulain with whom he came into contact; he also had dealings with a large number of Bambara. He founded a new capital in 1815 and called it Hamdullahi (which means 'praise be to God'). These wars waged by the Fulain were imitated by other Muslims in West Africa. The name of al-Hajj Umar Tall (1794? – 1864) has thus become famous. Born in a district of north Senegal he left on a twelve-year journey in December 1825. On his outward route he made a first contact with Sokoto, Cairo, etc. At Mecca he studied with a Moroccan who was closely acquainted with Ahmad al-Tijani, the founder of the Tijaniyya, whom he joined. On his return journey he stopped at Cairo and made contact with al-Azhar, the great centre of Muslim teaching. In 1830 he was again *en route* for Sokoto, where he remained, marrying a daughter of Muhammad Bello. When the latter died in 1837, he travelled on again. He returned to found a state near the present-day frontier between Senegal and Mali. He had contacts with the French, who were beginning to occupy Senegal. However, after a first clash he avoided coming into conflict with them and attacked the local kings further to the East (capturing the towns of Nyoro, Segu, and Hamdullahi, capital of Masina). A coalition was formed against him. He died (or committed suicide) in 1863 in the neighbourhood of Hamdullahi; it was under siege and he was trying to escape. He was supported by the brotherhood of the Tijaniyya, to which he belonged, and he worked to extend it around him.

In the same line one can also mention Samori Ture, born in 1746, who took Kankan (in Guinea) in 1873 and resisted the French.

Muslim penetration on the coasts of the Indian Ocean

The Arabs had had trade relationships with these coasts well before Islam. It seems that the Muslim presence began with groups of political refugees and traders who came from the Arabian-Persian gulf. It is to them that the foundation of towns like Mogadishu (908), Kilwa (975), Mombasa, Pate and Zanzibar is attributed. In the fourteenth century the Arabs disembarked on the Comoro islands and these islands continued to be connected with Zanzibar. The Comoro islands and Zanzibar were almost totally Islamicized. On the continent, except in the cases of Mogadishu and Somalia, the traders did not disseminate Islam because the kinds of operations in which they were engaged (above all trading in ivory and slaves) put their relations with the local populations on a very special level.

In the nineteenth century, the Arab establishments (Arab blood being in fact mixed a good deal with African blood in the veins of the inhabitants) formed staging posts on the routes leading into the interior of the country and Lake Tanganyika; these included the centres of Tabora and Ujiji. It was the suppression of slavery, combined with the fact that the Muslims were opposed to European education, which allowed Islam to spread in these areas.

The Muslims used a Bantu language for grammatical structures, but it included a large number of Arabic words, almost one in five or one in six.

In the vocabulary of civilization and in religious vocabulary most words are Arabic. The very name of this language, *kiswahili*, signifies 'language (one of the meanings of the Bantu prefix *ki*) of the coasts' (*swahili*, from *sawahil*, plural of *sahil*, meaning coast in Arabic) or, if one prefers, language of the eastern coasts of Africa, along the Indian ocean. The word civilization is either modelled on the corresponding Arabic word (*tamaddun*), or means 'become an Arab' (*usturab* modelled on *isti'rab*, to become Arab). This language is spoken in Kenya, in Tanzania, in the east of Zaire and in many other places.

At present (except in Somalia and in the islands of Zanzibar and the Comoros) Islam is still a minority faith in East Africa. Muslim colonies can also be found in Mozambique and Madagascar.

In Zaire, Islam penetrated at the end of the nineteenth century through the 'Arabs', the most celebrated of whom is Hamid bin Muhammad al-Murjibi (around 1840–1905), known under the name of Tippo Tip, who traded and collaborated with the explorers and later became governor of the Rapids District (later to be Stanleyville-Kisangani). Around 1925 movements towards conversion were noted. In the East, the district of Kasongo has a Muslim majority; in Kisangani their presence is tangible. How many are they in all? For a long time their number has been underestimated. While many were saying in 1967 that they were only 50,000, there were probably more than 300,000. By now they may well number over 500,000. Be this as it may, figures eight times greater than these, which are given by the Muslim authorities in Zaire, do not have any substantial basis.

Penetration through Ethiopia and the Sudan

This took several centuries to happen; as in Nubia (southern Egypt), the presence of Christian kingdoms which resisted the Muslim advance delayed the conquests. Islam came in by the port of Zayla, on the northern coast of Somalia, through the Gulf of Aden. Still Christian in the tenth century and subject to Ethiopia, two centuries later Zayla became the centre of a confederation of Muslim states which extended their rule through war. Harrar, now in Ethiopia, turned Muslim, and the role which it enjoyed made it a holy city of the region.

The distribution of religions in Ethiopia largely follows ethnic lines, though obviously with marked exceptions. Christianity (under its Coptic form, i.e. attached to the Patriarchate of Alexandria in Egypt), was practised by the ethnic groups living on the high ground, while Islam gradually penetrated those living at a lower altitude. However, the highlands were attacked by the Muslims in the sixteenth century, and thanks to the superiority of the firearms that the Turks had procured for them, the Muslims were on the point of winning. But the Ethiopians appealed to the Portuguese, who sent a contingent armed with muskets to help them. The attackers then had to withdraw.

At the beginning of the twentieth century the Christians dominated the country politically. During the 1914–1918 war an incident took place. The negus of the time, Lij Yasu, who was very well disposed towards the Muslims (and whom some said had been converted to Islam) and to the Central European powers (Germany allied to the Turks), was deposed by an opposition movement led by the clergy. Was Ethiopia at that time on the point of becoming Muslim?

The majority in southern Ethiopia, which was still pagan at the beginning of this century (ethnically the population was Galla), went over

Wooden tablet used by pupils in the Qur'anic school in Morocco around 1955. Passages from the Qur'an to be learned by heart were written on them.

This tablet contains Qur'an 3, 38–43, beginning:

Tell the unbelievers that if they mend their ways their past shall be forgiven;
but if they persist in sin,
let them reflect upon the face of their forefathers.
Make war on them until there are no more temptations[1]
and all religion is for God.[2]

1. For faith and for the existence of Muslims.
2. I.e. Islam.

to Islam between 1930 and 1950. At this time, the Italian occupation, which only lasted for a few years, relied on the Muslims against the Negus, who was Christian. The Galla also held against the Christians the fact that above all they represented the dominant race which had colonized them. The official statistics have long indicated an equal proportion of Christians to Muslims for Ethiopia (40%), but it is probable that the Muslims have now gone into the majority (i.e. over 50%). In the time of the negus, the Muslims said that they were neglected in comparison with the Christians; with the establishment of the revolutionary Marxist government there is no longer any favouritism for religious reasons and the problems are the same for Christians and Muslims.

Finally, we should note that after the disappearance of the Christian kingdoms of Nubia, on the Nile, north of present-day Sudan, and then with the Islamicization of the kingdoms situated between Khartoum and Lake Chad, all the countries surrounding the Sahara had become Muslim (by the seventeenth/eighteenth century). The Waday, the Darfur and the Kurdufan had all been touched by Islam by about 1600. In all these regions, the Muslim brotherhoods also played an important role in the spread of Islam. A Qadiri preacher who was particularly active exercised his ministry along the Nile valley around 1550; he was called Taj al-Din al-Bahari.

Conclusion

This survey of Muslim expansion has been very rapid. Many more dates and figures could have been cited. Moreover, these glimpses should above all have been supplemented by a picture of economic activities, and by a reminder of the role that Muslims played in spreading the technology, science and philosophy of the time. In dialogue, this simple recollection will prevent our forgetting that Muslims are proud of this expansion and of the power of the Muslim world.

However, one question does arise. Having been disseminated in a multitude of countries in which ancestral characteristics, climate and social tendencies are very different, has Islam always remained the same? It is certain that some specific affinities can be seen between believers in the same zone; the Muslim Arabs form a distinct group who do not react to events in the same way as Turkish Muslims. So within the Muslim world large groups can be distinguished: the Arab world, the Turkish world, the Iranian

world, the Indian sub-continent, Indonesia and Malaysia. Despite everything, however, the Muslims of today, like those of the past, the Muslims of the East like those of the West, have a common foundation. And voices are at present being raised in protest against expressions like 'black Islam'. These say that there is only one Islam.

Perhaps two distinctions can be made. First of all, educated Muslims who are aware of their religion have no doubt about their fundamental Muslim identity. And the works of a Pakistani like Abu'l Ala al-Maududi are translated and read in Arabic by traditionalist Muslims who rate them as highly as the works of Shaikh Hasan al-Banna or Sayyid Qutb; the type of person, whether traditionalist or progressive, counts more than the country of origin. Similarly, the classic objections addressed by Muslims to Christians are identical from Dakar to Indonesia. On the other hand, it can happen that newly converted populations or individuals remain very superficially Islamicized for several generations or even longer. Since Islam asks only for a simple profession of faith from the new convert, he and even his descendants often continue to think and act in ways which are very dubious. In West Africa for a long time all the population accepted the practices against which Uthman Dan Fodio, the master of Sokoto, unleashed his holy war at the beginning of the nineteenth century. However, in general the Islamicization of newly-converted families and groups goes on, and in time the situation returns to normality.

Secondly, this problem does not only arise with Islam; it exists everywhere. It is certain that the inhabitants of the world are both the same and different. The need for happiness and love, rivalries and jealousy, ambition and fear, to mention only these, exists everywhere, but the forms which they take vary a great deal. Islam, like all movements and all religions, is no exception to the rule.

The common heritage of all Muslims is first of all formed by a complex of dogmas and laws, fidelity to the Qur'an and to the memory of Muhammad, pride in belonging to the Muslim community and a feeling of superiority over those who are not part of it. That can be found everywhere. Islam is a clear stream, with well defined characteristics, which is the same everywhere. But the soil over which this stream flows can be very varied. Moreover, in each case the water will take on the colour of the stones, the sand or the earth which form its bed.

We shall first study the stream itself, i.e. the dogma and the law that Muslims still learn everywhere in all the schools of the world. Then we shall try to see the colouring that this stream has taken in the modern world; what Islam brings to the modern world and what response it has made to the great challenges of the day. In the course of doing this we shall stop here and there to note certain particularities of Islam in Africa.

4

The Dogma of Islam

The dogma of Islam has often been compared with that of Judaism and Christianity. For the Muslim, the question is clear: Moses and Jesus taught exactly the same things about God, human destiny, sin, death, the last things, heaven and hell, and Muhammad merely took up this teaching. For the Muslim, all the prophets brought the same religious doctrine, even if the legislation which God charged them with promulgating could be different. For Jews and Christians things are more complicated than that, and we shall be returning to the subject.

A first glance at the dogma of Islam shows it to be characterized both by a very great simplicity and by the insistence with which the faithful are reminded of it. Whether in prayer, in everyday life, in art or in preaching, advantage is immediately taken of every occasion by the devout Muslim to talk about dogma. Nor do the faithful just discuss it. Their sensibility has been impregnated with it, and all their existence is indelibly marked by it. This dogma is evoked either briefly, in lapidary formulae, or in a detailed way in more complete expositions.

The most concentrated profession of faith,

called the *shahada*, is as follows: 'There is no god but God (Allah) and Muhammad is his Prophet.'

This two-fold recognition of the Oneness of God and the role of the spokesman of the deity which has devolved on Muhammad underlies everything. It is demanded of anyone who wishes to become a Muslim; it is enough to recite it without any other ceremony. Since Islam has no sacraments, and therefore no baptism, no more is required, other than the presence of two official witnesses to legalize the confession.

There are other texts which express the faith of the Muslim. The Qur'an is full of them. However, the community retained some passages in preference to others because their content was more profound. Like this verse, which is very often quoted:

Believers, have faith in God and His Messenger, in the Book He has revealed to His Messenger, and in the scriptures He formerly revealed.
He that denies God, His angels, His scriptures, His Messengers,
and the Last Day, has strayed far from the truth.
(Qur'an 4, 6; the same text appears in Qur'an 2, 177).

These affirmations have been the origin of a whole literature which develops this doctrine. Then the example and the sentences of Muhammad (preserved in the stories [hadith] of the tradition [sunna]) show how the dogma has been lived out and interpreted authentically. Finally, Muslim theologians have produced works which expound the different points of this creed and comment on them. Their work extends from the very concentrated catechism to the voluminous treatise. Without being official, some of these works enjoy considerable fame. In West Africa the most widespread until recently was the little catechism called the 'Aqida of Muhammad bin Yusuf al-Sanusi (who died in Algeria in 1490).

Here I shall take up the five articles mentioned in the verse from the Qur'an which I have just quoted: belief in God, in the angels, in the revealed scriptures, in the Messengers of God and in the Last Day. And theologians add another article: belief in the divine Decree.

The Verse of the Throne

God, there is no god but Him,
the Living, the Eternal One.
Neither slumber nor sleep overtakes Him.
His is what the heavens and the earth contain.
Who can intercede with Him except by His permission?
He knows what is before and behind men.
They can grasp only that part of His knowledge which He wills.
His Throne is as vast as the heavens and the earth, and the preservation of them both does not weary him.
He is the Exalted, the Immense One.

Qur'an 2, 255

Belief in God

The Muslim believes in one God, eternal, creator, omnipotent, who sees all and knows all, infinitely good and merciful, who is harsh on those who oppose him, who forgives those who ask him but punishes the wicked severely.

We rediscover in Islam this faith which underlies Judaism and Christianity, even if the way each religion represents God may differ. But whereas Judaism and Christianity discovered God through sacred history and his pedagogy as much as, if not more than, in his power as Creator, the Muslim puts the stress on the God of creation. As for history, the Muslim sees it almost uniquely through the law of the triumph of the Messengers and the annihilation of those who oppose them. The rest of the allusions to the past are anecdotal and fragmentary. Muslims do not allow the anthropomorphic expressions or poetic imagery used to speak of God in the books of the Bible, and especially in Genesis. Their own dogma is clear and simple, presenting objections and responding to them. Our way of seeing things is completely alien to them because they take the Qur'an and only the Qur'an into account, excluding all other sacred books.

The existence of God is regarded as self-evident and the Qur'an does not seek to prove it. On the other hand, the Qur'an and Islam after it continually stress the oneness of God. A Muslim of our day, Dr Ismail al-Faruqi, a Palestinian who taught in the United States, wrote,

> The essence of Islam is its witness to the oneness of God (*tawhid*) or, if one prefers it, the affirmation that there is no god apart from God. This *tawhid* restores to man the dignity that certain religions have denied him by representing him as fallen or existentially wretched. In calling man to exercise these prerogatives given by God, Muslim preaching rehabilitates him and re-establishes him in his integrity, his innocence and his dignity. This moral vocation is the way to his success. Certainly the Muslim is called to a new theocentrism, but it will be that in which the cosmic dignity of man is applauded by God and by the angels (*International Review of Mission*, October 1976, 399).

This is how he presents Islam in contrast to what he thinks Christianity to be.

Creation is at the forefront of Muslim thought. It is the great subject put forward by the Qur'an for the continual meditation of the faithful. 'In the creation of the heavens and the earth, and in the alternation of night and day, there are signs for men of sense; those that remember God when standing, sitting and lying down, and reflect on the creation of the heavens and the earth, saying: "Lord, you have not created these in vain. Glory be to You! Save us from the torment of Hell-fire, Lord!"' (Qur'an 3, 188–191). In fact by its unity the creation shows that the Creator is one (cf. Qur'an 23, 93; 21, 22). It equally proves the vanity of the false gods, which are incapable of creating anything, even a fly (Qur'an 22, 73).

The Qur'an, which is very combative and apologetic, also makes use of every possible argument to affirm and reaffirm this oneness of God. At one point, for example, it relates a well-known story from rabbinic literature, that of Abraham breaking all his family idols save one, which he accuses of having broken the others. It's incapable of doing that, someone retorts. If it's incapable of doing that, then why do you worship it? Why do you worship an incapable object? (cf. Qur'an 21, 52–70).

The meaning of monotheism

For the Muslim, monotheism does not signify only the unity of God, because there can be several persons in the unity. Monotheism in Islam is the absolute oneness of God which formally does away with the notion of persons participating in the divinity.

The opposite of monotheism in Islam is designated by an Arab word *shirk,* i.e. the fact of giving God associates.

Shirk includes not only polytheism but also dualism and pantheism. All forms of philosophies of an incarnate God are excluded by the monotheism of Islam, as are blind obedience to dictators, to clergy or to one's own whims and desires.

Extract from a communication by al-Hajji U.N.S. Jah at an Islamic-Christian conference at Freetown, Sierra Leone, in 1986.

Furthermore, the creation reminds man of the mercy of God who frees him and supplies his needs. It also shows the power of God, which is capable of giving life and thus of restoring it on the day when he raises the dead.

Confronted with God, man is like a servant before his master. God is the 'Lord' of the universe; this truth is inscribed at the heart of human nature and man has no excuse if he does not recognize that (cf. Qur'an, 7, 172).

Muslim piety likes repeating the names or the attributes which the Qur'an or the tradition give to God. So the faithful repeat the same name or the same attribute dozens of times before going on to the next. In this way God is presented as the Sempiternal, the Maintainer, the Merciful, the All-Knowing, the Powerful, the All-Hearing, the Oft-Pardoning, the Avenger, and so on. Tradition has collected ninety-nine divine names, most of which are taken from the Qur'an. The believer submits of his own free will to the will of God; he entrusts himself to it with confidence, an attitude which is so characteristic of Muslim faith that it has given it its name, Islam, i.e. voluntary submission of one's own free will, active or not depending on circumstances, to God.

This attitude about the oneness of God is accompanied by attacks on any worship of anyone other than God. Islam fought fiercely against the religions which accepted other gods alongside the one God, the creator, for example pre-Islamic Arab polytheism. We too have in common with Muslims all that relates to the *De Deo uno*, the treatise on the divine oneness.

On the other hand Muslims accuse us either of wanting unduly to penetrate the hidden mystery of God or to divinize a prophet like Jesus and make him a god over against God. A well-known tradition orders the faithful to reflect on creation but to dispense with any reflection on the mystery of God in himself.

Some Muslims are persuaded that present-day Christians worship three Gods (either the triad God, Mary, Jesus or the three persons Father, Son and Holy Spirit). They are also opposed to the Christianity of the great church in the name of the divine Unity. They think that authentic primitive Christianity was a sort of Arianism or Unitarianism which regarded Jesus only as a prophet, a superior man to whom God entrusted a mission. For them, our Christianity is a distortion arising over time or as a result of the impious action of certain people. The name of St Paul is sometimes put forward as that of the one who corrupted the faith, although many Muslims have no knowledge of Paul. However, it is certain that the Muslims regard themselves as the true disciples of Jesus, the only ones who are still faithful to his teaching.

In our religious relations with the Muslims it would be very important to get to the point where they see that Christians, too, worship only one God, only one creative power, and that Jesus is not an 'other' god alongside God.

Belief in angels

Belief in angels seems to be experienced in different ways by Christians. But Muslims have a very lively faith in the invisible world; this is particularly marked in popular belief and that also used to be the case among women. The Qur'an speaks of angels; it also mentions the jinns or genies, a kind of being akin to spirits, who are organized into communities and among whom there are also Muslims and non-believers. In the Qur'an, the surahs Al-Ahqaf (46, verses 28–31) and the Jinn (72, passim) give some details about these beings with whom Muhammad is said to have had an encounter after his journey to Ta'if and the attempts he made to rally the nomads (around 620).

Muslim faith envisages angels in the strict sense in various circumstances. All accept that the angel Gabriel, called the Holy Spirit by the Muslims, has been the instrument of revelation, bringing the texts of the Qur'an from God to Muhammad as he did earlier texts to previous prophets. Similarly, everyone believes in the two guardian angels which a man always has with him to note his actions: he greets them to his right and to his left at the end of every ritual prayer. Heaven and hell are also places in which angels live, entrusted with God's praise or vengeance. This belief has often been amalgamated with vestiges of pre-Islamic beliefs. A certain number of notions about angelology appear in the making of talismans, the performing of cures, etc.

Basically, the main question to which the most well-disposed Muslims expect Christians to give a convincing answer is this: What difference is there between Muslim monotheism and Christian monotheism? And it must clearly emerge from the answer that Christians are truly monotheists, without any qualification.

The most beautiful names of God

This is an attempt to render into English these ninety-nine names of God.

When a particular name is often used with 'Abd as a masculine pronoun, I have indicated the Arabic word in a literal translation, e.g. *Abd al-Rahman*, servant of the Merciful God.

1. The Merciful (*Al-Rahman*)
2. The Compassionate (*Rahim*)
3. The Sovereign (*Al-Malik*)
4. The Holy (*Al-Quddus*)
5. The Consummate
6. The Guardian
7. The Masterful
8. The Almighty (*Al-Aziz*)
9. The Compeller
10. The Proud
11. The Creator (*Al-Khaliq*)
12. The Evolver
13. The Fashioner
14. The Oft-Forgiving
15. The Vanquisher
16. The Bestower (*Al-Wahhab*)
17. The Donor of Livelihood
18. The Revealer
19. The All-Knowing (*Al-Alim*)
20. The Constraining
21. The Munificent
22. The Degrading
23. The Enhancing
24. The Exalting
25. The Abasing
26. The All-Hearing (*As-Sami'*)
27. The All-Seeing
28. The Judge
29. The Just
30. The Subtle (*Al-Latif*)
31. The Ali-Cognizant
32. The Clement (*Al-Halim*)
33. The Supreme
34. The Remitter (*Al-Ghafur*)
35. The Prodigal
36. The Sublime
37. The Great
38. The Maintainer
39. The Sustainer
40. The Sufficer
41. The Majestical (*Al-Jalil*)
42. The Bounteous (*Al-Karim*)
43. The Vigilant
44. The Responder
45. The All-Embracing
46. The All-Wise
47. The Benevolent
48. The Glorious (*Al-Majid*)
49. The Resurrecter
50. The Witness
51. The Verity
52. The Champion
53. The All-Powerful
54. The Puissant
55. The Protector
56. The Laudable
57. The Reckoner
58. The Originator
59. The Restorer
60. The Life-Giver
61. The Life-Taker
62. The Omniscient (*Al-Hay*)
63. The Dominating (*Al-Qayyum*)
64. The Entire
65. The Illustrious
66. The One (*Al-Ahad*)
67. The Sanctuary
68. The Potent (*Al-Qadir*)
69. The Omnipotent
70. The Advancer
71. The Retarder
72. The First
73. The Last
74. The Evident
75. The Immanent
76. The Lord
77. The Transcendent
78. The Benefactor
79. Accepter of Repentance (*Al-Tawwab*)
80. The Avenger
81. The Oft-Pardoning
82. The Most Kind
83. The Owner of Sovereignty
84. The Lord of All Glory and all Honour
85. The Equitable
86. The Congregator
87. The Absolute
88. The Endower
89. The Averter
90. The Harming
91. The Useful
92. The Enricher
93. The Splendid
94. The Guide (*Al-Hadi*)
95. The Superb
96. The Sempiternal (*Al-Baqi*)
97. The Heir
98. The All-Wise
99. The Infinitely Patient (*As-Sabur*)

The revealed books

Note that for the Muslim, the sacred 'Book' comes before the Prophet in the list of articles of faith, for the Prophet's role is only that of the transmitter of a pre-existent Book. The communication of revealed 'Books' would appear to be the sum of the interventions of divine grace in favour of humanity.

Muslim theology hitherto has always held very traditional positions on the theory of revelation, and attempts at an *aggiornamento* on this point, which have been modest and rare, have always hitherto come up against a lack of receptivity. Perhaps the situation will change one day. At present, then, the revelation of holy Books is seen as the transmission of a pre-existent text coming down as it is from on high, without the Prophet playing the least active role in the operation. According to common teaching, he only receives the texts and repeats them. The revelation is a kind of dictation or, to put it another way, a lesson learned by heart. Only a few rare contemporary Muslim thinkers have gone further. One of them argued in 1966 that for him the Qur'an was entirely the Word of God and in a sense entirely the word of Muhammad. If such a position were accepted one day, we would rediscover the idea of the instrumental role played by the Prophet under the moving of

God. But we are still far from that.

For the Muslim, the great Messengers of God – Moses, David, Jesus, Muhammad – transmitted literally the respective books which were dictated to them: the Torah, the Psalms, the Gospel (in the singular), the Qur'an. Other older books (those of Adam, Seth, the leaves of Abraham) are sometimes mentioned by commentators on the Qur'an. However, regardless of whatever lip service may be paid to these books and the veneration that is due them, all, except the Qur'an, are in practice dismissed as not offering a sure text. And as the Qur'an contains *everything*, reading them cannot offer anything new. Those who read them do so on their own account, usually either with the apologetic purpose of finding mistakes and distortions in them or in order to discover in them an echo of the teaching of the Qur'an by choosing texts which can be reconciled with the Qur'an and then passing quickly over others which they judge to have been distorted. In the Arab world it may also be that the inferior stylistic quality of the translations of the Bible and the Gospels are a very serious obstacle to possible Muslim readers. In spite of everything, there are certain rare figures who have approached them objectively.

The Prophet-Messengers

Islam distinguishes between the inspired prophet (*nabi*) who has not received a particular mission, and the Messenger (*rasul*) who has. Every messenger is necessarily a prophet, but the reverse is not true. Furthermore, a small

number of these Messengers have been given the mission of handing down sacred books. The Qur'an gives the title of Messenger to the main figures of the Bible which it mentions between Adam and Jesus, including Noah, Moses, etc. To these it adds some Arabian Messengers, unknown to the Bible, like Salih, who was given a mission among the Tamudians, an Arabian people; Hud, sent to the people of Ad, in Southern Arabia; Shu'ayb, among the Midianites east of the gulf of Aqaba, north of the Red Sea. The role of the great biblical prophets between the ninth and the fifth century BCE is virtually passed over in silence. According to Islam, the Messengers all announced the same religious message, above all monotheism; for the religion which God wants is based on a dogma which is immutable and has been taught perfectly from the beginning, without any progress in revelation. Only legislation can vary.

The Messengers have all been sent to particular people; each of them has gone to 'his' people to whom he belongs and whose language he speaks. Thus from the Muslim point of view Jesus was sent only to the children of Israel. Only Muhammad, the seal of the Prophets, is the exception to this rule: he received a universal mission, valid for the whole of the last period of the history of the world.

In spite of all this, the role played by the Prophet-Messengers in the Qur'an poses a problem. It is seen in two quite different perspectives. The first is dominated by the great Qur'anic law of history, and the mention of the Prophet-Messengers seems to have been made to emphasize the fate which awaits the opposition. It is useless to look in the Qur'an for any information about the personality or history of Salih, Hud and Shu'ayb. We learn that Salih, sent to his Thamud people, exhorted them to respect the traditions about a sacred camel, which had to be given the drinking water it needed. Salih gave this message during a period of drought and the people refused to obey; they were therefore annihilated. The text does not say more than this. The mention of Abraham in certain surahs is made the occasion for the recitation of the passage about the 'guests' who destroy Lot's city; so again this is in connection with an instance of the application of the same law. And

The Sin of Adam

[Muslims] also believe that human nature is not 'fallen'. Adam certainly disobeyed God in the Garden of Eden; he was punished and repented; and that is one of the facts of the *discontinuous* history of humanity as Islam conceives it, the sole bond of which, as I have already said, consists in a simple recognition of the Oneness of Allah. Moreover, the descendants of the first man were condemned to be born outside the paradise in which their father had been created; but their present nature is identical to their original nature.

The Muslim will also be inclined to enjoy this world and not to 'depart from his smallness'; a natural tendency which is corrected by the moral sense of many Muslims and the profound spirituality of certain great spirits of Islam. It is equally true that, generally, Muslims are both freed from earthly things and trapped in them. Allah alone remains, it is true; but Allah too does not bear any resemblance to His creature and cannot in any way communicate himself to it to transform it and raise it up to Himself.

J.-M. Abd el-Jalil
L'Islam et Nous, Editions du Cerf, Paris 1981, pp. 62f.

sometimes, in connection with Moses, the text simply says that Pharaoh did not listen to him and was therefore punished terribly in the waters of the Red Sea. In Qur'an 89, 9 only Pharaoh is mentioned, without any allusion to Moses.

In this first perspective, talk of the Prophet Messengers derives from warnings to contemporaries who were opposed to Muhammad. If they do not stop, the same fate awaits them.

However, in a second perspective, some Prophet-Messengers preserve a degree of personality. Abraham, Moses and Jesus are not only examples intended to prove the truth of the Qur'anic law of history; they have some more positive features. Abraham obeys without reserve the God who demands his son. He fights for monotheism. He is the ancestor of the cult at Mecca; he has spoken so that God may feed the inhabitants of Mecca and send a Prophet to the Arabs. Moses with his role as a political prophet, the leader of the people, prefigures Muhammad. Jesus has his goodness, his filial piety, his miracles; he announces the future coming of Muhammad. Finally, Moses and Jesus received the Torah and the Gospel as Muhammad received the Qur'an. Their attitude confirms the teaching of the Qur'an on monotheism, total obedience to God, respect for parents unless they incite their children to unbelief, the struggle for truth, and so on. They are Muslims before the Muslims.

In the first case, the history of the past is fragmented into atomic moments, each people being called to live in its turn an adventure analogous to that of the others. The bond which exists *de facto* between the various people mentioned is hardly of interest and is not spoken of. In this context Islam appears as the Arab form of the eternal religion. In the second case, the stress is on the biblical line: Muhammad is presented as the reformer of Judaism and Christianity after Jews and Christians were unfaithful to Moses and Jesus.

Subsequently, Muslim theology developed the idea that the prophets were without sin and infallible. A special grace of God (the *'isma*) prevented them from doing wrong or sinning, and if sometimes the Qur'an refers to prophets who ask for forgiveness or to God who grants them his forgiveness (cf. the beginning of surah 48 for the sins of Muhammad), these are only peccadilloes or the beginnings of an impulse which is immediately restrained. In short, it is no more than a matter of falling short of the most perfect act that they could have accomplished. For a Muslim, for example, it is *a priori* impossible that Aaron should have been actively involved in the business of the Golden Calf or that David should have been guilty of adultery and murder. Commentators produce a multitude of hypotheses about the story in which David asks forgiveness after being presented with the story of the rich man who stole the poor man's sheep: in the worst case he would just have cast a rapid involuntary glance at the woman in question (cf. Qur'an 38, 23–24). In the case of Jesus the Qur'an has no allusion to any sin that he might have committed or that might have been forgiven, and a verse recalls that Mary's mother put her daughter and her descendants under the protection of God against Satan, who is stoned (Qur'an 3, 31–32). Some Muslims accept the Christian suggestion that this is a recognition of the 'immaculate' character of Mary, but others do not think that this text goes so far.

There are traditions which establish a hierarchy between the greatest Prophet-Messengers. In the story of Muhammad's journey to heaven, the text has him penetrating each of the seven heavens in succession. In each of them he meets one of the great Prophet-Messengers; the highest places are those of Abraham and Moses. Jesus is well below them. As for Muhammad himself, all Muslims put him at the head of all the prophets.

The case of the Prophet-Messengers poses another problem for theologians. How do these men prove the authenticity of their mission? Objections recalled that the prophets of old performed miracles to attest the divine origin of their mission, and they called on Muhammad to do the same. The Qur'an first protested against this demand by reiterating the affirmation of the divine origin of the Qur'an and then presented itself as the great miracle proving the authenticity of the revelation received by the Muslims. The professions of faith affirm that the Qur'an is of divine origin and has qualities the like of which no creature has or could have. The Qur'an challenges human beings and jinns to produce a single surah (chapter) which could be equal to the Qur'an. And as no one can take up the challenge, Muslims would hold this to be definitive proof of the divine origin of the Qur'an. Their faith in the authentic character of Muhammad's mission is tied up with this reasoning. We shall be speaking of this later, since it is an essential point of difference between Christians and Muslims.

The last things (resurrection, judgment, heaven and hell)

A good deal of Muslim dogma relates to the upheavals at the end of the world, the resurrection of the body, emerging from the tomb at the sound of the last trumpet, and then the judgment itself with the balance to weigh actions, the books which are opened, the verdict, and then paradise for some and hell for others. As among the millennarians, the description of future happiness gives a good deal of room to material promises, which include the promise of women of paradise (houris) who are reserved for the elect. These promises have sometimes been developed to a degree of crudity which is difficult to take in popular literature. However, the climax of this happiness will consist in knowing that one is accepted by God and in being happy with him.

The vision of God is mentioned in the Qur'an, but the commentators discuss it without being able to define it. A tiny minority think that the material descriptions of paradise are only the symbol of a more spiritual happiness, but the majority take them literally. As for the responsibility of human beings, it is clearly, though implicitly, accepted in the texts on the judgment. The wicked will be condemned for having done wrong.

In fact, human beings will be judged by their actions. The good Muslim wants the good works which he has done to weigh more than his wicked actions in the balance at the last judgment. The sin which cannot be forgiven, in fact the only mortal sin for most Muslim theologians, is *shirk*, the crime of setting other gods

After death

'The Qur'an teaches that life is a test, that life on this earth lasts only for a while (Qur'an 67, 2). The Muslim believes that there is reward and punishment, that there is a life after this one, and that reward or punishment are not necessarily kept for the Day of Judgment but begin immediately after the funeral. The Muslim believes in the resurrection, in human responsibility and in the Day of Judgment.'
Extract from a communication by al-Hajji U.N.S. Jah, at an Islamic-Christian conference in Freetown, Sierra Leone, 1986.

alongside God. The one who is guilty of this loses the benefit of all his good actions, which as a result no longer have any value. For the majority of Muslims, and following the position held by a theological school which has been dominant since the Middle Ages (that of the Ash'arites), hell will not be eternal for the believer. The intercession of Muhammad will secure release from hell, even if this may be after thousands of years of punishment, for those of his faithful in whose heart there is even an atom of faith. Several theologians, like al-Ghazali (1058–1111CE), accept that the infidel of good faith can be saved if he is not morally responsible for his unbelief and if he acts rightly. However, far more exclusivist positions on the damnation of infidels remain widespread.

There are traditions which class sins as 'great' and 'small'; however, this distinction does not coincide with that made by Christianity between mortal sins and venial sins. It is simply a matter of the relative importance of one or the other: not to respect the rights of parents, deliberately to kill a Muslim, to commit adultery, to calumniate a virtuous Muslim, to run away from the *jihad* (see box, p. 121), and for some groups to drink alcohol, are considered to be very grave sins.

This belief in other-worldly realities is to be set alongside the dearest family sentiments; it is evoked by the death of kinsfolk and friends, in different ways depending on the region, and is often associated with ancient local traditions. In Arab and Turkish countries one often finds this

---

The sin which cannot be forgiven

God will not forgive those who serve other gods beside Him; but He will forgive whom he will for other sins. He that serves other gods besides him is guilty of a heinous sin'.

Qur'an 4, 48

---

inscription engraved or painted on tombs:

All who live on earth are doomed to die. But the face of your Lord will abide for ever, in all its majesty and glory (Qur'an 55, 26).

Belief in the divine decree

This last article of faith is taught in two famous traditions; it has made a firm mark on Muslim spirituality. It is a matter of believing in 'the divine decree for good and evil, sweet and bitter', i.e. of believing that everything has been decided by God, that in one sense everything comes from Him. It is a way of entrusting oneself entirely to divine providence. Thus believing families in many countries down to our own day have taught their children to be content with what happens to them: we find this attitude especially in the face of tribulations, illness and death.

This belief in the divine decree cannot fail to cause a problem. For on the one hand it presupposes the Omnipotence of God who creates what he wills: 'God created you and created what you make' (Qur'an 37, 96). Furthermore, the Qur'an notes that He is the one who fixes the term of life, the term of nations, who provides the basis for all life, and so on. That is easily understandable in connection with anything that happens to a man and which does not depend either on him or on his like. Whatever human beings receive from nature comes from God.

But what do we say when human responsibility is involved? There are in fact very clear Qur'anic texts about human responsibility. Human beings are the masters of their actions and must give account of their conduct on the day of the last judgment. When the Qur'an calls for fighting against the enemy, it is addressing free men capable of acceptance or refusal.

In the Middle Ages, this question of human

freedom and divine decisions was discussed at length. Even now, one can often see Muslims asking whether man is free or whether his actions are dictated from elsewhere. One mediaeval theological school, the Mu'tazilites, proclaimed human freedom; however, this school was supplanted by another, that of the Ash'arites, who reduced human freedom in order to exalt the ominpotence of God.

By contrast, the Qur'an affirms the omnipotence of God and human freedom in parallel. Even now, all Muslim reformers stress action, the duty of action, while knowing that everything comes from God, the forces needed for action, human faculties and so on. Everything comes from God but men and women are responsible for what they do.

A comment on the magisterium

A last comment about dogma. Though Islam regards the Qur'an, read in the light of the traditions of the Prophet, as the source of dogma, it does not accord any of its followers a special power to interpret it. The caliph was the political leader of the Muslim community; he did not have any special religious power. There is no *magisterium* in Islam as there is in the Catholic Church, charged with supervising the conservation of the deposit of faith.

Where the dogma is simple, all is clear and everyone is in agreement. But opinions can be divided over delicate questions. In that case a certain number of individuals or more specialized bodies give their opinion. These can be doctors of the law; as this often happens in the absence of any priest, the authority devolves to those with religious knowledge. So there is a certain number of problems in connection with which jurists pass on lists of names of scholars who have given one solution and those of others who have given a different one. This happens in

deciding whether a particular mystical doctrine is acceptable.

Several organizations perform the role of giving legal judgments on the legitimacy of one position or another. Some simply hold their authority on the basis of the reputation of the body to which they belong, like the organization of legal consultations (called *fatwa* in Arabic) which is dependent on the great al-Azhar University in Cairo.

But as some decisions sometimes have consequences which affect the public life of a country (for example the dismissal of a particular professor whose teaching is unsound, and so on), an official organization for legal consultations, dependent on the government, is generally provided for. If one individual is the authority, he will be called the *mufti*, i.e. the one who gives *fatwa* or legal consultations. If the authority is a group, it is called the Dar al-Fatwa, the house of *fatwa*. In each Muslim country, the supreme authorities of Islam are therefore on the one hand the directors of institutes of Muslim studies or the president of the Muslim university if there is one, and on the other the supreme judge of the religious tribunals, i.e. the grand *qadi* and above all the grand *mufti*, the supreme *mufti* of the country, to whom the most important cases are submitted as a last resort.

To establish his decision, the *mufti* will have recourse to a certain number of principles which we shall consider shortly.

This situation makes it difficult to use the term 'orthodox' in connection with one position or another. Can one speak of an orthodox Islam as opposed to a form of Islam which is not orthodox? Many specialists challenge the validity of this expression. It is more correct to speak of positions in conformity with tradition. However, there is a consensus which is widely shared on essential positions: anyone who forgot it would soon find Muslims closing ranks against him.

5

The Law of Islam (The Five Pillars)

The Law of Islam (called *shari'a* in Arabic) has always occupied an important place in the Muslim world. In fact Islam is the religion of a law, a fact which, *mutatis mutandis*, in some respects recalls the Hebrew Bible. Moreover, since 1965–1970, this Muslim law has been very much in the news. The official doctors and movements supporting a return to authenticity call for the strictest application of it and stress that twentieth-century legislation is strongly marked by Western and not Muslim models, with the exception of certain sectors like that of personal status.

In fact the question is not a simple one, and first we should specify more clearly the significance attached to the expression 'Muslim law'. Is this an intangible code existing since the beginnings of Islam? To what degree is it legitimate to make amendments to this code? In what form has it already been applied? These are all important questions which it would be rash to evade.

The fundamentalist movements proclaim that the Qur'an is the constitution of the world. That is the way in which they refer to the commandments contained in this book. These commandments exist, but in fact not many of them relate to specific issues, while other verses evoke the general attitude to be adopted, for example the sense of justice in the question of relations between husbands and wives, in both marriage and divorce. Moreover, an examination of the practice of the primitive community shows that this legislation has some associations with very early customs, whether Arab, Judaeo-Christian, or even those observed in conquered countries.

With rare exceptions, Muslims themselves recognize that the Qur'an needs to be made more precise. The details of legislation on ritual prayer, marriage and inheritance, to take just these examples, is fixed by texts which complement what is said in the Qur'an. Similarly, a whole jurisprudence directs the application of the Qur'anic law. It has laid down the conditions on which particular measures are to be decided. For example, it is provided that someone guilty of adultery must be put to death. But as a Qur'anic text stipulates that no accusation in this sphere is valid unless based on the evidence of four men who caught the culprit *in flagrante delicto*, and as this condition is virtually never fulfilled, the death penalty is only imposed in the case of a confession.

The Qur'an contains verses about the veiling of women. In spite of that, some uncertainty remains, as there are two different traditions on this point. One requires that only the eyes of a woman of marriagable age should be visible and that the rest of her body should be hidden. The other allows her to keep her face, hands and feet free. Hence the possibility of discussions. Which text is to be chosen?

In the case of abortion, which is strictly forbidden from the moment when the foetus is a living being (all infanticide is normally prohibited), the question arises as to when animation begins. As the majority of Muslim scholars think that this is after 120 days, many Muslim doctors of the law allow abortion during the first three months of pregnancy, prohibiting it in the fourth month to be on the safe side.

Interpretations go even further. In the case of the thief whose hand has to be cut off, a failure to apply the penalty has been justified by the precedent of caliph 'Umar, who suspended this penalty during a famine; since masses of people do not have enough to eat, jurists have thought that the law should not be enforced.

In practice, some characteristic points of the *shari'ah* – women's dress, cutting of a thief's hand, the ban on alcoholic drinks and on loans at interest, and killing a Muslim who apostasizes – which have been abandoned throughout the Muslim world have continued to be observed where power was very traditionalist, as in Saudi Arabia. Today, fundamentalist Muslims demand that these laws should be applied again.

But in what form should the *shari'ah*, the Muslim Law, be revived? A look at the way in which this law is constituted will enable us to see the issue more clearly.

How is Muslim law constituted?

For the Muslim, it is quite evident that the Qur'an is, and must be, the essential basis of all Muslim law: where the Qur'an expresses a precept clearly, the obligation is absolute. But when is a precept expressed clearly? And in what cases does such a precept relate to particular circumstances which will not occur again later?

The Qur'an, composed in a very concise style, does not go into details, or does so only rarely; the words and examples of Muhammad in the first place, and sometimes those of his companions, have served to illuminate the legislation. These examples and these words have been systematically collected in a stereotyped form, that of the traditions or *hadith*, which have played a very major role in Muslim law, as in the spirituality of Islam.

The collections of traditions are presented as a series of texts juxtaposed and classified in accordance with their subject matter. These texts can differ in content; they range from the brief two- or three-line sentence to the account which takes up several pages. Each of them is called *matn*. Thus, for example, the famous affirmation, 'Intentions count more than actions'. Moreover, each text is accompanied by a kind of authentication. This consists in a list of names of persons who have handed down the text: one such has told me and another told him and another told that man, and so on, until the chain goes back either to Muhammad himself, to an eye-witness of the event in question, or to someone who heard the teaching. This sequence of names is called the *isnad*.

Nowadays these traditions are grouped together in classic books. This was not always the case, and to begin with they were transmitted orally, probably after being formed into small specific collections. It was only gradually that the science of *hadith*, or traditions, appeared. First of all they had to be collected. For that the Muslim scholars undertook very long journeys, going to consult those who knew about their local past.

Finally the collection of these scholars was set down in writing. Two and a half centuries after the beginnings of Islam, the Muslim community was in possession of the two most famous collections of traditions, which are still very authoritative and are regarded as the most substantial. These are the 'Authentic' ones (that is the meaning of the title in Arabic), the *Sahih* of the two scholars al-Bukhari (who died in 869) and Muslim (who died in 875). Other collections also enjoyed considerable renown. It is impossible to cite all of them.

The science of *hadith* was then enriched with much critical work. Even Muslims themselves confess that the literary genre of the traditions is not always certain. Many forgeries which sought to claim the patronage of the Prophet have gone through the mill of *hadith* criticism. Control over all the traditions in circulation was established; the Muslims also subjected them to a systematic examination. Their efforts were primarily concerned with external criticism: Is the chain of transmission probable? Could one reporter really have heard another? Can this reporter be trusted? The result was the composition of numerous biographical dictionaries, classifying the specialists on the traditions by successive generations.

The importance of the control of the authenticity of texts by lists of those who handed them down should be remembered in dialogue, since many Muslims would like Christians to be able to guarantee the authenticity of their Gospels by similar methods. Rather than follow the long and demanding researches of modern historical method, many of them would like to have a list of the names of those who handed down the Gospels from one person to another. Perhaps the place accorded by Muslims to those who handed down the traditions should be compared with the significance attached to lists of popes or bishops which have come down among Christians, safeguarding the deposit of faith and consecrating their successors.

However, the work of the jurists had to go further than that of the traditionalists. For though the Qur'an and the traditions provided ample material for legislation, not everything had been provided for, and decisions had to be taken on new points in the interest of the community. Some scholars, putting forward different principles, became the origins of different legal schools. Among these principles we should note: the universal accord of scholars living at a given period on a given question (in Arabic *ijma'*), common interest (*istisiah*), personal interpretation (*ra'y*), and reasoning by analogy (*qiyas*). The different positions taken over these principles were the origin of various schools; everything was discussed, explained and argued over vigorously. There was unbounded work both in the sphere of the legal principles (*usul al-fiqh*) and in that of casuistry which recalls that of the rabbis: it was exercised on numerous questions, some of which were vital.

For a long time theologians had discussed whether the major obligations of the Muslim Law were in conformity with an objective good or whether they depended only on the good will of God, who could say that evil was good and good evil. In the Middle Ages, the predominant theological school, that of the Ash'arites, who were concerned to safeguard the omnipotence and the absolute freedom of God, were of the opinion that good depended solely on the good will of God. Today, many Muslims following in the footsteps of the reformist movement from the beginning of the twentieth century accept the objectivity of the good.

The main legal schools

At present, following a secular tradition, Muslims are divided into several legal schools which are sometimes called 'rites' because they also specify details of liturgy. The differences are often minimal. For example, must one keep one's arms to the side when reciting the beginning of the ritual prayer or cross them over the chest? Is it or is it not permissible for non-Muslims to visit mosques? Does the fiancée of a Muslim have the right to have a clause included in her marriage contract authorizing a request for divorce if the marriage goes wrong? And so on.

At present the four main schools are:

– The Hanafite school (not to be confused with the term *hanif*, used to denote the independent monotheists of Arabia at the time of Muhammad, to whom Muhammad proclaimed his attachment). This school derives its name from its founder the imam Abu Hanifa (died 767) from Mesopotamia, who is buried in Baghdad. It was disseminated above all by the Turks and can now be found in Turkey, India, China and has adherents in countries once dominated by the Ottomans. Broad-minded without being lax, this school likes to appeal to reason (personal judgment, quest for the better, and so on).

– The Malikite school of the imam Malik, who died in 795 in the Hijaz, is implanted in Arabia, North and West Africa, Upper Egypt and the Sudan. It stresses a broad appeal to the principle of general utility, evoking among some people the idea of the common good.

– The Shafi'ite school of imam al-Shafi'i (died 855), who is buried in Cairo. It can be found in Lower Egypt, Syria and Southern Arabia, whence it spread to Malaysia, Indonesia and East Africa. This is an attempt to combine tradition and the consensus of the Muslim community (rather than the consensus of individual scholars) and results in a broad recourse to reasoning by analogy.

– The Hanbalite school of imam Ibn Hanbal (died 855), which is clearly marked by a return to a strict traditionalism and is virtually confined to Arabia. It has inspired the reform movement of the Wahhabites.

The legal sciences have continued to be the object of considerable activity. Those who know them best think that it is in the sphere of the *usul al-fiqh* or principles of Law that the most original aspects of Muslim thought are to be found. Free personal research or *ijtihad* in this area has been very limited. At present (or at any rate before the fundamentalist revival of recent years), there have been numerous calls for the reopening of the 'gates of the *ijtihad*'.

There was a trend at the beginning of the twentieth century to relativize the difference between the schools, and Egypt, for example, has used different ones in legislation depending on the needs of the moment, and borrowed from them all. Often one meets Muslims who refuse to say to what school they belong; they say that they are just Muslims.

The authorities I mentioned earlier in connection with the doctrinal control of the community also have a voice in these legal questions. This is where the officially nominated *mufti* or scholars exercise their knowledge and their wisdom most. Their opinions can have profound consequences when they say, for example, that a particular war is just and has to be carried on with vigour, or confirm the justification for a death penalty. These same opinions are sometimes tinged with politics, and it may happen that a *mufti* who refuses to approve a new law finds himself removed, to be replaced by another more docile *mufti*. This was the case in Tunisia when President Bourguiba wanted to pass laws relating to the practice of Ramadan or the prohibition of polygamy.

What obligations does Muslim law impose? Who is subject to it?

The Muslims recognize a universal moral law which largely corresponds to the moral part of the Decalogue (from the fourth to the tenth commandment): not to kill, not to commit adultery, not to steal, not to bear false witness, and so on. Its commandments appear throughout the texts of the Qur'an without there being any exhaustive official list comparable to the Ten Commandments. A long passage from the Surah of the Night Journey (Qur'an 17, 23–39) will give some idea of this.

There is also a strictly Muslim law which we have to note. It is at puberty that the Muslim is considered to be bound by this positive law on condition that he is of right mind – there are some other conditions in the case of slaves. But the custom is to prepare children and adolescents for it earlier, especially for ritual prayers and to some degree for the fast of Ramadan.

Muslims distinguish between obligations on all believers personally and obligations on believers collectively. For example, from puberty onwards, every individual must perform his five prayers ritually every day: he is personally under a kind of obligation called *fard 'ayni*. By contrast, the *jihad* (see below p. 121) is a collective obligation (*fard al kifaya*) incumbent on the community as such. The authorities then apportion specific tasks, organizing the army and services, including religious teaching, behind the front, which must not be abandoned. They resort to volunteers or conscription depending on what seems best to them.

The basic obligations of the specifically Muslim law are known under the name of the Five Pillars of Islam. They are an obligation on each individual Muslim after a certain age who is in a condition to be subject to the law. They are mentioned in the following tradition:

> The Messenger of God has said: Islam is built on five (foundations): the witness that there is no god apart from God and that Muhammad is the Messenger of God – the performing of ritual prayer – the payment of social taxation (or legal almsgiving) – the pilgrimage to Mecca – and the fast of Ramadan.

These religious values reappear under other forms as the basis of biblical monotheism: the Hebrew Bible knew the struggle for monotheism and belief in the Law and the Prophets. Pilgrimages to Jerusalem were provided for several times a year. And the Sermon on the Mount in the Gospel of Matthew contains teaching of Jesus on the triad of prayer, alms and fasting.

The first of the five pillars

Witness to the oneness of God and Muhammad as his Prophet

This witness (called *shahada* in Arabic) is formulated as follows: 'I bear witness that there is no god but God and that Muhammad is the Messenger of God.'

I have rendered the word Allah as God. Some Westerners (and sometimes even converts to Islam) keep the word Allah without translating it. Many Muslims dislike this style. Why not simply say God? Arab Christians use Allah in talking to or about God. This formulation of faith is so characteristic of Islam that it is enough to pronounce it to be considered a Muslim. It is proclaimed in a slightly different form by the muezzin, the official in charge of calling the faithful to prayer. It is taken up by the faithful in a more muted form (the *tashahhud*) in the course of ritual prayer and is made ceaselessly in everyday life. It underlies invocations which are repeated during the course of pilgrimages; and at the hour of death the believer tries to repeat it with special fervour. The Muslim is indeed a champion of the divine oneness.

His attachment to Muhammad can also be seen in the details of his existence. Ordinary believers praise their Prophet on many occasions in their lives. And even those who would seem to be most emancipated from religious ideas preserve at heart a very deep feeling which prompts them to react against anyone who slights the memory of Muhammad in their presence.

The use of a negative phrase (there is no god but God) in the *shahada* formula gives the expression a manifest clarity. It does away with that which is not God, but it preserves the question of the mystery of God in himself, a mystery which it does not penetrate, and which the believers keep themselves from touching on by virtue of a characteristic attitude of Islam. However, though the use of simple formulae has numerous advantages, it does carry with it the risk of making people forget in practice that even monotheism is mysterious, and that there is a mystery in God, because he is so inaccessible. In dialogue, if the one with whom we are talking is not aware of the mysterious character of God and His intimate life, we risk not being on the same plane.

This witness to the divine oneness has consequences in everyday life: it supports a refusal to submit to authorities who go against the Qur'an and against Islam. During the period of colonial occupation, this attitude encouraged national resistance movements to offer cultural resistance. Expressing the same idea in a different form, the formula *Allahu Akbar* ('God is the greatest, God alone is great') has been the war cry of the Muslim armies. On 6 October 1973, when the Egyptian army assaulted the Israeli fortifications on the Suez canal, the soldiers advanced shouting *Allahu Akbar*. Those who die in the holy war are also regarded as martyrs, witnesses to the divine oneness.

The same force has also inspired the action of numerous mystics within Islam, the supreme aim of whom has been to proclaim and live out in their lifetime the truth that there is no god but the one God and thus to do away with all the false gods whom men and women might follow, beginning with the 'self' whom we so often adore.

The second of the five pillars

Ritual prayer

Muslim faith is rooted in a series of observances, especially in ritual prayer and the fast of Ramadan. Even if not everyone accomplishes all that Islam asks on this point, there are enough faithful to do so, and the community bears their stamp. The discipline of prayer has made a special contribution towards maintaining the vitality of Islam. So what is this prayer?

From puberty on, and depending on some other conditions (notably being in a condition of legal purity), every Muslim man and woman is obliged to offer five daily prayers. These are the essentials of the Islamic liturgy. Moreover at noon on Friday men have to meet at the mosque for common prayer; this ceremony also includes a sermon. In addition to daily prayers and those on Friday, there is a special prayer for each of the two great festivals of the year and there are other prayers for various occasions (funerals, public disasters, and so on).

The Arabic word which denotes ritual prayer, and which has been taken over by many Muslim languages, is *salat*. Other types of prayers, invocations, requests and so on, are denoted by the word *du'a*. In talking with Muslims in English it is always important to know whether the person with whom one is talking is using the word 'prayer' to mean an individual ritual prayer, like *salat* in Arabic, or is talking of prayer in a wider sense; this will avoid a good deal of confusion.

'Lord, to You be the praise!'

(*Rabbana laka l-hamd*)

Invocation pronounced in the course of ritual prayer, on rising from the first deep bow.

Individual ritual prayers are said in private. Some of the faithful gather together in the mosques, but this is not absolutely necessary. The use of Arabic is compulsory (with the rarest exceptions which are provided for by the Hanafite school). Bodily postures and formulae are carefully specified. Although children are not yet under an obligation, they are often initiated into prayer from the age of seven to familiarize them with the ritual, and it is recommended that they should pray regularly from the age of ten. Men and women are equally obligated to offer private prayer; women are excused temporarily only during periods of legal impurity (e.g. during menstruation).

Prayer is performed in a state of ritual purity; hence ablutions beforehand if they are necessary. It is impossible here to go into the details of this observance. Suffice it to say that minor defilements are removed by minor ablutions (water on the feet, forearms and hands, face and head, mouth, nose and so on). These are the kind of defilements contracted on relieving oneself, breaking wind, bodily contact with the skin of a person of another sex who is not a close relation (even shaking hands), without some fabric as a barrier. Greater defilements, on the other hand, like those of sexual origin, call for complete ablutions of the whole body. Legal treatises provide a mass of details on this question, on the kind of water needed, on the clean sand which can replace water if none is available, and so on.

To pray, the Muslim stands on clean ground, without shoes or wearing clean shoes. The cleanliness of the ground is often provided by a special carpet. He faces Mecca, or the Ka'ba if he is in Mecca, and formulates his intention of reciting a particular prayer.

The gestures are regulated by each legal school but differ little from one school to another. At all events these variations do not change the general significance of this liturgy.

Each ritual prayer is composed of several similar elements which the faithful repeat. Each element is called *rak'a* or inclination. The time of the call to prayer is fixed ritually; as soon as the call to prayer ends (due account having been taken of foreseeable delays), the faithful present in the mosque line up facing the *mihrab*, the niche which indicates the direction of Mecca, and join together in pronouncing ritual formulae. This presence at the mosque is purely optional, except that men must be there at noon on Friday. Each individual is required only to pray in private, each prayer being made between the call to it and the call to the next prayer. It is not permissible to anticipate its recitation; to delay it after the time allowed by law is tolerated for good reasons.

55

The sentiments stressed in prayer

First is obedience to God. The Muslim obeys God's orders and loves to obey them. He comes to present himself before his Lord with fear and reverence, though at the same time trusting in the goodness of God.

Prayer is equally a proclamation of the greatness of God and of his oneness. Man prostrates himself before God and adores him. This aspect appears clearly in the gestures of bowing and prostration and in the frequency of the use of the formula *Allahu Akbar*, God alone is great, the greatest.

When Muslims speak of prayer, they also stress the fact that, like all observances, it brings human beings nearer to God.

> When My servants question you about Me, tell them that I am near. I answer the prayer of the supplant when he calls Me (Qur'an 2, 186).

Like all good actions, prayer contributes towards purifying the one who performs it and towards obtaining forgiveness for his sins. It gives him the strength to do his duty (Qur'an 2, 45) and to be steadfast in trials (Qur'an 2, 153).

The five daily ritual prayers

Each is made up of an elementary prayer repeated with minimal variations, twice, three times or four times

Dawn prayer (*al-fajr*)
– at the end of the dark night (repeated twice)

Noon prayer (*al-zuhr*)
– when the sun is past the zenith (repeated four times)

Afternoon prayer (*al-'asr*)
– after the middle of the afternoon (repeated four times)

Evening prayer (*al-maghrib*)
– immediately after sunset (repeated three times)

Night prayer (*al-'isha*)
– around an hour and a half after sunset repeated four times)

The call to prayer

This is made from the mosques before the ritual hour of each of the five daily prayers in order to remind the whole neighbourhood of everyone's duty. Sometimes it is broadcast on the radio in Muslim countries, at least at noon on Friday, and often throughout the month of Ramadan. For some years Egyptian Radio has retransmitted the calls at the time desired, interrupting normal broadcasts for them and resuming programmes when the call is over. In Muslim cities, at the hour of prayer the calls can be heard coming from all the minarets like the sound of bells in an Italian city on a Sunday morning.

The official in charge of giving the call is named the muezzin. The first muezzin in the history of Islam was the African Bilal; he ceased his functions on the death of Muhammad. When he was in Jerusalem some years later, at the capture of the city, he was asked to chant solemnly a new call to prayer. Nowadays the voice of the muezzin has been replaced by amplified voices from loudspeakers or even by tape recordings.

Everything is chanted in Arabic. When Turkey wanted to impose the Turkish language for this observance it came up against obstinate resistance and had to abandon the effort after a few years.

Here is the text of this appeal as given in the legal treatises. The number of repetitions of each phrase follows the practice of the Shafilite rite (or school). The Malikite rite of North and West Africa has fewer repetitions.

- God alone is great (*Allahu Akbar*, four times)
- I testify that there is no god but God (twice)
- I testify that Muhammad is the messenger of God (twice)
- Come to prayer (twice)
- Come to success (twice)
- God alone is great (*Allahu Akbar*, twice)
- There is no god but God (once)

At the time of the dawn prayer the muezzin adds: 'Prayer is better than sleep'.

The call to special prayers at the two great festivals (the end of the fast of Ramadan and pilgrimage sacrifices) is different and very short.

The faithful do not repeat the call. It is praiseworthy to respond in private to the formulae of the call by one traditional invocation or another.

The prayer itself

During the ritual prayer the faithful evoke the goodness of God; they thank him. For the formula 'Praise be to God' (*al-hamdu lillah*) that we shall encounter in the ritual is a common way of expressing gratitude. In everyday life it is the Arabic for 'thank-you'; and Muslims whose native language is other than Arabic use it without translating it. The faithful recognize the Lordship of God (an essential point in Islam), recall the last judgment and ask God to guide them.

Here is how each *rak'a* or element of prayer which I have just described is performed.

The believer stands facing Mecca or the Ka'ba with open hands, palms forward at head height, and recites the first *Allahu Akbar*. This is called the *Allahu Akbar* of sacralization, because it puts those who pronounce it in the sacred state of prayer. Then still standing, hands by his side or arms crossed, he recites the Fatiha, the first surah (chapter) of the Qur'an.

After the Fatiha it is usual (at least during the first two *rak'a* of each prayer) for the believer, still standing, to recite one or more verses of the Qur'an as he chooses. In very rare circumstances these verses are fixed by tradition.

Then begin the movements by which the believer's body expresses his adoration. First he makes a deep bow from the chest, stands upright again, prostrates himself (knees and forehead to the ground), and sits back on his heels with his knees still on the ground. Then he again prostrates himself with his head to the ground.

The invocations which punctuate these movements express praise and recognition of the greatness of God. I shall not mention all of them. By bowing and prostrating himself he affirms God's glory and greatness. By rising from his deep bow he says, 'God has mercy on those who praise him.' But there are above all five more *Allahu Akbars* which act as a command for (or accompaniment to) the gestures. Each of them is followed either by the beginning of the bow or the beginning or end of the prostrations.

Towards the end of the prayer, at a moment which the ritual provides for, on his knees, sitting on his heels, the believer silently recites a profession of faith called *tashahhud*. This simply develops ideas that we have already seen: the oneness of God, and Muhammad as his Messenger.

Otherwise there is no provision for an explicit request for pardon, but the ablutions can be understood in this sense. The request for pardon is often mentioned in the Qur'an and in the private prayers of the Muslim brotherhoods. In ritual prayer the help asked for from God is only to be evoked. However, in silence, during one of the moments provided for individual petitions, many of the faithful are accustomed to ask for pardon. At all events, they know that their prayer is a good work which blots out their evil deeds (cf. Qur'an 11, 114).

Communal prayer on Friday takes up the same ritual. However, a long public recitation of the Qur'an before prayer and a sermon further stress the Qur'anic character of the liturgy. The four *rak'a* of the prayers at Friday noon are thus spread out: two are performed by the believer individually on arrival if there is no exercise at this point, and two are performed communally after the sermon.

The great prayer of Islam

'In the name of God, the Compassionate, the Merciful
Praise be to God, Lord of the Creation,
The Compassionate, the Merciful,
King of Judgment-day!
You alone we worship, and to you alone we pray for help.
Guide us to the straight path
The path of those whom You have favoured,
Not of those who have incurred Your wrath,
Nor of those who have gone astray.'

This prayer is called the Fatiha, i.e. the 'Opening' of the Qur'an, of which it is the first chapter.

We should note the sober formulae in all the ritual prayers, and the role of the mention of God and the repetitions. These characteristics recur in other forms of Muslim devotion.

At the end of each prayer, after the last *rak'a* the believer, still with his knees on the ground and sitting on his heels, offers salutations to right and left, wishing peace to those next to him, and at least to his two guardian angels if he is alone. Once all are standing upright, this salutation of peace is often followed by a general exchange of handshakes as a sign of brotherhood.

The bow and the prostrations were customary among monks at the time of Muhammad. The Christian monks of Ethiopia still perform similar gestures.

The common prayers on Fridays, at festivals and those which are said on certain occasions (at funerals, when calling for God's help, and so on) have a marked social aspect. They are presided over by an imam (literally the one who is to the fore, the president), a literate person who has usually done a minimum of Qur'anic study. Any male Muslim (if there are males present), for a man does not pray behind a woman presiding over prayer, can take his place, Islam being a religion of lay people without priesthood. More precisely it is a society in which all the members enjoy equal religious status. The faithful of other so-called 'scriptural' religions have their place there as protégés and do not take part in either worship or prayer.

The Friday prayer also has a social and political aspect. The name of the ruling sovereign (formerly that of the caliph) was mentioned during the sermon: not to do so was an act of rebellion.

The esteem in which Muslim society holds prayer has an influence on the opinion that Muslims have of other religions. Not only do Muslims often accuse Christians of being impure (because they do not practise ablutions), but at present they are accused of not praying, or hardly praying at all.

The Muslim liturgical year

These daily and weekly liturgical prayers are set in the framework of a liturgical year which it is important to know.

The Muslim year follows the lunar calendar, i.e. it is composed of twelve lunar months, going from new moon to new moon. As each lunar month can comprise twenty-nine or thirty days, the whole year amounts to around 354 days. The pre-Islamic Arabs, like the Jews, had the same type of lunar year (see the mention of the festival of the new moon at the beginning of each lunar month in the Hebrew Bible), but they made corrections so that their calendar would not be too far removed from the natural cycle of the seasons. In Arabia a supplementary month was added every three years to compensate for the shift. Thus the great annual festivals always fell in the same seasons.

The Muslims have suppressed this intercalary month, and the Qur'an called it 'an excess of unbelief' (Qur'an 9, 36–37). So now the Muslim festivals recur each year eleven days earlier than in the previous year. Thus the month of fasting or the observances of the pilgrimage can coincide with the hottest times of the year and yet sixteen years later take place at the coldest times. After thirty-two or thirty-three years the lunar and solar years again coincide. Around 1945 the fast of Ramadan was in August; around 1955 it was in May; around 1965 it was in January; and in 1978 it had returned to its 1945 period, in August.

The festivals of the Muslim year

Not all these festivals are celebrated in the same way.

– The first of the year (the first day of the first month) is a holiday. It is the occasion for celebrating the remembrance of the Hijra, i.e. the exodus of Muhammad and his companions, who left Mecca for Medina in 622. There are devotional celebrations in the mosque in the evening. On that day the Eyptian newspapers usually have a drawing representing a pigeon's nest with eggs and a spider's web. Tradition records that during his exodus Muhammad, accompanied by Abu Bakr, took refuge in a cave in the desert. The

pigeon and the spider were put in the entrance to throw off his pursuers; on seeing them, the latter thought that no one could have entered the cave for a long time and went on their way.

– The twelfth day of the third month (the month of Rabi al-awwad, first) is the birth of Muhammad or maulid an-nabi. This is a very popular festival in which the brotherhoods are very active. The evening festivities begin a week or two before the last until the day of the festival, which is a holiday.

– The twenty-seventh day of the seventh month (the month of Rajab) recalls Muhammad's nocturnal ascension, his journey to heaven. In the evening there are devotional celebrations in the mosques.

– The fifteenth day of the eighth month (the month of Sha'ban) commemorates the change in the direction of prayer which was made in Medina in 623. There are devotional celebrations in the mosques on the eve of the festival.

– The month of Ramadan (the ninth month) was mentioned earlier in connection with fasting.

– The first day of the tenth month is the great festival of breaking the fast ('Id al-Fitr). There are several days of holiday, and popular rejoicing. In the morning, immediately after sunrise, there is festal prayer in which almost everyone takes part. This prayer is often held in the open air, on ground outside the cities.

– The tenth day of the twelfth month (the month of Dhu-l-Hijja, i.e. 'the month of pilgrimage') is the festival of sacrifices or of the sheep ('Id al-Adha). In West Africa it is called Tabaski. Everyone is united in spirit with the sacrifice of sheep and other animals which are killed for food on that day by the pilgrims in Mecca, at Mina, on the outskirts of Mecca. Most of the faithful think that this is a recollection of Abraham's sacrifice and the ram which was miraculously sent as a victim in his place. In the morning there is a great

The two great liturgical feasts of the year

The Feast of Sacrifices
(also called the Great Festival or Great Beyram),
the tenth day of the twelfth month (dhu-l-hijja),
in connection with the pilgrimage.

Feast of the breaking of the fast
(also called 'Id al-Fitr, lesser Beyram)
the first of the month of Shawwal (tenth month),
which follows Ramadan.

There is also a third festival which is less liturgical but very popular:

The birth of the prophet
(Maulid al-Nabi), the twelfth day of the third month, celebrated above all during the preceding days.

offering of prayer by the men as at the end of Ramadan. There are several days holiday, and popular rejoicing.

NB The dates of all these festivals pose a problem. Traditionally the beginning of a lunar month has to be determined as follows: one or two trustworthy men have to have seen with their own eyes the new, very slender crescent of the moon if the next day is to be declared to be the first day of the month. As a result, before sunset on the twenty-ninth day of every month, authorized witnesses begin their observation. If they see the crescent, all is clear and the next day is the new moon. But if they do not see it or cannot see it (because of cloud, etc.), the next day is declared the thirtieth day of the month and the following month begins the day after.

So the calendar could not be fixed exactly, and between 1945 and 1950 I noticed this twenty-four-hour fluctuation. Nowadays jurists accept that one sighting is sufficient for a whole zone, and the news is transmitted by radio. When the Jews, following Saadya Gaon, a mediaeval doctor of the law, accepted that the beginning of the month could be determined by astronomical calculations, Muslims still hesitated. Some countries accepted the calculation while others rejected it. Yet others had recourse to it if the moon could not be seen and if making the day after next the first day of the month would have had detrimental consequences for society.

The third of the five pillars

Social taxation

The Arabic term *zakat* is difficult to translate. The root signifies 'purification' and the word has taken on the sense of almsgiving. The link between purity and almsgiving is biblical, and the Gospels contain the saying: 'But give for alms those things which are within; and behold, everything is clean for you' (Luke 11.41).

However, the almsgiving in question here has become quasi-official and has been regulated by all kinds of laws. At the beginning of Islam, the tribes which were subjected but then refused to continue to pay the *zakat* were attacked by soldiers and forced to submit.

So the *zakat* is a kind of tithe meant to support the poor and those engaged in collecting it; alternatively, it might be seen as a charitable tax, also allowing the financing of certain enterprises in the public interest (like bridge-building in the Middle Ages, and so on). Nowadays it has lapsed except in very traditionalist countries like Saudi Arabia; elsewhere only Muslims who observe the law strictly practise it. Others consider that state taxation, part of which is directed towards the same social ends as the *zakat*, has replaced it. However, the present fundamentalist movement, with its return to the Muslim law, has restored the *zakat*. In countries in which it is not officially recognized, committees have been created which are skilled in collecting it and then distributing the aid which it makes possible.

In short, the *zakat* represents the financial dimension of primitive Muslim society; along with plunder, and the spoils of wars won without fighting a blow, it formed the major source of revenue for public expenses. This type of tithe can be found in the majority of societies, whether or not they are religious: thus we have the tithe in the Hebrew Bible, the tithe in the mediaeval European church, etc.

In Islam the *zakat* has been a factor of solidarity and unity.

The legal principle that the poor have a right to part of the property of the rich

This principle is stronger than that of a simple appeal to the generosity of those with possessions. This generosity, to be found in all religions, is also preached in the Qur'an. The

Qur'an teaches that it is good to give alms ostentatiously, but to give them in secret is better (cf. Qur'an 2, 271). But elsewhere the word 'right' is used formally: 'Give their right to the near of kin, to the needy, and to the wayfarers' (Qur'an 30, 38).

The *zakat* is constantly mentioned alongside prayer as having been taught by all the prophets before Muhammad. Furthermore, helping one's neighbour is frequently praised in the Qur'an. Those who have given alms will go to paradise. That is what is said in this text of the Qur'an, which speaks of the elect and describes their former life on earth which had brought them this eternal recompense:

> For they have done good works, sleeping but little in the night-time, praying at dawn for God's pardon, and sharing their goods with the beggars and the destitute (Qur'an 51, 16–19).

Similarly the brief surahs 93 and 94 recall Muhammad's poor childhood, the help that he received from God, and conclude:

> Did he not find you poor and enrich you?
> Therefore do not wrong the orphan, nor chide away the beggar. But proclaim the goodness of your Lord (Qur'an 93, 8–10).

Surah 76 is throughout a eulogy to acts of generosity, while Qur'an 74, 38–56 on the contrary consigns anyone who has refused to give alms to hell.

Despite everything, Muslim society has had its misers, as have all societies. They have been the object of the criticism of many writers, like al-Jahiz in his *Book of Misers*.

The amount of the *zakat* and those who benefit from it

The amount of the *zakat* has been scrupulously fixed by the doctors of the law. I shall not dwell on the details of their prescriptions but the general principle is that $2\frac{1}{2}\%$ should be given. However, there are special categories: thus it was provided that 10% should be given of the revenue of fields watered by rain and 5% of those with artificial irrigation. A similar principle is applied for herds of camels, account being taken of a difference in value depending on the age of the animals. For example, in certain cases one camel is to be given for every forty camels.

As for the beneficiaries of the *zakat*, they have long been listed in treatises of Muslim law. First of all, since the *zakat* is paid by Muslims, it can only benefit Muslims or Islam (only the almsgiving of Ramadan or *zakat al-fitr* can go to non-Muslims. Several verses of the Qur'an list possible beneficiaries: for example:

> Alms shall be used only for those who are in the way of God, for the ransom of slaves and debtors, and for distribution among the poor, the destitute, the wayfarers, those that are employed in collecting alms, and those that are converted to the faith (Qur'an 9, 60).

Who are these people for whom alms are destined? The meaning of several of the categories is clear: those who are in need, the poor, those personally charged with collecting these funds. Then there are those who have to be drawn to Islam or whose recent faith needs to be protected. The money in the *zakat* will provide, if need be, secret funds meant to pay for presents or gifts. Slaves: these are Muslims who have fallen into slavery or slaves converted to Islam. The funds of the *zakat* can be used to buy them back. The word 'debtors' denotes Muslims over-whelmed with debts; the funds are to help them free themselves from their creditors. Those in the way of God are those whom the *jihad* (see box on p. 121) has reduced to wretched material conditions. The traveller: if he is cut off from the source of his revenue, or even if he has no money for another worthwhile cause.

In short, for Muslims the important thing was to re-establish a new solidarity when the mercantile life of Mecca had broken up the ancient solidarity of the desert. The *zakat* was one of the elements in this process.

The *zakat* does not do away with private almsgiving, but supplements it.

One last remark. Nowadays, in an era of socialist societies, the theoreticians of Islam refer to the *zakat* to justify the intervention of the state or the community in the sharing of riches. While it is affirmed that the right to private property remains unaffected, the fact that the poor have rights over the property of the rich leads governments to redistribute property in the public interest. Some apologists even go so far as to say that the *zakat* made Islam a socialism before socialism. This assertion is too hasty, since it takes no account of the question of the private ownership of means of production nor does it note the other characteristics of socialist principles. It would be better to say that the Qur'an recalls the rights of the most disadvantaged and that the *zakat* was a way of gaining these rights for them.

The fourth of the five pillars

The fast of the month of Ramadan

The month of Ramadan is the ninth month of the Muslim lunar year. The fast called for during this month is an observance which marks not only the personal life of those who practise it but also the public life of Muslim societies. The physiognomy of a Muslim state is not the same during these twenty-nine or thirty days of effort, renunciation and collective festivals.

A long text from the Qur'an underlies the legislation on this fast. Here it is:

Believers, fasting is decreed for you as it was decreed for those before you; perchance you will guard yourself against evil. Fast a certain number of days, but if any one of you is ill or on a journey let him fast a similar number of days later on; and for those who can afford it there is a ransom: the feeding of a poor man. He that does good of his own account shall be well rewarded; but to fast is better for you, if you but knew it.

In the month of Ramadan the Qur'an was revealed, a book of guidance with proofs of guidance distinguishing right from wrong. Therefore whoever of you is present in that month, let him fast. But he who is ill or on a journey shall fast for a similar number of days later on.

God desires your well-being, not your discomfort. He desires you to fast the whole month so that you may magnify Him and render thanks to Him for giving you His guidance (Qur'an 2, 183–185).

The text then goes on to speak of God as being near to the one who prays. Then the text allows those who are legally married to have sexual intercourse at night during the fast, except those who are in retreat in the mosques. Finally comes the order:

Eat and drink until you can tell a white thread from a black one in the light of the coming dawn. Then resume the fast till nightfall (Qur'an 2, 187).

Commentary on this text

First of all this text shows how difficult it is to derive legislation solely from the Qur'an; hence the need to resort to traditions.

The Qur'an compares the fast which it prescribes with those of earlier religions. This can be done from two perspectives. First of all, how does one fast? As in the earlier religions, the faithful abstain from all food, drink and sexual intercourse throughout the day until sunset. The daily fast begins when a white thread can be distinguished from a black thread (is this an image to denote the line on the horizon which the dawn traces at the end of the night?). It finishes at sunset. However, there is a difference; Christians of the time abstained from sexual intercourse even during the night in the period of the fast. That is why the text of the Qur'an dwells specifically on this point further on.

On the other hand, it is impossible to see to which former religion the text could refer in connection with the duration of the period of fasting. The fast of a complete lunar month does not appear either in Jewish or in Christian tradition. The Christians of the earliest church fasted several days before Easter, and then they went directly to forty days, in remembrance of Christ's fast; but that did not include Sundays, and for some Christians Saturdays were not fast days either. Only the Manichaeans and the Sabaeans are known to have had a continuous fast of one lunar month. Did other sects in Arabia also act in this way?

The dispensations: the sick and wayfaring believers are excused from the fast on condition that they make it up later with as many days of fasting as they have missed. The jurists have spent a long time discussing the cases in which food given to a poor person was a substitute for a fast which it was impossible to perform. I shall not go into these discussions here. But it is certain that the major principle so far is that of replacing the days of fasting omitted by an equivalent number of days later.

The text clearly teaches that the month of Ramadan was that of the revelation of the Qur'an. Numerous traditions enlarge on the way in which the angel Gabriel taught Muhammad during these months and made him repeat the texts that he had learned earlier. One night of Ramadan, called the Night of Destiny, is regarded as having been that of the revelation of the Qur'an. It is celebrated quite specifically in the mosques. Some people say that it is one of the last ten days of the month without being able to specify which. Others fix it on 27 Ramadan (i.e. the night before the day of the 27th, since for Muslims the twenty-four hours of the day begin at sunset).

However, we should look at the question of fasting more systematically.

First of all the lunar month of Ramadan begins with an official declaration by the authorities (*mufti*) after its beginning has been observed in accordance with the procedures which I mentioned earlier (in connection with the annual festivals). At that time every Muslim who has attained the age of puberty is normally obliged to fast.

This fast consists of taking neither food nor drink (not even water) from sunrise to sunset. Tobacco, sexual intercourse and various other things are forbidden during these daylight hours. In the evening the prohibitions cease; the meal which breaks the fast after sunset is a sign of brotherhood, indeed almost a kind of sacrament. Towards the end of the night, those who are fasting usually take a light snack. They wake up for that, and in the cities a man goes from house to house arousing those who have asked for his services. In the major cities, the sound of a cannon often serves as a warning: one shot is fired at sunset, when all can begin to eat and drink, and another at the end of the night, when this is no longer allowed.

The jurists often discuss whether certain practices are allowed during Ramadan. In principle, nothing should enter from outside through the digestive tract and the intestine: enemas, for example, are forbidden. But what about that which enters the body otherwise? The jurist in Egypt allow eye-drops, ear-drops and vaccines, but do not accept other injections. Often people refuse anything. Many professions have to change their hours: the dentists have their Muslim patients at night, since swallowing water, blood, etc., breaks the fast.

The spirituality of Ramadan

As the month meant to celebrate the memory of the revelation of the Qur'an, Ramadan is also the month in which hunger reminds the rich of the existence of the poor, the month in which almsgiving is recommended. There is also provision for official almsgiving, the *zakat* of the breaking of the fast, so that all, even the most needy, may rejoice during the festival at the end of the fast.

This month is a month of self-mastery and the exercising of the will in order to control one's passions, resist hunger, thirst, the desire to smoke, and so on. For more devout Muslims, it is also a time of prayer and religious instruction (through mosques, radio, television, with numerous recitations of the Qur'an by reputed specialists). In the mosques there are special prayers (the *tarawih*) after the last of the five daily prayers, that of the dark night. The Qur'an is frequently recited either in the mosques or in private houses: a dawn recitation is particularly popular. Retreats at the mosque are now rare in Arab countries; it seems that they used to be more frequent.

A festival atmosphere reigns everywhere after sunset. Celebrations are quite private, however, because most people have limited resources and in any case they are tired. Celebrations are held above all in the sphere of the family, with visits from parents and friends, and dinners to break the fast which are the occasion for the exchanging of invitations and the sharing of vigils. Activity sometimes lasts quite late into the night. Work is affected by this, since the daily fast and the events at night exhaust everyone. Lack of sleep often makes itself felt as much as hunger. Except in individual cases, people only go through the motions of working. This led certain states like Tunisia to react in 1960. Comparing under-development with a state of war in the battle for development, President Bourguiba asked for work to take priority: those who could not both work and fast were to make use of the dispensations provided for those fighting in the Holy War.

For many people Ramadan is the occasion for

profound joy. Certainly there are also believers who fast only under the constraints of social pressure, and for whom this observance is a burden, but their number must not be exaggerated, since in general the others fast of their own free will. For many people the month of Ramadan is the occasion to return to practising their religion, either temporarily or permanently. The idea that good works purify those who perform them is frequently recalled, and preachers cite the *hadith* according to which those who practise their fast become as pure again as a newborn child.

The observance of Ramadan varies depending on the country. However, with the transformations brought about by modern life, the requirements of the industrial world and the possibilities of using the modern mass media for preaching, Ramadan may develop in an unforseen direction. As early as 1955 an authoritative voice in Egypt recalled that the West has its paid annual holidays during which industrial life comes to a standstill; Ramadan should be assimilated to them.

Ramadan, which is incomparably more demanding than what now remains of Lent among Western Christians, can best be compared to the fast of the Eastern Christian churches. But the atmosphere which prevails in Muslim countries during this month is not that of the Christian fast. Whereas the latter is entirely focused on the Easter mystery, serving as a preparation for Holy Week with its reminder of the human condition and of redemption, Ramadan has nothing to correspond to such a mystery. Besides, does not Islam itself claim to be a religion without mystery? At Ramadan, the accent is put on the exercise of the will and obedience to God, thanksgiving for the gift of the Qur'an, the nearness of God, Muslim brotherhood, awareness of the poor and spiritual purification.

The fifth of the five pillars

The pilgrimage to Mecca

The great pilgrimage or *hajj* has left a profound mark on Muslim society, since to make it once in a lifetime is an obligation on every free adult male Muslim who has the resources for the journey and for the support of his family during his absence – that is, provided that the route is safe (no war, bandits or epidemics). It is also obligatory for Muslim women if they can be escorted. Linked to Qur'an and the traditions which recall Abraham, it comprises two groups of ceremonies.

The first ceremonies are performed by individuals at Mecca itself, at a particular period of the year (during the tenth, eleventh and beginning of the twelfth months, this last being the month of Dhu-l-hijja or the month of pilgrimage). On arriving in the city, or later, the pilgrim goes round the Ka'ba ritually seven times, with it on his left. Then after a prayer which is prescribed, he 'runs' seven times (four times there and three times back) between the two sacred pillars called Safa and Marwa.

The second ceremonies take place on the same fixed date in the year for all, first in the neighbourhood of Mecca and then in the city itself. All the pilgrims (they used to number several hundred thousand, but in 1985 there were more than two million) meet in these wide tracts of desert. Then an immense gathering begins on the 9th of the month of Dhu-l-hijja, from mid-day until sunset, in a plain surrounded by mountains, about fifteen miles east of Mecca. This human

The plain of Arafat and the small Mount of Mercy, Jbl r-Rahma, in the foreground, with two million pilgrims massed in tents during the afternoon of the ninth day of the month. This is the great central ceremony of the pilgrimage.

sea of pilgrims dressed in white, with tents for shelter, presses up against a small rocky height in the centre of the immense plain of Arafat, towards which all eyes are turned: an official sermon is given and personal private prayers are offered. Everyone asks pardon for their sins. For some years pilgrims have brought transistor radios and follow the sermon on them; before that it was inaudible.

On the return to Mecca, a night stop is provided for, to pray and sleep in a place called Muzdalifa; the next day, the 10th, everyone meets at Mina (or Muna in some pronunciations), between four and five miles east of Mecca, spending at least two full days there (until the 12th). The 10th is the day when countless sacrifices are offered at Mina (individually by all those who wish to or have to, depending on what is prescribed by the law). A brief return to Mecca to circumambulate the Ka'ba another seven times, and various rites of desacralization, are followed by a return to Mina. On the 10th, 11th, and 12th days at Mina the pilgrims throw stones at pillars symbolizing the demon (there are three). On the 10th only one pillar is stoned, immediately on arrival. The three pillars are stoned (by throwing seven stones at each pillar) on the 11th and the 12th. People used to stay another day at Mina, until the 13th, but leaving on the 12th, which has always been acceptable, is now the general rule.

Formerly, any meat from the sacrifices which was neither eaten nor taken away was left exposed to the open air, smelling strongly and decomposing very rapidly under the effect of the sun and the flies. Nowadays the Saudi government resorts to modern means to cope with this problem of health and hygiene. Recently, some of the meat has even been sent to various areas of the Muslim world by plane or refrigerator ship.

Ritual clothing

This ritual clothing, called *ihram*, is obligatory only for males. It consists of a loincloth covering the legs and a sash; neither may have seams. The loincloth is held up by a broad leather belt with a pocket for personal papers and money. In addition the pilgrim often carries a leather bag with a shoulder strap. On his feet he wears open-toed sandals. The head has to be bare, but in fact many people use a parasol.

The pilgrim performs ablutions when he puts on this dress, which is the same for all males and therefore a symbol of equality before God, irrespective of social situation, in a religion without priests. Particular points are provided on the itineraries for putting on the *ihram*. Arriving by ship does not change the ritual in any way; the ceremony takes place on board as the ship passes a certain point north or south of Jedda. If the pilgrim is coming by air, he arranges to be in *ihram* when he gets into the plane that is taking him on the last stage to Jedda. So at the time of the pilgrimage Cairo airport is full of pilgrims in ritual dress. The women enter the sacral state without special clothing; they are required to wear dresses with sleeves and long skirts and a high neck.

The sacred state, which involves the observance of certain prohibitions, lasts for at least the time needed to perform the two groups of ritual practices mentioned above. If there is an interval of several days between the performance of these two groups of actions, the pilgrim is free either to remain in the sacred state or to return to the worldly state until he puts on the *ihram* again.

When he has put on the *ihram*, the pilgrim constantly repeats the invocation:

You call us, we are here, O God! We are here!
We are here, there is no one beside You! We are
    here!
Praise and good deeds belong to You, and the
    empire!
There is none but You!

Note that the ritual clothing of men must once have been the customary dress of the country. The nomads in the torrid deserts near Djibouti still wear it today.

The meaning of the pilgrimage

The pilgrimage is a great penitential act which, if it is performed well, secures the remission of all former sins. It is an immense gathering which makes those who take part in it aware of the force of Islam, and though only a minority is in a position to make real contacts and have discussions, at least the majority of peoples who have embraced Islam can assemble together. The pilgrim ceaselessly repeats and hears invocations to the glory of God, the One, and to Muhammad. The essentials of Islamic dogma are thus constantly repeated for him. He lives in a setting which saw the birth of Islam, and many educated Muslims also try on this journey to discover and visit all the holy places from the beginnings of Islam. Recollections of the victory of the first Muslims over polytheism are present everywhere. The pilgrim returns with the envied title of *hajj* or *hajji*.

Circumstances have changed. When the caliph at Medina was the head of a rising empire, the pilgrimage was the occasion for bringing together the governors of provinces and sorting out affairs of state with them. Similarly, up to the beginning of the nineteenth century and the introduction of steam navigation, the pilgrimage was the occasion for a substantial trade fair (on the commercial route between India and the Mediterranean); by the fifteenth century the transactions which took place there over the space of two or three weeks were estimated at being worth two million gold pieces. Merchandise from India and later coffee were bartered there for coin or merchandise coming from Europe. Nowadays the commercial activity is that of a world centre of pilgrimage, sometimes with the sale of precious objects brought by pilgrims in lieu of travellers cheques (precious stones, carpets, and so on). Some pilgrims are also concerned to buy objects which are taxed less than elsewhere, or to exchange currency. The preachers castigate those who come on pilgrimage for primarily material reasons, and public opinion is fully with them on this point.

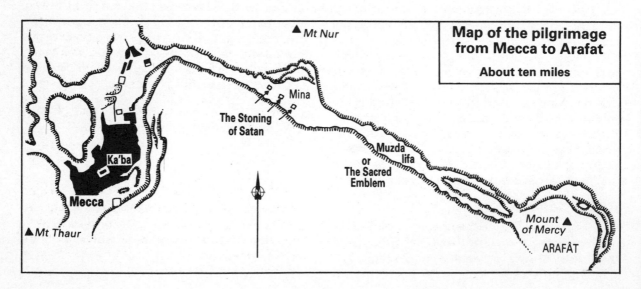

▲ Mt Nur

Mina

The Stoning of Satan

Muzdalifa
or
The Sacred Emblem

Ka'ba

Mecca

▲ Mt Thaur

Mount ▲
of Mercy

ARAFÂT

Map of the pilgrimage from Mecca to Arafat

About ten miles

Biblical or para-biblical remembrances on the pilgrimage

While they perform the pilgrimage because it is an order from God, Muslims associate a series of remembrances or traditional stories with the observance. As I already indicated in passing, at the beginning of the book, the Qur'an teaches that Abraham himself called men to pilgrimage after he had built (or, as some traditions say, only rebuilt) the Ka'ba. As these statements appear in the Qur'an, no Muslim would dispute them. Perhaps the traditions were already current before Islam in the Jewish milieu of the African Diaspora, just as nowadays a whole series of traditions about the coming of the holy family to Egypt is current among Egyptian Christians.

A series of traditions is associated with Hagar, the mother of Ismail, and her flight between Safa and Marwa. On the point of dying of thirst with her child (cf. Genesis 21.14–19), Hagar is said to have run off, maddened. An angel is then said to have shown her the well of Zam-Zam, at the foot of the place on which the Ka'ba was rebuilt, and its water saved her and her child. Hagar and Ismail are then said to have settled at Mecca, where Abraham came to visit them at regular intervals. A relic, a stone on which Abraham's feet are said to have left a trace, is still venerated in a golden reliquary a few paces from the Ka'ba; the whole site is called the *Maqam Ibrahim*, or station of Abraham.

When it recounts the sacrifice of Abraham, the Qur'an does not mention the name of the son: was this Isaac, as in Genesis, or was it Ismail? At the beginning of Islam, commentators were hesitant and many thought that it was Isaac. However, little by little the idea spread that the sacrifice was of Ismail and that it took place in the environs of Mecca. Nowadays the supporters of Isaac are a tiny minority. The result is that the ceremonies of the 10th Dhu-l-hijja are directly associated with Abraham and his sacrifice. Moreover, the stonings of the three pillars have been presented as a repetition of actions performed by the patriarch. Tempted by the demon who suggested that he should turn a deaf ear and let his son live, Abraham is said to have reacted by throwing stones three times at the tempter. Hence, on this view, the present-day stonings of the three carved pillars.

69

The sense of the sacred and semitic customs

The Muslim pilgrim practises observances many of which recall the Hebrew Bible and have their roots in the same semitic soil.

Hebrew Bible

1. Like all temples, the temple of Jerusalem is called the *house of God*. God is present in a particular way.

Three times a year the faithful go up to Jerusalem for the festivals called *hag* in Hebrew (cf. Numbers 16.16, where the three festivals are listed and the word *hag* is repeated three times).

The role of sacred stones in the earliest form of the cult.

2. The obligation to be in a state of ritual purity in order to approach God. Before the theophany on Sinai God tells Moses that the people must wash their garments (Exodus 19.10).

3. God tells Moses to mark out the boundaries of a sacred area which no one is to enter (Exodus 19.12). Part of the Jerusalem temple was banned to all non-Jews on pain of death.

4. Moses tells his people before the theophany on Sinai to abstain from women (Exodus 19.15).

5. The believer who makes a special vow of consecration to God (the nazir, cf. Numbers 6.5) allows his hair to grow freely, without cutting it. When he returns to his everyday state, his hair is cut at an official ceremony (cf. St Paul in Acts 21.23f.).

Muslim pilgrimage

1. The Ka'ba in Mecca is called the *house of God*. The pilgrims are the guests of God, the delegation to God, so there is the sense of a very powerful divine presence.

Mecca is in fact the new Jerusalem for Muslims, although they never use this expression. Once in a lifetime they have the obligation to go on a pilgrimage called *Hajj*.

The role of the Black Stone which many pilgrims try to kiss.

2. The obligation of ritual purity. Sacred clothing for males, called *ihram*, which they don at a specific place before arriving in the area of Mecca. The prohibitions to be observed apply equally to Muslim women, although they wear no uniform, but only a discreet garment, covering arms and legs, but not face.

3. The existence of a territory around Mecca, utterly and permanently forbidden to anyone who is not a Muslim. The sacred character of the territory obliges Muslims who enter it to observe certain prohibitions (neither hunting nor fighting except to repel aggressors, etc.)

4. The sexual prohibitions observed by the pilgrim while he is in a sacred state (while he is wearing the sacred garment of the *ihram*).

5. While he is in a state of *ihram*, wearing his sacred garment (or for women, even without such a garment), the pilgrim may neither cut or let fall any hair from the body. In addition, perfumes are banned. The ceremony of desacralization includes the ceremonial cutting of some locks of hair.

<table>
<tr><td>6. The sacrifice of Passover corresponding to a Semitic spring sacrifice.</td><td>6. On the pilgrimage we also have a sacrifice, the only official sacrifice in Islam.</td></tr>
<tr><td>7. The sacred character of the figure seven in the Hebrew Bible, from the seven wells of Beersheba to Joshua's seven circuits round Jericho.</td><td>7. The fact of going round the Ka'ba seven times and 'running' seven times between as-Safa and al-Marwa.</td></tr>
</table>

Some examples of invocations pronounced by the pilgrims

A certain number of modern Christian writers have translated the prayers recited by the pilgrims. It is worth pointing out that some of these prayers are purely devotional and vary, depending on the author. That is the case with the texts collected by the famous spiritual master of Islam, al-Ghazali (who died in 1111), in his treatise on the revival of the sciences of religion. By contrast, others are spoken by all, indefatigably, like the invocation quoted earlier: 'We are here, O God, We are here!', etc.

Another text which can be heard continually, by itself, or preceded by a few other phrases, from the station of Arafat (on the 9th Dhu-l-hijja) onwards. It recalls that the pilgrimage could take place only after the complete triumph of Islam over the pagans of Mecca and proclaims that God alone has been the cause of the victory:

> There is no god but God, the One, and there is none beside him. To him be the dominion! To him be the praise! He is powerful over all things. There is no god but God, the One. He has fulfilled his promise: he has given victory to his servant and to Himself, He has put the confederates to rout.

A last example will show one of the numerous prayers of devotion suggested to the faithful, which is also repeated often.

> There is no god but God, the One, and there is none beside him. To him be the dominion and the praise; he is powerful over all things. O God, put a light in my heart and a light in my ears and a light in my sight and make what I have to do easy for me.

The speakers on the radios which broadcast the ceremonies, or those presiding over the prayers, improvise requests for Muslims all over the world, without forgetting their victory and the political needs of various peoples. So around 1960 I heard invocations for the victory of the Algerians (in their war of independence), for that of the Arabs and Muslims against Israel, and for Muslims living under non-Muslim leaders in certain countries, although they were in the majority in that country. I heard prayers for the Muslims of Ethiopia and the USSR. The Philippines are now mentioned also.

Furthermore, numerous invocations involve Muhammad, and the sermons recall the way in which he performed his last pilgrimage and what he said on it.

The influence of the pilgrimage on Islam in Africa south of the Sahara

I should note briefly that for many Muslims in this area contacts with the rest of the Muslim world are made at Mecca on the occasion of the pilgrimage. This journey makes it clear to all that one has become a Muslim; so as soon as they are converted, many African princes have been concerned to show their support for their new faith by going on pilgrimage. Furthermore, the pilgrimage is now a source of prestige. Ideologically, it seems that pilgrimages have favoured many positions more in conformity with dogma, and opposition to practices inherited from paganism has been favoured as a result of pilgrimages. Cases are known in which reflections heard at the holy places of Arabia have made individual pilgrims think, and have changed them.

Finally, the leaders of the brotherhoods have had meetings at Mecca with other officials of their brotherhood: for example the Hajj 'Umar Tal, which I mentioned earlier. But all, whether or not they are members of brotherhoods, return impressed by these moments of intense religious emotion. They have been marked by the atmosphere of fervour, the sense of a presence of God. They have noted the power of Islam, whose faithful come from everywhere.

The men are all dressed the same, and those whom the pilgrims meet are of all kinds, generous as well as greedy. In time, the memories of the exploitation of pilgrims by many traders fades, and only the good memories are left. Besides, is it not important for the inhabitants of Mecca to earn their living for the year during the few crowded weeks? Some recall the prayer of Abraham, praying for his descendants settled in Mecca.

> Put in the hearts of men kindness towards them, and provide them with the earth's fruits, so that they may give thanks (Qur'an 14, 37).

The visit to the tomb of Muhammad at Medina

This visit is not required by the Muslim law, but a large number of pilgrims take advantage of their journey to make a detour to Medina and go to pray at the tomb of their Prophet, buried where he spent the last years of his life, in the mosque which was that of the first Muslims.

Similarly, some (even fewer) go to Jerusalem, or at least did so before it was occupied by Israel. For Islam, Jerusalem is 'the third of the two holy cities', as a famous *hadith* teaches. Muhammad is said to have gone through it at the time of his nocturnal ascent, and at Medina, for several months after the Hijra, ritual prayer is offered in the direction of Jerusalem. A visit to the holy places of Jerusalem (the al-Aqsa mosque built on the esplanade of the old temple) is also traditional. A *hadith* even affirms that it is only permissible to travel as a pilgrim to Mecca, Medina and Jerusalem.

To return to Mecca, apart from the great pilgrimage which has just been described at length and which takes place at a particular time each year, it is always possible for the rest of the year to perform the lesser pilgrimage or Umra. The ritual of this latter gathering is similar to that of the first part of the *hajj* (wearing sacred clothing, performing the seven circumambulations of the Ka'ba and then the seven 'runnings' between Safa and Marwa).

Finally, we should not forget that though he does not do so officially, the pilgrim feels that he is representing his family on pilgrimage. If he often asks forgiveness for his own sins, he also prays for all his family, and does not fail to buy numerous souvenirs for his kinsfolk and friends. Their welcome when he returns home will be warm and unforgettable.

6

The Law of Islam and Social Life

The development of the modern world has left a clear mark on Muslim society in the twentieth century, even if not all its members have been affected to the same degree. There is an enormous difference between a Nigerian Muslim graduate from the University of Ibadan or Zaria and his compatriot who remains in a distant village, but both are caught up in a new system. The most visible outward sign of this is the invasion of items which were once unknown, ranging from the truck or plastic objects to the transistor radio. The possibility of more widespread education and the attraction of the great cities should also be noted. But even more profoundly, the great economic laws which govern the world set the prices of raw materials, and as I have said, distant struggles between progressive and conservative countries have repercussions almost everywhere.

However, in spite of everything, a certain number of institutions inherited from the past and called for by the religious law still give Muslim societies their characteristic aspect. It can also happen that the disappointments replacing the enthusiasm over the rediscovery of political independence and decolonization have driven large elements of the population to rediscover salvation in a form of revolution based on a fundamentalist view of Islam.

Recourse to technology and the need for industrialization are no longer questioned at the level of application and implementation, but there has not always been an answer to the question whether technology and industrialization do not presuppose a certain spiritual shift and therefore a different kind of civilization.

Everything goes on as if Islam, proud of its mediaeval achievements in the sphere of the sciences and the arts, had arrived at the modern world dreaming above all of its own human values which it seeks to preserve at any price and trusting in its ancestral qualities which have been put to the test in the past in the acquisition of science and technology. Perhaps, too, Islam feels the ambitions of Western society to be overweening, unacceptable to a believer because of their

Promethean dimension. Instinctively the mass of ordinary workers refuses to be enthusiastic about the demands of the new technologies with their absolute imperatives of firm planning, exactness, precision, maintenance. Might we not have here a vital act of rejection, because of a feeling that it is impossible ever to enter wholly into this world unless it has been profoundly modified and humanized? Or is this only a temporary pause in the march forward?

In fact Muslim society is based on a certain number of values to which believers have an emotional attachment. First is the place of God in this society. Men and women have been created to worship and serve God (Qur'an 51, 56). Their first duty is to recognize the lordship of God over all the universe, and therefore also over themselves (Qur'an 7, 172). But at the same time, Muslim faith makes the believer a member of the people or the party of God, with a mission to the whole of humankind. By virtue of belonging to this society, Muslims enjoy an egalitarian religious status, since the society does not have any priests, though it does in fact have a class of clergy, men of religion whom their knowledge distinguishes from others.

In this society, human relations are primarily regulated by a small number of commandments. These recall those of the Decalogue, with their recognition of the sanctity of human life within the limits of the law (do not kill), of the right to private property (do not steal, do not take another's spouse), the duty to speak the truth in a certain number of specific instances where it is indispensable for the progress of the community (prohibition of false witness). The basic nucleus is the family (respect for parents, their rights and their duties, love and affection between husbands and wives).

We shall look quickly at the principal features of this society, beginning with the family nucleus, individuals (the marriage regime), possessions (property, inheritance, lending at interest, games of chance), and end with political power, peace and war.

The family nucleus

The basic nucleus of Muslim society is the family. So far, in most Muslim countries, this has been the extended family, ruled over by the paterfamilias or an uncle, in which all have their place. With modern city life and scanty accommodation, the idea of the family restricted to the father, mother and children is in process of becoming established. Perhaps the social security regulations will equally reduce the importance of the extended family which hitherto was the basic nucleus of solidarity and welfare, especially in sickness or old age.

In this family, theoretically everyone is equal before God and their eternal destiny, with the same duties: the supporters of this basic equality are fond of citing a verse of the Qur'an which lists side by side Muslim men and women who practise their religion equally (Qur'an 3, 36). However, in earthly life, a dominant role has developed upon the male within society; he is head of the family. In some respects Muslim society is a male society, or at least it has been down the centuries. Hitherto the rule was that the head of the family, i.e. the man, should provide the money needed to keep his family. Paid work for women, a characteristic of modern urban society, risks modifying these perspectives.

What are the main features of family life in Islamic lands? Let us look at them in order, taking one by one the stages through which Muslim men and women pass in the course of their family life.

First of all the child is considered to be born good by nature. A *hadith* says that he or she is by nature a Muslim, and it is the parents who make him or her a Christian, Jew or Zoroastrian as the case may be. Names are given by the parents; among these, some are characteristic of Islam, while others are neutral and could be borne by the faithful of other religions. A whole series of these names is derived from the names of the Prophet of Islam – Muhammad, Ahmed, Mustapha, Mahmud – or his first companions. Others recall the great figures of the past mentioned in the Qur'an; Ibrahim, Ismail, Yussuf, etc. For girls the names are often those of the first Muslim women: Amina, Khadija, Umm Kulthum, 'A'isha, Zaynab, etc.

The role of the mother in a child's very first upbringing is very great, even if the father's example also leaves a stamp on the child. Thus an Egyptian writer, recalling memories of his earliest childhood, can see his mother teaching him by heart the words of the Fatiha, the first surah of the Qur'an which is at the heart of all ritual prayers. Or there was a woman who said that she had been very impressed in her childhood by the seriousness with which her father read and recited the Qur'an.

Circumcision for boys is a universal custom throughout Islam. Despite this, the texts do not say much about it. Doctrinally it does not hold the place which it has among the Jews, according to the pages devoted to it in the book of Genesis in connection with the covenant between God and Abraham.

The age at which circumcision is performed is not specified. In Arab countries, relatives usually wait until a boy is seven or eight; the circumcision is not accompanied by any ceremony of initiation, but is a family festival. I have sometimes been asked whether in Africa south of the Sahara the ancient traditions which linked initiation and circumcision have left any traces in Islam; I have found it impossible to reply.

'Female "circumcision"' is sometimes practised, but it is a local tradition and Islam does not call for it.

Islam stresses the respect due to parents (to the father and the mother) and in particular recalls that pregnancy and breast-feeding have cost the mother effort and are wearying (cf. Qur'an 46, 15–16). The Qur'an suggests this prayer for children who have grown up and whose parents are old:

Treat them with humility and tenderness and say, 'Lord, be merciful to them; they nursed me when I was an infant' (Qur'an 17, 24).

Not to give one's parents all their due is considered to be one of the 'great sins'. The only exception is where parents want to withdraw their child from the faith: the duty of fidelity to Islam is absolute, and comes before obedience to parents. The Qur'an rules that in this case children must not obey.

When the children are small, they can go anywhere, with men and women, without anyone forbidding them or imposing on them. The question of the separation of male and female only begins to arise with growth and the approach of puberty. It is associated with veiling.

Hitherto in certain traditional Muslim countries and up to the 1930s of this century in many others, a woman of marriageable age might show her face only to her father or her husband, or to those of her closest male kin whom she was forbidden to marry. In public she wore a veil which hid her face. A simple net veil in Egypt, this veil was absolutely impenetrable in any respect in Afghanistan or in northern India. It could even become a kind of mask in southern Arabia. As marriage is clearly prohibited in direct line, and between a man and his aunts, his father's other wives, his own sister's nieces, great-nieces and so on, the simultaneous presence of men and women connected by these degrees of kinship, including those of relatives of both sexes by marriage to the same degree of kinship, remained quite legal. In this context, a male and female first cousin had to be separated at puberty, even if they had played together in their infancy. Marriage is in fact allowed at this degree of kinship.

This strict position was based on a verse of the Qur'an and on a *hadith*. The verse runs: 'Prophet, enjoin your wives, your daughters, and the wives of true believers to draw their veils close round them. That is more proper, so that they may be recognized and not molested' (Qur'an 33, 59). Supplementing this verse with the *hadith* which says that the whole of a woman is nudity, to be hidden save for her eyes, formed the legal foundation for the practice of veiling the face completely. So it is that the Jalalayn commentary on the Qur'an (fifteenth century CE) specifies that women have to hide the whole face except for one eye. In the countryside, the modesty of the women is shown more simply; they wear no veil and just live separately from the men. However, in the cities, for a long time custom has required Muslim women to veil themselves from the first symptoms of puberty, except within the family circle comprising the men with whom marriage has been forbidden them by reason of kinship, and the spouses of their sisters, nieces etc.

At the beginning of the twentieth century the question of the veil became the symbol of whether the status of women was developing or remaining fixed. In educational establishments (male and female students together in universities), for working women and even purely for social reasons, a certain number of writers championed the suppression of the veil. In Egypt and the Near East the veil has almost disappeared. It can still be seen in certain areas of North Africa, India and Pakistan. It does not exist in Africa south of the Sahara. About other places, I do not know. It is strictly worn in Saudi Arabia.

However, with the appearance of fundamentalist movements, a reaction can be noted. It became evident when the imitation of Western miniskirts began around 1968. In student circles, women began to wear long dresses (maxis), long sleeves, high necks and a kind of cowl which left all the face uncovered. In spite of everything this form of dress was limited to a small minority in 1980. Since then, the emergence of fundamentalist trends has been the cause of a return to high-necked dresses and particularly to cowls. In Iran, however, after the revolution of the Ayatollah Khomeni, wearing a veil has once more regained all its importance.

It should be noted, though, that except in Westernized or secular spheres, even after the suppression of the veil, the presence of women in male society remained very discreet.

Marriage and celibacy

In Muslim society, marriage is considered the normal situation of the adult man or woman. A tradition going back to Muhammad teaches that 'marriage is half religion'. The general opinion is that men and women only attain the fullness of their personalities in parenthood. That is even more true of the mother than of the father and it is specifically said in a *hadith* that 'paradise is at the feet of the mothers'.

The idea of remaining voluntarily celibate is alien to Muslim thought, though it recognizes the virginity of Mary, the virgin birth of Jesus (cf. pp. 104f.) and the fact that neither John the Baptist nor Jesus married.

However, continence is the rule before marriage. If a man cannot get married for the time being because of financial difficulties, business, etc., a tradition requires him to fast for self-control. For men, Muslim society (though not Muslim law) is in fact more permissive than many other societies, but it requires young women to come to marriage virgins. In Arab countries and others this is a matter of family honour, and customs are very strict on this point.

Motherhood in marriage used to be the sole aim of a Muslim woman's life, or at least everything was subordinated to this. The qualities of feminine intelligence were recognized in specific areas, and the woman was not the man's rival in all spheres. Certainly we are not to believe that the opinion of the pagan Arabs reported by Qur'an was accepted unreservedly by all. These considered women to be beings who 'adorn themselves with trinkets and are powerless in disputation' (Qur'an 43, 18).

In the history of Islam there are certainly precedents which allow modern Muslim women not to be content with the role which more traditionalist Muslims would assign to them, that of wife and mother. Various memories of the earliest times of Islam, of the desert life in which the woman was freer than her successors in subsequent centuries, are examples used to justify this evolution. Quite apart from Khadija, who made her fortune bear fruit, cases are known of women who looked after the wounded in one of the first battles, or there is that of Asma, the daughter of Abu Bakr, who provided food for Muhammad and his father in their hiding place at the time of the emigration in 622, when they were being sought by the pagans, and so on.

This development is evident in the recognition of the possibility for girls to engage in middle and higher education and then to do paid work outside their homes. The only difference between Muslim trends on this point is that the traditionalists require this work to accord with the feminine vocation (teaching children, women's and children's medicines, for example) and sometimes require male and female students to be separated at school and in universities, and in public transport.

The development is also evident above all in the conception of marriage, which in many places is orientated on monogamy and the regulation of divorce. Those who want to give marriage more significance recall a verse of the Qur'an in which it is said that God put 'love and kindness' between husbands and their spouses (Qur'an 30, 21). From the beginning of the century, outside Arabia, Africa south of the Sahara and some remote regions, polygamy has

---

Some Muslim women's names

Amina, the mother of the Prophet
Halima, his nurse
Khadija, his first wife (died 619)
'A'isha, daughter of Abu Bakr, whom Muhammad married after the death of Khadija
Hafsah, another wife, daughter of Umar
Zaynab, the name of one of his wives and one of his daughters

Ruqayya, **Umm Kulthum**, **Fatima**, his three other daughters: all four had Khadija as their mother.
Only Fatima gave him grandchildren.
The names of his other wives are less used.

We should also note the name **Maryam** (mother of Jesus – with two *a*s).

Finally there are names which have a generalized meaning and which are also born by non-Muslims:
Hudah, the direction that God gives;
Jadila, the beautiful;
Farida, the only one, the pearl of great value;
Rashida, endowed with honesty; **Layla**, the night; **Ihsan**, the one who does well; this last name is borne equally by men and women.

---

been restricted to exceptional cases. The fundamentalist movements of recent years have only declared that nothing in the new legislation may go against Muslim law.

77

Marriage legislation

The norm is the marriage of a Muslim man to a Muslim woman. This is possible between first cousins and *a fortiori* with or between the descendants of first cousins. If the ties of affinity are closer, it is forbidden. The fact of having been breast-fed by a woman other than one's own mother (if there are five feeds or more) creates a degree of kinship analogous to blood relationship; the bans between foster brothers and sisters are the same as those between brothers and sisters of the same blood.

The age of marriage was formerly left free. So unions between minors were arranged, creating a real couple from the time the contract was signed, even if the consummation was postponed until later. Nowadays most states have promulgated laws prescribing a minimum age for marriage.

Customs vary depending on the country, and the betrothal or engagement has more or less importance, depending on the area. Marriage itself takes place in two stages, and can be blocked between them if need be. A contract is first signed between the husband and the legal representative of his future wife (usually the father or brother or the closest male relative). For the contract to be valid, the woman has to give her consent, although for a long time it has been agreed that her silence is sufficient. Since marriage is not only a union between husband and wife but also between two families, these intervene in the choice of spouse. At the time of separate women's quarters, this intervention was indispensable. Now even those who are most traditionalist no longer allow marriage to be concluded before the two interested parties have met; however, the strictest traditionalists require the interview to take place in the presence of other members of the families. The consent of the fiancée is indispensable. It used to be very difficult for her to refuse, but now customs have changed, and many young women say no either to marriage at a very early age if it is going to interrupt their studies, or to the partner proposed to them.

The contract is specific about matters of property, notably that of the dowry which the husband pays in whole or in part; in the latter case, the rest must automatically be given to the wife if her husband repudiates her. Once the contract is signed, the two parties are considered to be married and the breaking of this bond counts as divorce.

The marriage is not complete until after the wedding night, which is celebrated solemnly; during its course husband and wife go off to consummate their union. In Arab countries, to demonstrate the virginity of a woman marrying for the first time, the blood which flows on deflowering was mopped up with linen which was solemnly shown to those present (cf. Deuteronomy 22.13–29).

Repudiation (*talaq*)

The Arab word used in this case means 'send back'. It is the husband who is free to send back his wife. He does not have to account for such a decision to anyone but God if he takes it, but he knows that relations between the families will probably be affected by it. The right to ask for a divorce can also be given to the woman if she asked for it and it was written into the contract, and if the legal school under whom the marriage was concluded allows it. In the case of a divorce pronounced by the husband, the husband lets his wife go with all the dowry that she has received from him together with the remainder still due (see above).

However, the law does not encourage this repudiation at all. A well-known tradition states that 'repudiation is the most hateful of lawful things'. Futhermore the Qur'an stresses the rules of justice to be obeyed, the procedure for reconciliation in case of trouble or threats of a breaking of the matrimonial bond. In the case of divorce or widowhood the wife must wait several months before remarrying, so that her new husband may be sure that she is not pregnant and so that the paternity of the child can be established with certainty. During this delay (*'idda*), and if she is pregnant, up to the birth of the child and its weaning, the husband who repudiates his wife has to supply her material needs at his own expense.

In a repudiation, if the husband regrets his decision, he may take his wife back. But if he repudiates her for the third time he may not take her back until she has remarried and has then become free again. Compare with this the contrary position in Deuteronomy 24.1–4, where a man is forbidden to take back his divorced wife if meanwhile she has married another man.

In cases of divorce, custody of the children below a certain age (seven years, for example) is always entrusted to the mother, unless she is unworthy. Then the children automatically go back to the father. Here again some people would like the maximum age of custody to be raised. In 1979 Egypt promulgated amendments to the law of personal status in this direction. They were not universally accepted and were abrogated some years later.

Temporary marriage

During the Prophet's lifetime, the Arabs recognized a type of marriage concluded for a limited period. It was called *mut'a*, which means rejoicing. The Sunnites, i.e. the vast majority of Muslims, teach that though Muhammad accepted this type of union to begin with, he then forbade it. So the Sunnites still prohibit it. However, the Shi'ites consider it still lawful as a form of marriage and there are allusions to such unions in the works of Ayatollah Khomeini, i.e. in the 1970s. At one point the text speaks of marriage concluded for ten days. The Ayatollah would even see temporary marriage as a solution to the moral disorder which follows from men and women living together in universities and establishments of higher education. The Sunnites do not share these views.

Polygamy

Islam allows polygamy without ever imposing it, but on two conditions: first that the number of wives does not exceed four, and secondly, that the husband treats his wives equally, without favouring one at the expense of others (Qur'an 4.2–4). It should be noted that the number four had already been proposed in rabbinic circles. Some rabbis taught that in polygamy (permitted in the Hebrew Bible without any condition about numbers) the number of four wives was not normally to be exceeded. Muhammad is a special case which is directly regulated in the Qur'an. On the other hand, the same text (Qur'an 4, 2–4) allows other women in addition to these four wives with senior status; it calls them those 'whom your right hand possesses', i.e. concubine slaves. The text does not mention any number in this connection.

The question of polygamy did not cause difficulties until the last century. At that time, in a desire to see Muslim countries become powerful again, and noting the dire domestic consequences of rivalry between wives and their respective children, Muslim reformers like Qasim Amin, Muhammad Abduh (who died in 1905) and others reacted firmly. They clashed with the traditionalists of the time, who were often men of religion or men from a feudal background.

Here, briefly, are the main arguments which were put forward during this polemic.

The main arguments in favour of polygamy were:
– the practice of Muhammad and his first companions;

– the fact that physiologically the sexual needs of the male are more demanding than those of the woman and last to an advanced age;
– when a catastrophe like a war has reduced the proportion of men to women, only polygamy allows all the women to marry legally;
– open and free polygamy is better than all the hypocrisies of monogamists who practise adultery in secret or have mistresses.

It is indisputable that permission for polygamy has much favoured the expansion of Islam in Africa. Finally, if anyone attacks the matrimonial behaviour of the Prophet in front of Muslims, many of them will reply: 'And how many wives did the prophet David have?'

Furthermore, it is worth remarking that in many countries polygamy is practised only by a tiny minority. In Egypt not more than four per cent of the male population is polygamous, and the majority of these cases are bigamists who have taken a second wife to have male children (or indeed children of either sex) which their first wife has not given them.

One can also find an opposite attitude which, without condemning the practice of polygamy (since the Qur'an allows it), would want to restrict it to quite exceptional cases.
– A first argument in favour of monogamy as the norm for marriage is a concern for political power and modern development. Those who want the Muslim countries to become great and who note that polygamy often divides homes and thus ruins children's education, see salvation only in a solid education for future citizens, education which calls for united and monogamous homes. One of the most famous Egyptian Muslim reformers, Muhammad Abduh, wrote: 'There is no way of educating a nation in which polygamy has become widespread.'
– A second justification of monogamy comes from the idea of justice. The Qur'an requires the husband to be 'just' to his wives if he has several (Qur'an 4, 3). Now another verse of the same surah seems to say that justice is impossible in this case (Qur'an 4, 128–129). So, nowadays those who support monogamy note that in the modern world a husband can no longer be just with his wives if he has several of them. And according to the Qur'an itself polygamy has to be the exception (Qur'an 4, 39).

The seriousness of marriage

In the case of polygamy, as in the case of repudiations, many Muslims nowadays take the family seriously. Traditionalists protest openly against a custom which is all too well known. After the third repudiation, the husband can only take his wife back if she has married a third party and this third party has repudiated her in turn. It may happen that a husband pronounces the three repudiations too quickly and then regrets them: he goes to an obliging man who marries the woman in question for form's sake and then repudiates her. This shadow of a marriage is stigmatized by writers. I have seen a pamphlet in which the man who is too obliging in this respect was regarded as a 'hired buck'.

Some writers claim that certain words pronounced lightly cannot be regarded as legally valid. Some formulae which can be found relatively often cannot be regarded as valid, e.g.: 'I commit myself to doing this or that and my wife is repudiated if I don't.' Similarly, many writers stipulate that a threefold repudiation (the kind that entails the prohibition against taking back one's wife unconditionally) may be considered threefold only if it has been made on three different dates. To say 'I repudiate you' three times must be considered a single repudiation, and so on.

In general the feminist movements are in favour of these limitations on polygamy and divorce. But many Muslim women are content to say, as I heard one of them saying, 'You can't ask too much of men.'

It is sometimes suggested that the decisions in these spheres, which are so important for the future of the home, should go before judges and not be left to the initiative of the husband or relatives. However, this proposal comes up against the letter of the Muslim law and is rejected by many *'ulama* (learned men).

The new marriage legislation in many Muslim countries seeks to guarantee the seriousness of commitments (the fixing of a minimum age for marriage, requirement of the woman's consent, and so on). Only Tunisia and Turkey have gone so far as to prohibit polygamy by law.

Mixed marriages

The previous paragraphs only relate to marriages between Muslim men and Muslim women. What happens if one of the parties is not a Muslim?

In the first place, only the Muslim man can marry a non-Muslim woman, and even then only on condition that this is a woman taken from the 'people of scripture', i.e. above all Christians and Jews. The Muslim is prohibited from marrying a woman of traditional religion unless she becomes a Muslim.

Secondly, the Muslim woman can only marry a Muslim husband. The Christian or Jew who wants to marry her has to become a Muslim.

The Christian or Jewish woman who marries a Muslim can keep her faith and practise her religion, but the children have to be Muslims. In the case of a divorce or the death of the husband, small children whose care is normally entrusted to the mother will be taken from her unless she becomes a Muslim. Similarly, she will not receive the part of the inheritance normally provided for a widow unless she is converted. This double pressure causes many women to renounce their Jewish or Christian faith. Mixed marriages have also been a great occasion for Islamization.

In Africa south of the Sahara there is some tolerance on this point and the law is not always strictly applied, but elsewhere the Muslim community exerts such pressure that it is difficult for the Muslim partner to go against the law.

Abortion and birth control

These questions are as topical in Islamic countries as they are elsewhere. There is much discussion of birth control by non-natural means. Some are against it in the name of expansion and the numerical power of Islam, and also in the name of life. Others allow it, recalling that certain companions of Muhammad used contraceptives to enjoy women captured in war without diminishing their market value. The Prophet knew about this and allowed it.

The law prohibits abortion when the foetus is animated and is considered a living being. The Qur'an knows of a case in which, confronted with an unwanted birth, the pre-Islamic Arabs killed the child: it formally condemns this practice:

> You shall not kill your children for fear of want. We will provide for them and for you. To kill them is a great sin (Qur'an 17, 31).

But as the doctors of the law think that the foetus is only a human being after the fourth month, abortion is allowed in general during the first ninety days of pregnancy, and out of prudence is prohibited immediately afterwards.

So far, except in the middle classes and even then not always, these measures have come up against the deeply-rooted desire to have children, either because family values are most alive among the people or because the woman fears that her husband will leave her if she does not give him the children he wants, and either take a second wife or even repudiate her.

Adultery

To end this broad survey I should mention the question of adultery, for which the Muslim law prescribes the death penalty provided that the act has been confirmed either by confession or by the evidence of four male witnesses. The legislation is applied only in very traditional countries.

However, there are regions (for example the Arab world) where it has long been accepted that the oldest brother may put his sister to death for misconduct. I have been told that in West Africa the practice is not observed so rigidly since here, as in other matters, ancient custom is also involved.

Mention should also be made of prostitution, which poses the same problem as it does anywhere in the world. It is forbidden. The Qur'an prohibits a master from prostituting his female slaves, and also requires that the debauched should marry among themselves and not with normal men and women.

The Muslim law, dietary prohibitions, the economy

Dietary prohibitions

In Muslim doctrine beings are divided into the clean and the unclean. They can be clean in themselves but unclean as a consequence of a failure to observe the laws of purification. Thus for the Sunnites, Christians and Jews are clean in themselves, but unclean in that they do not purify themselves. Similarly, for Sunnites those who associate other gods with God are unclean in themselves. For the Shi'ites, even Christians and Jews are unclean in themselves. Consequences follow from this as to what food prepared by non-Muslims may lawfully be eaten by Muslims.

Sunnites will eat with Christians and Jews on condition that the dishes offered them contain only clean food. Among the Shi'ites matters are more delicate, and there was a time when schools going on outings had to provide two separate types of food, one for Christians and one for the Shi'ites. The question of meat products has also been raised; the Egyptian Reformists, following a *fatwa* (decision) of Muhammad Abduh at the beginning of this century, have accepted meat killed in abattoirs by Christians. But not everyone is so broad-minded.

In the sphere of utensils, for example, a plate from which a dog has eaten is unclean. It has to be washed six times in water and cleaned once with earth. Pigs are unclean but cats are not.

These dietary prohibitions recall those of the Hebrew Bible. Some are the same (the prohibition against eating pork). On the other hand, certain animals the meat of which is prohibited in the Hebrew Bible, like the camel, are permitted in Islam. Generally speaking we should note that the blood (including any animal the blood of which has not been let at the time of its death), pork, alcoholic drinks and a whole series of animals and reptiles, including the ass, are considered unclean and are forbidden. It is acceptable to eat them in times of famine, when it is impossible to survive otherwise.

By contrast, fish are eaten with their blood, so a fish thrown up by the sea can be eaten.

These questions of prohibitions and purity have been the origin of a vast casuistic literature, studying a mass of possibilities and proposing solutions. Finally, we should not forget that the meat of animals sacrificed in the name of another than God is formally prohibited to Muslims.

Possessions and property

While recognizing the right to property, Islam does not make it an intangible absolute. The exercise of this right is subject to a certain number of limitations. At one time, according to the Qur'an itself, the prophets' opponents reproached them for restricting their freedom at this point:

> 'Shu'ayb,' they replied, 'did your prayers teach you that we should renounce the gods of our fathers and that we ought not to conduct our affairs in the manner we pleased?' (Qur'an 11, 87).

Some modern writers explain this position by saying that for Muslims riches entail social service. We have already seen how private almsgiving is recommended, and the official organization of a collection for benevolent purposes in the form of the *zakat*. Various other measures thus regulate the use that a man may make of his property. The principle of expropriation and nationalization with indemnification is accepted in the name of the public good.

Theft

Theft is forbidden. The Qur'an prescribes that the thief shall have his hand cut off. A whole legislation specifies which, and what to cut off in the case of someone who offends more than once. Does this penalty apply in cases above a certain sum, and if so what is that sum?, etc.

This law is only applied in a few countries at present, but the fundamentalist movements want to make it general. However, such a measure does not in any way affect the whole category of those who steal by trading influence, by corruption and by sophisticated misappropriation. In the old Bedouin society the measure was in line with the situation. Nowadays, it is irrelevent to the problems posed for the establishment of a just and honest society.

Inheritance

The Qur'an itself contains a large number of indications on this issue; the jurists then harmonized them all. Muslim law provides for a fortune left at the time of death to be divided into two parts. The first and more important is automatically shared between the heirs in accordance with the proportions which the Qur'an has laid down in advance. The second, which cannot exceed a third of the property, can be left by will to the individual or individuals whom the testator has chosen freely.

Where property is shared out in proportions fixed in advance, the proportions go by degrees of kinship, but where such degrees are equal the woman receives a part equivalent to half that of the man. The reason for this is that in the family the man is the one who has the responsibility of feeding his family and paying their expenses. The portions laid down automatically can only go to Muslims: a convert from Islam loses his right to inherit, just as he is automatically divorced from his Muslim wife. Only the laicized legislation of Turkey no longer takes conversion into account.

Some doctors of the law like Muhammad Abduh (but not all) say that if the Christian widow of a Muslim official does not receive anything in the automatic share-out she should receive a portion provided by her husband in his will (in addition to the third that anyone can leave by personal preference). In fact, the practice of many Muslim countries (but again not all) is that she receives the pension of the widow of an official or retired official without the question of her religious allegiance being raised.

Lending at interest

The Qur'an, like the Hebrew Bible, formally prohibits lending at interest. The difference between the two cases is that the Hebrew Bible prohibited loans at interest when the Israelite was lending to another Israelite but did not prohibit it if the loan was made to a non-Israelite.

In the Qur'an the ban is absolute, no matter to whom the loan is made. The word used, *riba*, often translated usury, has been understood to cover even loans at very modest interest. The reasons given to justify the prohibition are usually as follows:

1. The fact that the usurer profits from a person's need in order to exploit him.

2. Islam does not accept that the lending of money should be remunerated solely as a function of the loan without the lender sharing in the risks of the operation.

In reality, lending at interest is so closely bound up with banking practices that it has not been possible to reject it totally. The Aswan dam was financed with a Russian loan at a symbolic interest rate of 2%. Only certain rigorists have rejected the difference between shares and debentures. Debentures which produce a fixed interest each year are rejected. By contrast, shares are seen as participation in the capital of a limited company the variable benefits of which are distributed annually among the shareholders once all the expenses and costs of the operation have been covered. They are acceptable.

Since 1975 Islamic banks have been founded with support from certain Arab governments and wealthy individuals. The intention was for the Islamic law to be respected in its entirety, so that any question of interest was ruled out. In fact the bank lends without interest and calls only for 'expenses' to cover the costs of its operations.

Games of chance

Games of chance in which money is involved, including cards, lotteries, etc., are banned by Islam. However, this ban is not always observed.

Slavery

Slavery was long considered an economic necessity, given the state of means of production in Muslim countries.

Islam accepted slavery as a social fact and no one felt the need to react against it immediately.

Christianity, too, did not initially react against slavery. At one point the Qur'an takes the inequality between the slave and the free man as an illustration of how things are (Qur'an 16, 71). But the question has been inflamed by an anti-Muslim apologetic which seeks to heap on Islam all the shame for a practice which has now been abolished. It may indeed have been the case that the raids of Muslim slavers were the last to take place when elsewhere this kind of traffic had already disappeared. However, it is for those whose ancestors have never practised slavery to cast the first stone.

It is true that, like Christianity, Islam for a long time accepted slavery, but both religions contained principles of brotherhood which, little by little, have made the suppression of this institution seem normal. The main difference between Christianity and Islam was that in Islam sexual relations with female slaves are officially permitted in addition to legitimate marriage; hence there was a supplementary traffic to supply the harems. By contrast, Christian slave trading was engaged in supplying labour. In the eighteenth and nineteenth centuries the adventurers of Europe and America had more powerful means of transport and their relatively modern ships took cargoes of slaves to the plantations of the American colonies.

Quite frequently the Muslim tried to free other Muslims from slavery (while accepting the service of a Muslim slave to a Muslim). This liberation is prescribed for as an expiation for multiple failures to observe the law; the *zakat* can also be used for this purpose. However, neither the Muslim nor the Christian adventurers, nor certain kings of Africa, were restrained by moral considerations in this sphere, and once the movement had been launched, people's pockets profited directly from it (or did not) without their either asking questions or realizing the situation.

The history of Islam contains a formidable revolt of slaves from East Africa who were used in the government plantations of Iraq. It took place in the ninth century and is known as the

Zanj revolt (the word Zanj in Arabic denotes the inhabitants of Ethiopia and East Africa. The island of Zanzibar is called Zanjiba in Arabic, i.e. the country of the Zanj). The catalyst for this revolt was the intrigue of a Shi'ite and it was supported by the mass of rebel slaves. A whole area of Iraq, from Basra to the vicinity of Wasit, thus escaped the authority of the caliph of Baghdad. The caliph, hindered in his movements by the secession of Egypt, which had just made itself independent, could not really react for about fifteen years. The revolt was then put down. These events have recently been the object of several studies, and like the revolt of Spartacus in Rome have been seen as the tremors heralding future world revolutions.

We should note that female slaves who gave a child to their masters were put in a separate legal category. They are called *umm walad* (mother of a child) and cannot be sold. They have to be freed on the death of their master. Compare this with Deuteronomy 21.10–14, where the woman prisoner of war is married as a wife; if she ceases to please and is repudiated, she is treated as a free woman and cannot be sold.

However, the child of a slave couple belonging to the same master also belongs to him.

We should note, finally, what a difference there was between the domestic slave, who was often considered an inferior member of the family, and the slave working in the plantations or in industrial enterprises, whose lot was very harsh and who remained at the mercy of overseers who were often irresponsible. When slavery was suppressed in Egypt in the nineteenth century, many 'dadas' or African nurses who had brought up children preferred to stay with the families in which they had always worked. On the other hand, eye-witnesses have spoken of the unenviable lot of agricultural slave workers in the Sahara oases around 1910.

At present the press sometimes runs campaigns about the remnants of slavery in Muslim countries. This is often a way of making people forget other more blatant social injustices. The time when slavery was the great means of exploiting men and women is now over. Unfortunately economic and racial injustice, oppression by the police and the international trade in women for prostitution rank well above it now.

The laws of peace and war

The history of Islam contains enough wars for the governing principles in this sphere to appear clearly. Furthermore it is very easy to compare practice with theory, as there are many legal texts on the subject.

The original Muslims faced two kinds of situation which in turn led to two very well-defined attitudes.

First, initially the Muslims had to adopt defensive positions and oppose those who wanted to remove them from power in Mecca. To escape persecution, the first faithful took refuge in Medina in 622 under the leadership of Muhammad himself. This exodus was considered to be in effect an expulsion of the Muslims. The right of Muslims to recover their citizenship and their goods is also loudly proclaimed in the Qur'an. Hence the first kind of text, which seeks to justify any defensive war and to recover anything plundered from Islam:

> Fight for the sake of God those that fight against you, but do not attack them first. God does not love the aggressors. Kill them wherever you find them. Drive them out of the places from which they drove you. Idolatry is worse than carnage (Qur'an 2, 190).

The Arabic word translated aggressor can also mean transgressor. So there are two types of commentary. Some, like the Jalalayn commentary, interpret this as meaning 'Do not be aggressors by being the first to fight.' But others see in this verse an obligation for the war to remain within certain limits: for example, noncombatants are not to be killed and certain basic necessities are not to be looted, etc.

The reference to idolatry relates to the risk of Muslim apostasy. If the Muslims are put in circumstances that endanger their faith, war becomes a legitimate means of maintaining this faith.

This text from the Qur'an is the basis for theories about a first kind of war which is called a defensive war. During the last two centuries of struggle against the Western colonialist powers, the Muslims publicized it to stress their rights, and now it applies perfectly to the conflict between Palestine and Israel.

Secondly, there is the offensive war. We meet this when the position of the Muslims at Medina had been consolidated. At that time the Muslims turned their arms against the rest of Arabia and even against the exterior. These wars of conquest were presented as follows: Muhammad is said to have written to a certain number of rulers or political figures (the king of Persia, the emperor of Byzantium, the governor of Egypt, etc.) letters inviting them to become Muslims. Is this an authentic tradition? At all events it is classic Muslim tradition. Anyway, when those who had received letters did not obey, the Muslims attacked them. This allows them to justify any offensive war against a neighbour who rejects Islam.

The earlier views allow all kinds of theories about war which respect a certain number of humanitarian principles. In fact Muslims often took the initiative in attacks up to the colonial era. At this point, as the victims of aggression, they passed over into the opposite camp and became anti-imperialists.

What will happen in the future? Modern technology has completely changed the way in which wars are fought. It is probable that in the future justification will always be found for unforseeable *de facto* situations, if only on the principle of protecting Muslim minorities, which can be stretched a very long way. At present, Muslim countries conform to the verse of the Qur'an which calls on believers to arm themselves (cf. Qur'an 8, 60). In 1979, when there was a strong rumour that Pakistan had made an atomic bomb, triumphant voices were raised in

Characteristics of Islam

It continues to be dominated by an attitude of defensive struggle. First persecuted because it claimed exclusiveness of worship (*'ibada*) for Allah, God 'without associate', 'without rival', or 'son', or 'daughters', or 'wives', it ended up making itself an aggressive collective, precisely because it was on the defensive: within against the 'hypocrites' and the Jews, and on the outside against the 'associationists' (the polytheists of Mecca). Having proved victorious over both of these, it formed a fighting community animated by a strong sense of brotherhood in the faith and with a mission of promoting and defending the 'rights of God' and the 'rights of the servants' (of God). Touchy about these 'rights' (above all those of God), and believing itself always to be threatened, it took refuge in struggle by polemic or by force of arms. So Islam will not just be a religion: it will also be a political organization and a separate cultural world, and will be all this at the same time. This conception of the role of Islam must be always kept in mind if one is to avoid the all too current contempt which consists in judging it from a Western point of view which emerged from Christianity. Also because of this, it still remains the religion of the masses, of the collectivity, more than the affair of the individual towards his God.

J.-M. Abd el-Jalil, *Islam et nous*, pp.89f.

the Muslim world to celebrate what they called the first Muslim atomic bomb.

In spite of everything, Islam favours peace, and when our contemporaries study the contribution of religion to the cause of peace, Islam claims a peaceful aspect. First of all there will be the peace of paradise, that place of happiness called 'Dar es Salaam' ('the dwelling place of peace') in the Qur'an, but also that peace which must reign between Muslims, the sign of which is the greeting with which Muslims address one another (*as-salamu 'alaykum*, peace be upon you). Non-Muslims will experience this as the peace of the strong, peace after victory. Between Muslims it will be a relative peace.

For the Muslim rarely forgets the duty incumbent on him: that of extending the reign of the Muslim law, first by peaceful means but also, if need be, by warlike means.

Pride is evidenced everywhere in the Muslim world when Islam is extended. By contrast, attitudes over lost territory vary. When the loss was in the past and there is no question of going back, these are regrets and nostalgia, as in the case of the memories of Muslim Spain and its glories. When the recuperation of what has been lost is still possible, the struggle is carried on (liberation from colonialism or the war against Israel).

In modern times Muslims have adopted all the ways of fighting that can be used by oppressed people: guerilla war, the taking of hostages, hijacking aircraft regardless of international disapproval. However, not all Muslims agree on the suitability of some of these means, even if there is agreement over the main ones, for example the oil war. Nevertheless a universal aspiration to unity regularly emerges, despite the persistent schisms within the Muslim world. Marx's slogan, 'Workers of the world unite', in fact corresponds to another slogan which is formulated less often, but which inspires many leaders: 'Muslims of the world unite'.

Plunder

With questions about war are associated questions about plunder (or to speak more modestly, about what is captured in war). The Qur'an and Muslim law contain numerous regulations on this question, distinguishing between plunder taken in the course of fighting and that which the community has gained by other means (for example the property of Jewish tribes driven out of Medina). A fifth of the plunder taken in fighting went to the Prophet.

The treatment of conquered countries

It was after wars and conquests that Muslim society took on its contours. Inhabitants of a country who had kept their old religion gradually came under the thumb of the new masters who little by little came to be in the majority as a result of regular conversions to Islam. The status of these inhabitants varied, depending on the region.

In principle, only Muslims live in the Hijaz (the province of Arabia which includes Mecca and Medina), even if nowadays non-Muslim groups can be found there outside the two sacred territories of Mecca and Medina. At the beginning of Islam, after several years during which Christians and Muslims continued to live there, it was decided that only the Muslims would have the right of permanent residence, and the caliphate of 'Umar saw the exodus to Iraq of the Christians of the Hijaz. The sacred territories of Mecca and Medina and even more the two cities themselves are in principle totally forbidden to non-Muslims. However, several exceptions are known. In the seventh century, the father of two converts to Islam lived with them in Mecca while remaining a Christian, and similarly, in the seventeenth and eighteenth centuries, pilgrims took Christian slaves with them as servants during the pilgrimage.

In the other conquered countries, the Muslims who were full citizens had pride of place, and these were normally the ones in charge. Second came the 'people of scripture', i.e. those whom the Qur'an mentions as monotheists, having received the revealed scriptures. These were above all Jews, Christians and those who took the name of Sabaeans, mentioned in the Qur'an, to enjoy a protected status (they were known as *dhimmi*). The Qur'an rules that the peoples of scripture will be attacked unless they pay a special tax for protection and maintain an inferior place (see Qur'an 9, 29). They have rights in Muslim society, and in the Middle Ages many of them contributed to the splendour of Muslim civilization. In practice, marriage apart, many non-Muslims have been given this kind of protected status.

Finally, there is a third group in Muslim society, that of the 'associators' (*mushrikun*), who do not profess pure monotheism and worship associated deities alongside God. Their status is not clear. In fact they were never given much responsibility and sometimes were segregated.

In the Middle Ages those under 'protection' were discriminated against; they wore clothing of a special colour, could not ride horses, and so on, measures which were applied more or less strictly depending on time and place.

Nowadays the constitutions of most Muslim countries provide for all citizens to be equal. The respective positions of Muslims and non-Muslims are determined much more by whichever party has a majority (or is the ruling group) than by strictly religious questions. The situation is different in countries in which there are almost no indigenous Christians (for example, in North Africa) and in those which have Christianity rooted in the area (Middle Eastern Christians, for example, or African Christian countries).

It is quite difficult to appreciate the situation of Christian minorities in Islamic countries since outwardly everyone will say that all is well and no one wants foreigners interfering in their affairs. In fact there are several delicate areas, primarily that of nominations to important posts. A Muslim fundamentalist leader like Abu'l Ala al-Maududi of Pakistan (who died in 1979) wrote in connection with the Qur'an verse on the tax for protection (Qur'an 9, 29) that those under protection must not be entrusted with posts of leadership which rightly belong to Muslims. The rulers of Muslim countries are not as exclusivist, but despite everything there is a latent tendency in this direction.

A second matter is the building of churches. In 1972 there were clashes in Egypt between Copts and Muslims in a small town about twenty miles from Cairo where a room which served as a

'No constraint in religion'
Qur'an 2, 256

Traditionally (cf. the commentary on the Qur'an below) this verse has been interpreted in two different senses:

* Sometimes in a general sense, but it has then been abrogated by this verse: *'Make war on the unbelievers and the hypocrites and deal rigorously with them'* (Qur'an 9, 73).

* Or in a specific sense relating to the people of the Book. According to one tradition a Muslim of Medina, one of the Ansar (helpers), had two sons who had embraced Christianity before Islam; they had then gone to Medina and their father had joined them saying: 'I will not leave you until you become Muslims.' They refused, and took their difference to the Messenger of God: the verse was then revealed (Baydawi on Qur'an 2, 256).

Nowadays this verse is understood as prohibiting the use of constraint in persuading an adult to embrace Islam: entrance into Islam must be of a person's own free will.

A minor must follow the religion of his father or his mother if they are to become Muslims.

Furthermore, a certain number of thinkers would like this principle to inspire a more open interpretation of the Muslim law.

This position would have important consequences if it were followed.

church and had been used for worship without official permission was burned down. The government immediately intervened out of a concern for national unity and understanding between all citizens. An official commission of enquiry was nominated and the report was published in the great Cairo daily *al-Ahram*. Among the causes of friction listed was this. The Copts were building churches without permission because when they bought land to build a church and asked permission to do so, others would rush to build a mosque on the nearest free land (which needed no permission) and permission was refused to the Christians because the church would be too near to a mosque. Hence the temptation to build without a permit in order to avoid this trap.

A last delicate point is that of the apostate Muslim. Those under protection in Islamic territory are tolerated on condition that they do not engage in any kind of proselytism. While thousands of Christians pass over to Islam each year and are fêted, it is never admitted that a Muslim has left Islam to become a Christian. A strong tradition known in the Middle Ages said that to shed the blood of a Muslim (to kill him) is lawful only in three cases: the blood of a Muslim who has killed a Muslim; one who has committed adultery; and the apostate Muslim. This last point remained in force up to the last century.

Apostasy is in fact to be envisaged in the perspectives of the wars which marked the beginnings of Islam. The apostate was a deserter who went over to the enemy, and in all armies such an action is punishable by death. The situation then changed. At the end of the nineteenth century thinkers like Muhammad Abduh in Egypt observed that since the state of war no longer existed, the convert should not be disturbed if he did not attack Islam. However, not all are of his opinion, and the tradition in question is still taught unreservedly in the school books on Muslim religion in Egypt.

Contemporary fundamentalist movements want to re-establish the Muslim law in its entirety, including putting to death the apostate Muslim. In Egypt the Orthodox Copt Patriarch Amba Shenuda made a personal approach to President Anwar Sadat in 1977 to ask for such a law not to be passed. If it were accepted, numerous Copts who had become Muslims in order to marry and regretted this action would be subject to the death penalty if they went back and resumed their Christian faith, as frequently happens. The law was not passed at that time, but it was adopted some years later. And the problem arises all over the Muslim world, with the same pressure from the fundamentalists for official recognition of the Muslim law in its entirety and under its strict mediaeval form.

Only God knows what the future will bring.

7

Piety, Muslim Mysticism and the Brotherhoods

The previous pages have sought to present the main points of the dogma and law of Islam as they appear through official teaching. In fact religious experience is inseparable from theory and more than once I have reported testimonies or impressions from experience. With the subject of this chapter, piety and mysticism, we enter more into the sphere of religious experience. Islam is at present contributing to the preservation of a certain number of basic religious values which are not exclusive to it but which are endangered by the cares and pleasures of the consumer society. So there are Muslims who are concerned to interiorize their faith and not to keep solely to the ritual of obligatory prayers and a legalist mentality.

This movement, which tends to develop more of an experiential relationship between human beings and God is called sufism. According to the most widespread view, this word is derived from the Arabic *suf*, wool, a recollection of the dress worn by the first sufis in imitation of monks, whether Christian or of other faiths. The

term sufism covers a broader area than mysticism. It embraces every aspect of the desire for interiorization or a more sensitive expression than the mere formality of prayer, ranging from the adoption of collective practices of piety in the popular brotherhoods to the poems and teachings of the great spiritual masters. It is especially important not to oppose sufism systematically to activism, since on many occasions in history the sufis have been engaged in political action, like Uthman Dan Fodio, the founder of the Sokoto empire in the nineteenth century.

The sense of the presence of God

One of the elements on which sufism is based is the sense of the presence of God. This presence is not as intimate as that of God in Christianity, but is the presence of a beloved master whose demands are linked with very great kindness towards anyone who obeys him.

A series of interviews carried out by an Egyptian Muslim in 1969 included the question: At what moment do you feel closest to God? Here

are some of the most characteristic replies:
- Whenever a man reads the Qur'an he is close to God.
- I feel closest to God during prayers in the last part of the night.
- I believe that God is very close to me.
- I never for a moment feel that I am far from God.

This belief in the presence of God (especially in prayer or when reciting the Qur'an) underlies a whole life-style or at least a certain type of piety.

There are texts in the Qur'an and the traditions (*hadith*) which teach this proximity to God. Thus:

> When My servants question you about Me, tell them that I am near (Qur'an 2, 186).

A tradition explains vividly that if a man goes an inch towards God, God will come a yard towards him. If he goes a yard towards God, God will come a furlong towards him. In short, if a man makes an effort to approach God, God will respond to an even greater degree in coming to meet him (compare the same idea expressed more concisely in the Letter of James 4.8).

Or there is the famous text: 'Serve God as if you saw Him, and if you do not see Him, He sees you.'

The whole of the doctrine of the Qur'an rests on this sense of the presence of God. God sees everything and knows everything; nothing escapes him. And the best Muslims live out this idea. Many of them repeat formulae, or spontaneous prayers, counting them on their beads, and these prayers help them to live in the presence of God.

This repetition of brief formulae can be found especially in the offices of the brotherhoods. One of the greatest Muslim mystics, Jalal ad-Din al-Rumi (who died at Konia in Asia Minor – the Iconium of St Paul's journeys – in 1273) has an excellent image for stressing the value of such repetitions. He speaks of it in his work entitled *The Masnavi*. A man was repeating the name of God, 'Allah, Allah . . .' One day Satan appeared to him and asked him what benefit he gained from such a prayer, since God did not reply to

him. The man then stopped repeating his invocation 'Allah, Allah'. But God made him understand that to say 'Allah' was at the same time both a call and a response, and that God was present when the man pronounced His name (this story can be found in *Teachings of Rumi: The Masnavi*, abridged and translated by E. H. Whinfield, The Octagon Press 1979, p. 114).

The great dates in the history of Muslim mysticism

Here are a few landmarks against which to set the names I shall be mentioning.

Sufism sees the beginnings of Islam as having been particularly marked by two factors. On the one hand, austerity of life, prayers directed towards Mecca and nocturnal vigils, and the poverty of the earliest community at Medina, have left memories which the Sufis were fond of recalling later.

However, above all when the conquests and the mass of plunder enriched the first Muslims to an unbelievable degree (one need only look in Ibn Sa'd's book of biographies at the list of the fortunes which certain companions left on their deaths, which were colossal), there were sincere and upright Muslims who refused to abandon the more austere ideal of the first years and rejected the easy life of their fortunate fellow-religionists.

One name to remember a century later is al-Hasan of Basra, who died in 728 and who lived amongst his contemporaries without taking part in the conflicts which set them one against another. The Sufis and certain thinkers claim him as their ancestor. The Sufis often still have a document or chain of initiation mentioning the name of the master who initiated them, the master of this master and so on. Now in most cases the spiritual line goes back to Muhammad, but passes through al-Hasan of Basra. At the same time there was an ascetic movement in Khurasan, a province celebrated for its civiliza-tion, which lasted until the country was devastated by Mongol invaders in the thirteenth century. Khurasan covered the north-east of what is now Iran: it bordered on part of Afghanistan and in the north on territory which now belongs to the Soviet Union.

Between 750 and 950 we see the golden age of Muslim mysticism, especially at the school of Baghdad.

Then with the end of the tenth and the eleventh century there begins the period of the theorists of the spiritual life; these composed treatises analysing the different stages of this life and the notions that it prompts. Among these

treatises is the famous work by al-Ghazali, who died in 1111, entitled *The Revival of the Religious Sciences*.

The most characteristic feature of the twelfth and thirteenth centuries is the appearance of movements of popular piety or brotherhoods (*ilturuq as-sufiyya*) each of which developed in the wake of a holy figure.

Finally, from the same period, there developed a mysticism rooted in a philosophy with a whole theory of the world emanating from God yet resting in Him.

Attitudes towards God: the theme of the love of God

The notion of the love of God is far from being alien to Muslim mystic literature. The very word 'love' is accepted by Islam, though the doctors of the law often restrict its meaning. It can be found several times in the Qur'an.

First it expresses the satisfaction or rebuke of God over certain human attitudes:

God does not love the unbelievers (Qur'an 3, 32).

God loves those who fear him (Qur'an 3, 76).

We met this idea of the Muslim who obeys and loves to obey the orders of God earlier.

However, some texts of the Qur'an are even more explicit, and it is on them that the mystics rely when they go further, despite the opposition of the jurists. They include this verse, the

words of which are attributed to Muhammad:

If you love God follow me. God will love you and forgive you your sins (Qur'an 3, 31).

Believers, if any of you renounce the faith, Allah will replace them by others who love Him and are loved by Him (Qur'an 5, 59).

In fact the notion of the love of God is increasingly mentioned by Muslims, perhaps under the influence of the brotherhoods or in competition with Christianity. It figures largely in Muslim schoolbooks in Egypt and Syria, but is rarely to be found in old texts except among the mystics. A devotional book published recently in Cairo and entitled 'With God' (*ma'a Allah*) has a whole chapter devoted to the love of God (*mahabbat Allah*).

For many people, the expression is in fact about merciful goodness or *rahma*. Thus the pages about the love of God in the book *ma'a Allah* recall the gifts of God, his creation, all he gives to humankind, his forgiveness for sins. This notion is truly at the heart of Islam. This love is mingled with the goodness of an infinitely good master towards his servants; 'Tell my servants that I am the one who pardons, who is merciful' (Qur'an 15, 29).

For all present-day Muslims, love is basically a modern word to denote what their ancestors called mercy or the goodness of the infinitely good God. However, it is also certain that a number of believers have been fascinated by this love of God and have felt in themselves a call to respond to it unreservedly, to give themselves and their life entirely to the one who was everything to them. This is the whole question of the love of humankind for God; what does it signify? Strict jurists say that human beings cannot love God in himself but only his law, his service, his will, but many mystics have largely gone beyond this position. An example will allow us to see this better.

Rabi'a al-Adawiyya (713–801) and the pure love of God

The notion of the love of God has been highlighted in a more specific way by a famous Muslim woman whose memory has been popularized in a film. Her mysticism was centred on the notion of pure love. This was that fascination for God who alone counts in the eyes of the faithful, towards whom all life, all thought and all being are orientated.

Born in a poor home, Rabi'a was stolen as a child and sold as a slave. But her holiness brought her freedom. A flute player, she abandoned her career and withdrew to live a life of prayer and celibacy. First she lived in the desert, south of Iraq, and then at Basra, where the circle of disciples formed around her.

She taught the pure love of God. God has to be loved for himself and not for other reasons. We have some very fine prayers which are attributed to her, like this one:

Lord! The stars shine and men's eyes are closed. The kings have closed their gates and every lover is alone with his beloved. Here I am alone with You.

One day Rabi'a went out into the streets of the town with a jug of water in one hand and a flaming torch in the other. 'Where are you going?', someone asked her. 'I am going to quench hell and set fire to paradise so that God may be adored and loved for himself and not for his rewards.'

This woman's detachment from all that was not God was absolute; she regarded as insignificant, compared with the love of God, even that which those around her regarded as being eminently religious, like the religious sciences, and even the Ka'ba or love of the Prophet. This view is the fruit of her personal religious experience and of the radiance of God in her life. There are no direct external influences, Christian or otherwise. The Qur'an gives her the sense of a divine absolute, of the vanity of all creatures compared with God. She loves God as one who is absent from him here below and scarcely speaks of the love of God for her. Christians may be struck by both what seems to be her absolute sincerity in her relation to God and the lack of precision in the way in which she expresses it. But to say that she envisaged God as something that she is lacking would be completely wrong.

Rabi'a's attitude can be explained by the tension which is evident in Islam between the absoluteness of God and the place which is given in practice to all that is not God, even paradise. If God is all, how is paradise not centred on God himself? And why is such an important place given to the joys of the senses? It is against giving such a place to that which is not God that Rabi'a rebels. As her conduct puts in question the equilibrium of Islam, she was criticized by those who saw this as a danger.

The love of God and mystical poetry

The idea of the love of God recurs in mystical poetry, but we cannot say that it occupies pride of place there. In these poems, the religion of love is contrasted with that of the law. A whole symbolism serves to express this love of God: wine, the beloved, and so on. Certain poems thus contrast the cabaret with the mosque to signify the religion of love and the religion of the law. Love is conceived of as a response to the attraction of beauty, and one tradition which stresses the beauty of God is often cited in mystical circles. However, there has been too much vagueness in the cult of beauty, and it can be impossible to know whether love really extends to God or whether it stops as its symbol, a particular kind of earthly beauty. The philosophical tendency to see the world as an emanation of God increases the danger. The distinction between the Creator and creatures became blurred; one can also understand how such an attribute has provoked a good deal of opposition, simply because of its equivocal nature. The danger of aestheticism and amoralism was not imaginary, nor even that of the occasional use of drugs to create artificial states of mind.

> One spring day Rabi'a went into her room and bowed her head in meditation.
>
> Her maidservant said to her: 'Mistress, come outside and see the marvellous works of God.'
>
> 'No,' she replied, 'come in, so that you can contemplate their Creator.
>
> Contemplation of the Creator prevents me from contemplating what he has created.'
>
> *Anthology of Sufism*

Attitudes towards God: the theme of the divine Oneness

In fact the real primary theme of Muslim mysticism is that of the divine Oneness. It is the central theme of the Qur'an. Islam is the religion of the *tawhid*, the proclamation of the divine Oneness. God is all and human beings are nothing. As a consequence, life, prayer or contemplation are a matter of proclaiming by one's attitude that God alone is everything.

Human beings must annihilate themselves. They can do so:
• by annihilating their wills in obeying the orders of God. For the doctors of the Law this is the highest form;
• by annihilating themselves in contemplation, bearing witness that there is no god but God. So the oneness is a oneness of witness. Men and women confess that God alone counts and that all his creatures are nothing in comparison with him.

'Your place in my heart is my whole heart' says the mystic al-Hallaj (who was crucified in Baghdad in 922). For many mystics this way of annihilation is the highest;
• Finally, there is a more philosophical conception of annihilation, which affirms that the world has no existence and that God alone is. From this point of view by nature human beings are nothing and their duty is to become aware of this situation. This position rests on the idea that the world proceeds from God by emanation.

This last position, which was especially held by the mystic Ibn al-'Arabi (who was born in Murcia, in southern Spain, in 1116 and died in 1240 at Damascus in Syria, where he is buried), provoked numerous controversies in the Muslim world. In the Near East, his attitude has been periodically challenged, but there are always voices in his defence. Ibn al-'Arabi's position is also to be found in India, where the rulers of the Mogul dynasty (sixteenth and seventeenth century) used his doctrines to justify a policy of *rapprochement* between the religions, especially between Muslims, Christians, Hindus and Buddhists. Around 1975, in Egypt, the statesubsidized publication of one of Ibn al-'Arabi's main (and voluminous) works led to disturbances which even produced a ban from the People's Assembly on continuing the printing. However, this measure was withdrawn some weeks later after competent figures had protested and demonstrated that it went beyond the powers of this assembly.

This position has sometimes been described as pantheism, but that accusation is unfair. Fundamentally we find here the same problem as that of Meister Eckhart and the Rhineland mystics at the end of the Middle Ages, who dreamed above all of the greatness of God. If God is everything, what becomes of the creature?

From the eighteenth century on, mystics like al-Nabulusi in Syria and Shah Wali Allah in India expounded this position in quite an acceptable way. God alone exists in himself (*per se*, as Latin scholars would say) and creatures exist only through him. But in the Middle Ages, what was the position? It is difficult to know, since it is expressed in poems and the significance of the poetry is not always easy to determine. It is certain that some figures were engaged in a form of intellectual or intellectualist gnosis, with the creation of esoteric chapels and groups.

The basic idea of this trend is that man's true homeland, from which he comes and towards which he will return, is not this world but the world of God, the world of the spirits. The *Masnavi*, that magnificent poem by Jalal ad-Din al-Rumi, begins with the poem of the reed flute. The sound of the flute is the lamentation of the reed which is nostalgic for its home, those distant marshes where it was cut and carried away. Thus the plaint of the mystic, expressed by the flute, is that of a being cut off from his true home.

The annihilation of the self

The Muslim mystics understood that if God was everything, the human self had to be annihilated before him. The *Masnavi* expresses this idea in the story of the friend who replies 'It is I'.

> Once a man came and knocked at the door of his friend.
> His friend said, 'Who art thou, O faithful one?'
> He said, ''Tis I.' He answered, 'There is no admittance.
> There is no room for the "raw" at my well-cooked feast.
> Naught but fire of separation and absence
> Can cook the raw one and free him from hypocrisy!
> Since thy "self" has not yet left thee,
> Thou must be burned in fiery flames.'
> The poor man went away, and for one whole year
> Journeyed burning with grief for his friend's absence.
> His heart burned till it was cooked; then he went again
> And drew near to the house of his friend.
> He knocked at the door in fear and trepidation
> Lest some careless word might fall from his lips.
> His friend shouted, 'Who is that at the door?'
> He answered, ''Tis Thou who art at the door, O Beloved!'
> The friend said, 'Since 'tis I, let me come in,
> There is not room for two "I's" in one house.'

from *Teachings of Rumi: The Masnavi*, abridged and translated by E. H. Whinfield, The Octagon Press 1979, pp. 47f.

Is this metaphysical poetry which would be difficult to accept? Is it not rather a lesson in psychology? The literary genre of the poem does not lend itself to over-firm interpretations.

The lesson of this story is clear. Do we not have the same problem in Christianity with the annihilation of the self? As St Paul wrote: 'It is no longer I who live but Christ who lives in me.'

The sense of God and the Muslim brotherhoods

Up to the twelfth century the schools of Muslim mysticism were the real centres of mysticism: they reached a small number of people, several disciples grouped each time around a spiritual master. With the rise of the brotherhoods, for the most part we pass to a simpler piety, although some great spiritual figures have emerged within the brotherhoods. In general we find the emergence of popular groups, well-structured and bringing together a large number of brothers.

Doctrinally, the brotherhoods do not get lost in major philosophical considerations; the only possible exception would be certain esoteric groups. In general, most of the founders of the brotherhoods were orthodox men. The charge made against the brotherhoods was above all that of complacency and stagnation, ignorance and often superstitious practices. The heads of the brotherhoods were criticized for the place that they claimed in the life of their disciples (veneration, obedience and so on). In the colonial period they were accused of playing political games with the enemies of Islam, whereas on the contrary some of them were fighting against the invaders. In Algeria a local leader of the brotherhood of the Qadiriyya, the emir 'Abd al-Qadar was from 1832–1847 the soul of the resistance to the French conquest. Elsewhere the Sanusiyya resisted the Italians. But the brotherhoods were accused of taking refuge in passivity instead of struggling, of allowing themselves to be bought by gifts and honours. Nevertheless, these charges do not apply at all places and all times. And it would be better to say that the brotherhoods played an important role in the life of Islam over the centuries.

I shall be discussing here only the two main brotherhoods which contributed to the Islamization of Africa south of the Sahara. There were many others. I might instance the Mirghaniyya, who were so important in the Sudan, or various branches of the Shadhiliyya, for example the Yashrutiyya, who split off from the Darqawiyya, who themselves had split off from the Shadhiliyya. The Yashrutiyya were established on the Comoro islands by Sheik Muhammad Ma'ruf ben Sheikh Ahmad ibn Abi Bakr, who lived from 1853–1905. He had to go into exile for years and used the period to develop his brotherhood. He returned to the Comoros, where he built a centre (*zawiya*) from which he extended his influence over the continent. He headed his brotherhood as *khalifa* on the Isle of Anjouan and on Moroni.

The two brotherhoods I shall concentrate on are the Qadiriyya and the Tijaniyya.

The brotherhood of the Qadiriyya (with numerous branches)

This is connected with a Muslim saint, Abd alQadir al-Jilani (1078–1167/9), who was the superior of a Muslim monastery in Baghdad and director of a school of Muslim law following the Hanbali rite. His talents as a preacher were famous and during his life he had disciples who made his teaching known in various countries. A certain number of books on spirituality are attributed to him. Islam has often canonized 'sages'; Abd al-Qadir is one example. He gave courses on Qur'anic exegesis, tradition and Muslim law. He is said to have converted numerous Jews and Christians to Islam.

He was a perfectly orthodox master. He stressed obedience to the Muslim law and the entire acceptance of the message of Muhammad. He taught that the perfect man, the saint, is the one who has transcended his accidental (or superficial) self to attain his real and interior self.

The second point that he noted was a struggle against hidden *shirk* (polytheism). Fighting against this hidden polytheism consists in seeing the will of God in whatever happens, the best and the worst, and submitting to his will in accordance with the law.

Abd al-Qadir al-Jilani is buried in Baghdad and his tomb is a celebrated place of pilgrimage. At present his brotherhood is spread over a number of countries, from Indonesia to West Africa. In West Africa it is one of the two orders which have contributed most to the conversion of the Pygmies; a large number of believers from this area belong either to the Qadiriyya or to the other order, the Tijaniyya.

The brotherhood of the Qadiriyya world-wide is under the authority of a descendant of Abd alQadir al-Jilani living in Baghdad (the supreme sheikh); it comprises heads of zones (*khalifa*), members (*ikhwan*), i.e. 'brothers' in Arabic, and a mass of novices and initiates (*muridun*).

The brotherhoods hold prayer meetings with their members once or more a week, and we shall discuss these later. At the same time, however, members are accustomed to recite a certain number of invocations each day in private. At the end of the last century the Qadiriyya of North Africa had a kind of daily office in private.

The prayers include:
– one hundred times: I ask pardon from God (*astaghfir Allah*);
– one hundred times: praise to the transcendent God (*subhan Allah*);
– one hundred times: a formula of praise in honour of Muhammad;
– five hundred times: there is no god but God (*la ilah illa llah*).

Down to the period of colonial occupation the brotherhoods often played a political role in many Muslim countries, especially in Africa south of the Sahara. I said earlier that Usman Dan Fodio, the master of Sokoto, who founded an empire extending from the Niger to the North Cameroons, was a member of the brotherhood of the Qadiriyya.

The brotherhood of the Tijaniyya

This brotherhood is younger than the previous one and is also less widespread. However, its role in West and Central Africa has been considerable. Its founder, Ahmad at-Tijani (1747–1815), was a North African Muslim. Born in a small town in the south of Nigeria, on the edge of the desert, he studied there before going to Fez (Morocco) and then continued his studies in other cities. At the age of thirty-six he left to make the pilgrimage to Mecca and went through Cairo. He travelled for ten years and made contact with several brotherhoods. The Tijani declare that their founder took the best from these various brotherhoods. On his return to Algeria he founded his own movement at the instigation of the Prophet of Islam, Muhammad, who is said to have appeared to him in a dream. After a number of years, in 1798 he chose Fez as the centre of his brotherhood. He travelled a good deal, but kept Fez as his base. It was there that he was buried after his death.

This brotherhood has a simpler ritual than the previous one. It stresses the duty of thanking God for all that he has given but rarely speaks of asceticism. It has neither long retreats nor repeated fasts, and its prayers are easy and shorter. It is also said in particular to have attracted well-to-do people as well as the simple faithful. This is how one witness describes the prayer at which he was present. This is the shortest office, since the Tijani also have their solemn meetings with a communal liturgy. Note, too, that the ritual also has variants.

Once or twice a day, in addition to their five daily ritual prayers, the brothers must recite:
– one hundred times: I ask pardon from God (*astaghfir Allah*);
– one hundred times: a short prayer in honour of Muhammad;
– one hundred times: *La ilah illa llah* (there is no god but God).

The more solemn liturgies include recitations of the Qur'an and often religious poems. The brotherhood has a special prayer in honour of Muhammad which is called *al-Fateh*. It is famous among the brothers, and members say that it makes those who recite it sure of entering paradise. This last point has been the occasion for polemic with rival brotherhoods who deny that a prayer can automatically have such an effect, and oppose such pretentions.

Earlier we came across the figure of al-Hajj Umar al-Tall who, on returning from his pilgrimage to Mecca, had passed through Sokoto, staying there between 1831 and 1837 and marrying a daughter of Bello, the successor of Dan Fodio. Umar al-Tall extended the Tijani brotherhood over the kingdom that he founded. In northern Nigeria the city of Kano is now an important centre of the Tijaniyya.

While this is not true of all brotherhoods, many sway rhythmically in their solemn worship; it is likely that this practice has an African origin. While a brother slowly chants a religious poem with long silent pauses between the verses, the assembly of brothers, standing and with bare feet, sways to the rhythm of words like Allah repeated indefinitely (this is pronounced with a stress on both syllables, which are well separated): there is either Al-lah, which means God; or Allah Hayy (two shorts and a long, meaning God is alive), or just Hayy Hayy (living, living), or even Hu Hu (He, He).

If you live in a Muslim area, though your attention may be drawn to the problem of the brotherhoods, it should not be forgotten that these in no way play their former role. They now contribute towards maintaining a sense of God and brotherhood among the people. But many Muslims do not join them, saying that there is only one Islam, that of the Muslim law and the observances that it provides, without any addition.

At present, more modern forms of association are emerging. They seek to be purely Muslim, and include the 'Muslim brothers' or the various 'Islamic Associations' (al-jama'at al-islamiyya), which combine prayer and political action. The new *tabligh* movement (faith and practice) has, however, so far represented a combination of preaching and propaganda along classical Islamic lines. Originating in India, it spread to Western Europe, particularly to England and France, in immigrant areas, and by its apostolate contributes to the religious revival among Muslims from the Maghreb who have long been disorientated by their new environment. Their influence emanates from mosques, which serve as their centres.

Groups which are not to be confused with the brotherhoods

The Ahmadiyya

The Ahmadiyya claim to be Muslim, though one of their two branches is attacked by strict Sunnite Muslims. We shall come across them shortly in connection with the crucifixion of Jesus. Contrary to the other Muslims, they accept that Jesus was really nailed to the cross, but claim that he was still alive when he came down from it. He recovered, and left for Kashmir in northern India where he preached, died and was buried. The

Ahmadiyya are one of the most active movements in propaganda and study in the contemporary Muslim world. They are divided into two branches. One of these, the Qadiyani, is especially criticized by Sunnite Muslims. They take this name from the place of origin of their founder, in the Punjab, on the border between India and Pakistan. For them this founder, called Mirza Ghulam Ahmad, who was born in 1839, is a prophet, but a prophet inspired to interpret the message of Muhammad and entirely subject to him. After writing a substantial work, in 1889 this man announced that God had authorized him to gather disciples. From then until his death in 1908 he worked and struggled in the face of much criticism.

One of his most important ideas was that the time of holy war by force of arms had come to an end. The struggle now had to be carried on by propaganda and by peaceful means. His disciples also developed a varied apparatus of journals, books and broadcasts which recalls the activity of the biblical societies. They also opened schools and held meetings.

The Qadiyani (the Ahmadiyya movement in Islam) number more than half a million members, half of whom are in Pakistan. They can be found in Nigeria and Indonesia, and there are some converts in Great Britain, Europe and the United States. Before the opening of mosques for immigrant Muslim workers in Europe, several mosques were built by these Ahmadiyya.

The second group, the Lahore group (*Ahmadiyya Anjuman Isha'at Islam*) regards Ghulam Ahmad as a reformer and not as a prophet. Their missionary activity favours Islam generally. They have a centre in England from which they publish an English journal.

In East Africa, where they have a number of centres (e.g. in Nairobi and Tabora), it has been noted that their objections to Christianity were taken up by almost all Muslims. Even those who did not belong to their groups used their publications. They translated the Qur'an into Swahili, but the Sunnite Muslims went on to make a new translation. So there are two translations of the Qur'an into Swahili.

Babists

At this point we now leave Muslim ground, but as both Babists and Baha'is, whom we shall consider next, have detached themselves from Islam, they may be thought to fall within the framework of this book. There are not many Babists at present; by contrast, the Baha'is can now be found in a variety of countries. They have centres not only in Iran but in Britain and the United States, and their activity is markedly philanthropic.

The first of these movements, Babism, was founded by a Shi'ite Muslim called Sayyid 'Ali Muhammad. Born in Shiraz, in Iran, in 1819 or 1820, an orphan brought up by an uncle, he made contact with a Muslim nobleman who had sent emissaries in search of the Mahdi, the figure expected at the end of time. He himself was recognized as the Mahdi by one of these emissaries.

In 1844, 'Ali Muhammad began his activity, made the pilgrimage to Mecca, attacked the Muslim clergy of his country and proclaimed himself to be the Mahdi. But his standpoint was unacceptable to the Muslim world. He was arrested by the governor of Shiraz and expelled from the city. Under the protection of the governor of Isfahan, he remained there until the death of his protector. His disciples were persecuted, and he himself was arrested and finally shot in Tabriz in 1850. The title Bab (gate) is an honorific title by which he was known at a very early state. His body was later transported to Acre (in Palestine), where he was buried.

His teaching appears in various letters and writings. The most famous of the writings is called the Bayan (in Arabic and in Persian), the sacred book of the new religion. For this is certainly a new religion which aimed at displacing Islam. The Bab affirmed that the cycle of Muhammad's prophecy had ended in 1844 and that now it was his own time. He abolished certain Qur'anic laws and had his own system of penalties. Prayer was no longer offered towards Mecca (and the Ka'ba) but towards the Bab's house. He encouraged bodily cleanliness. The calendar was changed. The year was made up of nineteen months, each of nineteen days. The last month was the month of fasting. Many other measures were taken.

The Babist religion was violently persecuted.

In 1852 there was an incident which further inflamed the situation. The Shah of Persia, Nasir al-Din, was assassinated by two Babists who had been deranged by persecution. The persecution then became a real reign of terror. A poetess, the Egeria of the movement, Qurrat al-'Ayn, was assassinated in prison at that time. The Babist tradition speaks of twenty thousand martyrs.

Then everything calmed down. Meanwhile there had been a schism between the disciples loyal to the memory of Bab and his sacred book, the Bayan, and those who followed Baha Allah, a disciple of Bab, who founded his own religion soon afterwards.

Baha'is

The disciple who parted company with Babism was Mirza Hussein Ali Nuri. Born in 1817, he had been an adherent of Babism; indeed he had been considered one of the main disciples of Bab and even a possible successor. In fact Bab was succeeded by Hussan Ali's half-brother, Mirza Yahya Nuri (surnamed Subh-i Azal).

In 1852, after the assassination of the Shah, Hussein Ali left prison, but was then exiled. He went to Baghdad in 1852, and there his half-brother rejoined him. In fact the influence of the latter gradually decreased. Yahya was arrested by the Turks, deported, and interned at Famagusta in Cyprus.

By contrast, the position of Mirza Hussein Ali became increasingly established, although on several occasions he was interned in various Turkish villages. Finally, he was deported to St John of Acre (Acco) in Palestine, where he arrived in 1868. Initially imprisoned in the citadel, he then lived in freedom in the city and later in its suburbs. Between 1871 and 1874 he wrote the basic book of his religion, the *Kitab-i Aqdas*, the Most Holy Book. He himself was called Baha Allah, the splendour of God; hence the name of his movement. He died in 1892. He left behind several works; some of his

collected teaching has been translated and published under the title *Lessons of St John of Acre*.

On his death his oldest son, Abbas Efendi Abd al-Baha, succeeded him; he too was imprisoned. Finally the Young Turks freed him. Abd al-Baha then embarked on a series of journeys. His movement had made considerable progress: the first group of American Baha'is dates from 1894. He visited his faithful, made contacts in Egypt, then in Europe, and then in America (1910–1913), preaching where he could. He died in Haifa in Palestine in 1921, and was buried near to Bab.

This religion now has features which can be found among numerous sects. It claims to be a prophetic movement in the line of former prophetic movements, each religion summarizing and taking up in its entirety all the values of the earlier religions which it supplants. Other prophets will come after Baha Allah, but not for a thousand years.

It then uses the great fashionable words: it claims to be a scientific, anti-dogmatic religion, and so on. It is for the unity of the human race, the equality of man and woman, world peace, etc. And God is one.

There are prayer meetings and readings of sacred texts, including the Bible and the Qur'an. Prayers are offered three times a day in any language. No fermented drinks are consumed, and there is fasting for a month of nineteen days (between 2 and 21 March), on the eve of the new Baha'i year, which begins in the Persian Nauruz, at the spring equinox. Monogamy was proclaimed initially and then abrogated by Abd al-Baha.

The sect proclaims obedience to local political authorities but allows the possibility of conscientious objection. It forbids membership of secret societies or political parties and condemns spiritualism. It commands the opening of temples which welcome believers of all religions. Each individual prays as he or she wills. Colleges, hospitals and orphanages are often attached to temples. So the Baha'is have a large temple near Chicago on Lake Michigan. They distribute tracts stressing their spiritual and social objectives, recalling that they are born out of persecution.

How many are there of them world-wide? In Iran the central nucleus must have been around a million before the Ayatollah Khomeini's revolution. Since then, the press has from time to time reported the difficulties encountered by the Baha'is in their own country. In the United States there are more than ten thousand of them; there are several thousand in Germany, and above all in Uganda and East Africa, and in Indonesia. A discreet but effective propaganda will recently have increased these figures.

A world appeal, distributed in the form of a tract, presents Baha Allah as the divine messenger for our social and scientific era. The Baha'i faith claims to be in the line of former religions in demonstrating their unity and restoring the purity of their teaching. The world centre is in the Holy Land.

It is understandable that such an appeal is formally rejected by Muslims, for whom Islam is the eternal religion which nothing may supplant, and who also claim to demonstrate the unity and restore the purity of former religions. This is the same kind of logic, but applied to two contrasting realities.

8

Christianity as Islam Sees It

A later chapter will be devoted to the relations between Christians and Muslims. Before this, however, we need to look at what Islam thinks of Christianity in order to prepare the ground.

At first sight, it might seem that Christianity would be a subject which brought us together. The Muslims want to be faithful to the message of Jesus, of which they speak with emotion. They recognize a whole series of biblical prophets whom the Qur'an cites. They have a great respect for the persons of Jesus and Mary, and they believe in the virgin birth of Jesus, which the angel Gabriel announced to Mary. They recall the immense goodness of Jesus, his miracles, his forgiveness, his love of his enemies. And on the occasion of a festival like Christmas, Muslims sometimes recite the passages of the Qur'an about Jesus and Mary to please Christians.

However, once we have gone beyond first impressions, the subject proves to be a very tricky one, full of traps. The accounts which Christians are given from their partners in dialogue are part of a strongly structured whole, coherent and with a seamless logic once the postulates on which Islam is built are accepted.

In fact, everything is dominated by certain basic presuppositions, so it is useless to talk about documents or facts; nothing is taken into consideration unless it conforms rigorously with these presuppositions. Anything that goes against them is immediately rejected, and arguments are then accumulated to justify the rejection.

The first principle is that the only true source which allows a knowledge of Christianity is the Qur'an. Recent Muslim lives of Jesus, written in Arabic, present what they call the Jesus of history. In fact, their account is based exclusively on Qur'anic sources; what is taken from elsewhere is there only as a supplement or for illustration. The authors explain this by saying that only the Qur'an has an absolute value: its witness is enough. Our canonical Gospels are sometimes used, but only to the degree that they fill the gaps in the Muslim description of Jesus and only so long as they say nothing which is not in harmony with the teaching of the Qur'an. Moreover, those who use our Gospels have no scruples when it comes to suppressing a phrase, jumping a paragraph, and so on. They do not feel that they must keep to the texts, which they believe to have no value.

The second principle is that the Muslim Jesus has his place in the religious history of the world as the Qur'an describes it. In other words, he does not introduce anything on a strictly dogmatic level which had not been taught by earlier prophets, nor anything more than Muhammad was to teach later. The religious message of all the prophets is the same, and in this sphere Adam had as much knowledge as Jesus or Muhammad. Hence when suspicion is thrown on earlier scriptures, Torah or Gospel, and they are accused of distortion, only the Qur'an counts. A professor, a well-known man of religion, teaching future graduates in a Muslim state university around 1955, said in his course: 'If you want to know Judaism or Christianity, do not read the Bible or the Gospels; they are forged. Read the Qur'an; it contains everything.' And the practice of many teachers up to the present day shows that this rule of conduct is still current.

The third principle is that since Jesus falls into the category of prophet, he must be considered one of them. The main features of his personality must conform with the model type of prophet. Sent by God to preach a strict monotheism, himself a mere creature like the others, without any role as mediator (since the Qur'an rejects any principle of mediation), he teaches what the others taught. He also announces the coming of Muhammad. As God has promised victory to believers, he is concerned that his Messengers should triumph, as in the case of Noah, Lot and Moses, whose enemies he destroyed. So Jesus escaped crucifixion. God saved him from the hands of the Jews, who wanted to put him to death, and another victim was substituted for him. His only distinctive features are seen within this general framework.

The fact that Christianity is seen by Muslims in the light of these three principles must be taken very seriously, regardless of what one may think of the validity of such a position. At root we find ourselves confronted with a difficulty which some will say is unsurmountable; it is a psychological difficulty and relates to that total influence of the environment which is exerted on the sensibilities of the faithful from their childhood. The fact of knowing texts of the Qur'an by heart and repeating them ceaselessly; the place reserved for them in public and private life – all that gives them an authority, an evidential value, which is quite beyond discussion. Reality is seen through some principles of an ideology: the clarity of ideas is surpassed only by their simplicity. There is no trace of the complexity of life. Everything is easy; everything is crystal clear. On God the creator and providence, the Qur'an expresses general views on which all believers are in agreement. But as soon as it comes to the religious history of the world, and particularly that of Jesus, the situation changes, and Muslims move in a world of their own.

Here we find an attitude which is well known in the history of religions. On a particular point, a gnosis (i.e. theoretical knowledge) determines *a priori* what must be reality. The clarity which results from this still proves to be seductive, while the humble materiality of facts is no longer interesting.

Christianity as Islam sees it is essentially the form of the unique religion, eternal and immutable, which God willed to be valid for the children of Israel at a particular moment in history. It was preached by Jesus, but little by little his disciples moved away from his message and God sent Muhammad to remedy the situation.

In this sort of perspective, Judaism, Christianity and Islam are just one and the same unique religion with the same dogma. Since the coming of Muhammad, Islam has taken up the riches of the two earlier religions, and their time has come to an end.

Truth to say, this very schematic position, which has now been disseminated over all Muslim lands, only took shape gradually. At the beginning of Qur'anic preaching, the accent was put elsewhere. The scene was dominated by the fundamental law of world religious history: 'Anyone who opposes God's Messenger is destroyed.' History appeared as a discontinuous series of flashbacks on peoples punished by God for having rejected God's Messengers: the peoples of Noah, Lot, Moses, Salin, 'Ad and Shu'ayb. A prophet had been sent to each people, taken from among its members and speaking their language. In this context Muhammad was the prophet of the Arabs, himself an Arab, and sent to the Arab to announce the Arab form of the eternal religion. He was compared with Moses sent to Pharaoh (Qur'an 73, 15). At this stage the Qur'an speaks of Jesus without putting particular emphasis on his mission. Jesus is offered as an 'example' to the children of Israel (Qur'an 45, 59). And the Qur'an mentions him along with Mary his mother, among the remarkable figures of this people, alongside Zechariah and John the Baptist (Yahya), Abraham, Moses and Ismail (cf. the surah Mary 19, 1–58). He also appears in the long list of figures taken from within the people of Israel, chosen and guided by God in the right way (cf. Qur'an 6, 84–90).

The very name of Jesus ('Isa in the Qur'an) appears relatively little in the Qur'anic texts from Mecca (four times as compared with twenty-one times in those of Medina). The name Mary itself appears only five times at Mecca as compared with twenty-nine times at Medina. On another occasion, at Mecca the Qur'an still mentions 'she who remained virgin' and her son (Qur'an 21, 91). The expression Messiah, son of Mary, is purely restricted to Medina.

However, at Medina Islam was essentially confronted with Judaism and Christianity; its believers encountered Jews and Christians in the oasis and therefore spoke of these faiths with more precision. It presented itself as the reform of these two religions to which Jews and Christians had been unfaithful. It described Jesus as the Messenger to the children of Israel. Since

then, Islam has stressed the limited character of the mission of Jesus according to the Qur'an, while Muhammad was sent to the whole world and Islam is valid to the end of time.

One very often comes across a simplified summary of the question. Muslims write that Judaism was a materialist religion: Jesus was sent to redress the situation and for the moment, because of circumstances, had to stress a spiritual religion. Finally Muhammad received the mission to preach definitively the right balance between materialism and pure spiritualism.

Jesus is described by the Qur'an without any allusion to the setting in which he lived. He appears outside space and time. Everything begins with the mother of Mary (the wife of 'Imran). She brings Mary into the world and entrusts her and her descendants to the Lord to be protected against Satan, the one who is stoned. The childhood of Mary in the temple is narrated with features which appear in the apocryphal infancy gospels, above all the Protevangelium of James. Zachariah looks after her.

Then the angel Gabriel announces the future virgin birth of Jesus. This takes place in the desert, far away from any human habitation. The text stresses the miracle of the conception without a father and Mary's absolute purity. The miracle, which is contested by the people whom Mary rejoins on her return after the birth, is confirmed by another miracle: the infant Jesus speaks, though he is only a baby in a cradle. This is how Jesus explains his own situation:

I am the servant of God. He has given me the Scripture and ordained me a prophet. His blessing is upon me wherever I go, and He has commanded me to be steadfast in prayer and to give alms to the poor as long as I shall live. He has exhorted me to honour my mother and has purged me of vanity and wickedness. I was blessed on the day I was born, and blessed I shall be on the day of my death; and may peace be upon me on the day when I shall be raised to life' (Qur'an 19, 30–34).

Everything is bathed in an atmosphere of

The meeting between St Francis of Assisi and the Sultan of Egypt in 1219. Codex *Legenda Major*, 1457 manuscript, Brescia (Library of the Capucin Historical Institute in Rome).

miracle. The miracle of the palm tree which bends over to give its fruit and the water which springs up at its foot, a miracle told by the infancy gospels in connection with the flight into Egypt, recurs in the Qur'an with slight modifications, at the moment of Jesus' birth. One detail to note is that Mary feels the pain of giving birth. When one thinks of what was written in the Middle Ages and beforehand, about whether or not Mary felt pain when giving birth, associating these points with theological positions, this precision of the Qur'an can help us to rediscover the sphere in which these narratives circulated. Furthermore, Mary is the only woman whose name is given explicitly in the Qur'an; all the others are designated by the name of their husband: the wife of Adam, the wife of Noah, the wife of Pharaoh, etc.

Joseph the husband of Mary does not appear in the Qur'an, but an ancient legend is taken up by certain commentators. It makes Joseph Mary's cousin, and her comrade in the service of the temple. He is the first to notice that she is pregnant. Troubled, he speaks about this to Mary in very delicate terms and she replies by recalling that the laws of life are in the hands of God and that the first trees of creation were produced without seeds and Adam, the first man, without a father.

A few more details are added in the Medina texts. The general word scripture as a term to denote the texts which God entrusts to Jesus is replaced by Gospel. Jesus receives the Gospel, and the whole Muslim tradition teaches that he receives it from heaven, just as Moses received the Torah and Muhammad the Qur'an. Muslim theology, at least up to this point, has seen the three cases as the revelation of books dictated to the prophets down to the least detail.

The Medina texts describe the miracles performed by Jesus: giving life to birds modelled in clay, curing the lepers and those who were blind from birth, raising the dead, seeing hidden things and perhaps even securing from God by his prayers the descent to earth of a table laden with food. Is this the multiplication of loaves or a reminiscence of the eucharist? The text does not allow us to say. At all events, the Qur'an says specifically each time that it is 'with the permission of God' that he performs his miracles.

Jesus had disciples, and asks their help when he comes up against the resistance and unbelief of the Jews. He allows certain things that the law of Moses prohibited; i.e. God entrusted him with the announcement of a legislation different from that which had been current previously. He instilled kindness and mercy in the heart of his disciples. And later Muslim tradition has stressed the ascetical spirit of Jesus, who had nowhere to lay his head.

In a second account of the annunciation, this time dating from Medina, the personality of Jesus is described like this:

> The angels said to Mary: 'God bids you rejoice in a Word from Him. His name is the Messiah, Jesus son of Mary. He shall be noble in this world and in the next, and shall be favoured by God. He shall preach to men in his cradle and in the prime of his manhood, and shall lead a righteous life' (Qur'an 3, 44–45).

And in a text still later than this:

> The Messiah, Jesus the son of Mary, was no more than God's Messenger and His Word which he conveyed to Mary: a spirit from Him. So believe in God and his messengers and do not say 'Three'! Forbear, and it shall be better for you (Qur'an 4, 171).

The title Messiah is explained in different ways by the commentators, but for all the faithful it is an honorific title without the historic resonances that it had in Holy Scripture. The term Word is interpreted by saying that God created Jesus by a direct word and not according to the ordinary processes of nature.

Like all the prophets, Jesus is bound by the pact which links him to God. After the covenant with Jesus, Muhammad came to confirm the truth of the earlier messages received by the children of Israel, and the Qur'an adds:

Page of the surah Mary in the
Qur'an, narrating these events.

The birth of Jesus. Mary shaking
the date palm (after a Persian
manuscript).

Believe in him and help him (Qur'an 3, 81).

The covenant between God and the children of Israel was already described in the following way;

> I shall be with you. If you attend to your prayers and pay the alms-tax (*zakat*); if you believe in my Messengers and assist them and give God a generous loan' (Qur'an 5, 12).

Prayer, almsgiving and personal commitment are always called for in the struggle alongside the prophets.

The principle of respect for the former Messengers and the sacred books which they brought is absolute and allows of no reserve:

> God's Messenger (Muhammad) believed in what had been revealed to him from on high, by his Lord, and so do the faithful. They all believe in God and His angels, His scriptures and His messengers. They said: 'We discriminate against none of his Messengers. We have heard and we have obeyed' (Qur'an 2, 285).

Jesus, too, announces the future coming of Muhammad by virtue of this solidarity (Qur'an 61, 6).

However, this very clear profession of faith has been the cause of scorn and equivocation. I am not afraid of being more specific here. In fact, in Muslim thought the Judaism was an ideal Judaism, in conformity with the Qur'an, and not that of real-life Jews; the Christianity was also an ideal Christianity: there was an ideal Torah and an ideal gospel. It is possible that the Christian community of which Waraqa bin Nawfal was one of the leading figures represented the type of true Christianity in Muslim eyes. Nevertheless, it is certain that the other Jewish and Christian communities encountered elsewhere did not conform to the Qur'anic model. Hence a certain number of clashes which are reflected in the Qur'an. With whom did they take place? With the Christians of the mainstream church or with members of marginal sects? It is difficult to say. When Jesus refutes the charge of ever having

The Old Testament Covenant as presented by the Qur'an

God made a covenant with the Israelites
and raised among them twelve chieftains.
He said: 'I shall be with you.
If you attend to your prayers and pay the alms-tax (*zakat*);
if you believe in my Messengers and assist them,
and give God a generous loan,
I shall forgive you your sins
and admit you to gardens watered by running streams.
But he that hereafter denies me
shall stray from the right path. .

Qur'an 5, 12

asked his followers to worship him and his mother as two deities apart from God (Qur'an 5, 116), it is almost impossible to know whether this is a general remark or whether on the contrary it has in mind a specific sect which deified Mary.

The one thing that is clear is that now the Muslims are convinced that they are the only true disciples of Jesus who are faithful to his doctrine. They think that only the Qur'an provides all the indispensable knowledge about Jesus. Like the Unitarians, for whom Jesus is only a man, Muslims feel a profound repulsion over the specifically Christian dogmas of the Trinity and the Incarnation. Only a small number of them accept that we are really monotheists.

With very rare exceptions indeed, a tiny number, Muslims reject the crucifixion of Jesus on the basis of the traditional exegesis of an extremely concise verse in the Qur'an:

> They did not kill him, nor did they crucify him, but they thought they did (Qur'an 4, 156).

Traditionally Muslim exegesis has seen this as the indication of the substitution for Jesus of a double to whom God had given all the physical attributes of the Messiah. This traditional exegesis follows the line of the second-century Christian docetists who also believed that Jesus only seemed to have been crucified, and that in fact Jesus himself escaped death. We have already seen that the Ahmadiyya of Pakistan accept that Jesus was really nailed to the cross, but they believe that he was still alive when he was taken down. He cured people, left for India and was buried near Srinagar, in Kashmir. They are really the only Muslims to hold such a position: no other Muslim has ever shared it with them.

However, regardless of this verse and its interpretation, since in Islam God gives his forgiveness directly to anyone who asks for it, without the intervention of any mediator, the cross no longer has a place in the history of salvation. Meanwhile God has raised Jesus up to heaven, where he dwells and whence he will return just before the end of the world.

There are also other traditions about Jesus; one of them presents him as returning to Jerusalem at the end of time and proclaiming his Islam publicly. But although these stories are popular, they are far from having the same authority as the Qur'an texts.

Attempts have been made from both the Christian and the Jewish side to interpret the Qur'an in a way which accords with the respective beliefs of each side. The theorists of one particular sect sought to reconcile the prophecy of Muhammad with their own position. These people, who are mentioned in Muslim documents, affirm that Muhammad was sent only to pagan Arabs, and not to Christians and Jews. He was prophet in a limited sense. Muslims generally have never accepted this restriction, and anyone who opens the Qur'an can only say that

Some dominant psychological features
(of the Muslim)

Above all, they feel 'elect', chosen, called to witness, and perhaps to fight, to be champions, 'martyrs' of the One God . . .

Christianity, to speak here only of the religion which we know best, is judged and classified. Without any doubt it originates in a 'revelation', and therefore comes from God; at least where it still preserves its authenticity, that which has not been changed, in which it has not been falsified and altered by its sectarians. But this religion has been either taken up, adopted and continued by Islam, or abrogated, corrected and overtaken by it. For Muslims, conversion to Christianity is nonsense; it is a regression. Even the young or less young 'rationalists' conceive that a Muslim can cease to believe in Allah (provided that he does not cry this out from the rooftops), but not that he should retrace his steps towards an outmoded religion.

So the problem is settled; the solution is there, simple and convenient . . . Hence the great pride, the disconcerting assurance, what has been called the 'superiority complex', that kind of inaccessibility that one meets among the least educated Muslim, the one who is most illiterate and most down to earth from a moral point of view.

K.-M. Abd el-Jail, *L'Islam et nous*, pp.57–9.

they are right. The Qur'an affirms that the prophetic authority of Muhammad extends to both Christians and Jews. And Muslims explain that since Christianity and Judaism were corrupt, it was he whom God charged with re-establishing the religion in all its purity.

People of the Book! Our Messenger has come to reveal to you Our will after an interval during which there were no Messengers, lest you should say: 'No one has come to give us good news or to warn us.' Now one has come to give you good news and to warn you (Qur'an 5, 19).

Or again:

People of the Book! Our messenger has come to reveal to you much of what you have hidden of the scriptures, and to forgive you much (Qur'an 5, 15)

This call to Christians and Jews to act in accordance with their scriptures is classic in Islam. They are accused in particular of having suppressed passages announcing the coming of Muhammad, since the Qur'an itself declares that Jesus spoke of this coming.

The divisions among Christians of which Muslims have heard once they have had even a small amount of education in the Qur'an are associated with a divine curse. Because they forgot part of the covenant which God had given them, the Qur'an explains, putting the words into the mouth of God:

We stirred up among them enmity and hatred, which shall endure until the Day of Resurrection (Qur'an 5, 14).

Whatever one makes of these theoretical affirmations, the fact remains that for centuries Christians and Muslims have lived together in the same cities. Although Muslims did not recognize contemporary Christians and Jews as the true disciples of Moses and Jesus, they gave them a place in their public life. Apart from the Hijaz and Central Arabia, where only Muslims were allowed to live from the time of the first caliphs, Christians and Jews were free to organize themselves into communities, to practise their worship and to look to their own personal affairs. They were simply required to abstain from all proselytism towards Muslims and not to prevent those who showed a desire to become Muslims from doing so. Various additional restrictions (ghettoes, clothing, a prohibition against riding on horseback, etc.) were also imposed in the Middle Ages. And despite all this, from the moment when they agreed to pay a special poll tax or recognized that they were no longer the masters, the Muslims left them in peace.

With modern ideas about the equality of all citizens, the situation has changed, but since human beings are human beings everywhere, the frameworks of religious differences still serve as a pretext for opposition, and the strongest are still the strongest. The history of Muslim-Christian relations would be too long to tell here. It varies, depending on countries and periods. However, one fact is certain: the Christian churches have always figured, and still figure, in the countryside of Muslim lands. They are an integral part of it, where the old Christianities have subsisted for centuries alongside Islam as well as where Islam and Christianity are both more recent. They have only disappeared in the vast territories which were once Christian and in which the faith has gradually become extinct or from which it has had to emigrate.

It remains equally true that Christian and Jewish scholars, artists and craftsmen have collaborated with Muslims over the centuries within the same unique civilization.

9

Islam in the Modern World

Now that we have considered various historical and religious aspects of Islam, the time has come to touch on the subject of Muslim society in the modern world. Islam is in fact a political and religious movement which seeks to secure happiness for its faithful in this world and the next. And as happiness in this world presupposes a social organization and social success, traditional Islam has always wanted to have its say in the matter.

That is all the more the case since the last one hundred and fifty years, with the profound transformations of all the societies which have followed scientific discoveries and the birth of major industry, the problem has arisen of the role that religions can or should play in developments. The most varied opinions can be found in these areas. They range from materialism or atheistic scientism, which see all religion as illusions retarding progress, to the positions of believers who are concerned to work at building a world in which that which is God's and that which is man's is identified and respected.

In the West, voices can still be heard affirming that Islam is against progress, but Muslims have always protested loudly at such assertions. They are hurt by them, for if reasoned criticism from strangers is difficult enough to bear, calumny from them will be even less so. Be this as it may, a problem arises which could be put in these terms: what is the situation of Islam in the modern world? Or again, how can the technology which has allowed the scientific and industrial rise of the West be adopted while preserving the distinctive values of the Muslim heritage? For several decades Japan has been a source of hope. This country seems to have been able to modernize its production and become one of the two or three major industrial countries in the world while preserving its 'authenticity' over against the West. It offered the most striking example of success in this area. What was the attitude of the Muslim world to this challenge from history?

At the beginning of the twentieth century, the situation of Islam in the modern world seemed to be all the more abnormal to Muslim élites, since these were very well aware of the point when their past had been a brilliant one.

The glories of former Muslim civilization

To evoke past glories one need only mention Baghdad in the time of Abbassid caliphs, just two centuries after the death of Muhammad. At this time this city had been the focal point of a remarkable cultural activity in every sphere. The riches of the ruling classes produced many wealthy patrons and attracted brains as the United States does today. Muslims, Christians, Jews and Sabaeans participated in this activity. In the spheres of literature and philosophy, but also in a wide range of sciences like mathematics, algebra, chemistry, medicine, astronomy and many others, the Muslim civilization of Baghdad shone with great splendour. And what took place in Baghdad was reproduced in other courts throughout the Muslim world.

Taking up the Greek heritage, attentive to the contributions of India (which provided decimal numbering with figures which are called Arabic in the West and Hindu and Arab countries) and Persia, the workers of this civilization could develop and complete what they had received. Algebra, invented by a Greek of Alexandria, took its definitive form with the Arabs. Similarly, in medicine and in astronomy the observations of the Arabs considerably enriched the heritage they had received from the Greeks. Discoveries like that of paper, the compass and gunpowder may have come from China, but it was through the Arabs, who also developed them (for example using cotton instead of silk for paper), that they arrived in Europe.

Independently of all these aspects, one would also have to cite the vast Arab and Muslim literature with its poems and contributions to the humanities, about history, geography, travel and agriculture; or the architecture of the magnificent monuments of Andalusia, North Africa, Cairo, Jerusalem, Damascus, Istanbul, Ispahan, Russian Turkestan, India, etc.

The vocabulary of European languages still bears traces of the Arabic and Muslim influence which was exerted in the Middle Ages on the centres of thought in Europe and the growing universities. Did not Thomas Aquinas have the distinction of adopting the riches of this Graeco-Arabic thought and making it serve the development of theology? In science, to take just a few characteristic words, algebra (denoting 'reduction' in Arabic, in the sense in which a surgeon reduces a fracture), logarithms (the distortion of the proper name of a Muslim scholar alKhawarizmi), cipher, zero, the names of many stars, the zenith, and so on, parts of the body, the names of plants, games, some of the vocabulary of heraldry, and hundreds of others (ogive in architecture) show the impact of this Muslim civilization.

It would be naive to attribute all the scientific achievements of the West to the influence of Arab-Muslim culture. This influence was one of the determining factors in the intellectual renaissance at the end of the Middle Ages. It prepared the ground, but then the Europeans themselves made further inventions. Had there not been a complete reversal of perspectives with the Copernican revolution and the new world system, with the massive use of the measure in chemistry, etc., the sciences would have remained no more than crafts. In fact one can see a discontinuity between qualitative ancient science, in which Arab-Muslim mediaeval science still plays a major role, and quantitative modern science. It does not seem that those in charge of the Muslim city understood the significance of this shift at the time (which was in fact a complete break) and the totally new character of modern scientific and industrial thought.

Nevertheless, a concern to maintain the authentic Muslim character and religious values led Muslims to react to this West that science had made so powerful. Confronted with the threat to their own values, Muslims found in Islam the heart of a cultural resistance to Western penetration. One has only to think of what religious circles did to preserve the Arabic language during the time of colonial occupation. Even now, negative attitudes to various demands of the modern working world can be explained as profound hostility to a kind of society in which believers cannot see a place for their faith.

So it was that gradually the clearest thinkers realized that to be strong and prepare for an independent future, Muslim countries had to accept modern science. They too moved to the creation of a network of schools and universities, to the adoption of an infrastructure which allows economic development. How did all that happen?

Practice before theory

When the West was developing modern industry and science, the Muslim countries were continuing on the momentum of their past glories. Though they had been at the head of mediaeval civilization, they had not renewed themselves. Despite the splendour of certain late dynasties which were remarkable for the development of the arts and thought, like those of the Great Moghuls in the north of India (sixteenth and seventeenth centuries) or of Iran in the seventeenth centuries, and despite the Ottoman Turks with their military conquests in Europe and the refinement of their court life in the fifteenth and sixteenth centuries, the gap between the West and the rest of the world increased. Discoveries in the realm of science and industry led to the enslavement of stationary peoples, and this situation in turn paralysed cultural activity. The colonial tide overran everything; an overwhelming technological superiority for the moment overcame all resistance.

At that time one can see a progressive transformation of life in Muslim countries not only by internal evolution but also by the introduction of external factors, material and cultural. The construction of railways and roads, education distilled drop by drop to train the personnel needed for the colonies to function, and international links all gradually had their effect. Countries on the way towards recovering their independence adopted many points of Western legislation. The equality of all citizens before the law, taxation and military service became customary, replacing the mediaeval practice of the semisegregation of Jews and Christians.

The city continues to shelter the traditional Muslim authorities, but civil authorities, fashioned on a Western model, have developed alongside them. The caliph, the political head of the Muslim community, has ceased to exist; though his function was real during the first two centuries of Islam, it progressively lost its importance. The caliphate disappeared in 1924, suppressed by the Turks themselves, who had been its final resting place, and the Muslim world no longer has a caliph at its head.

Legislation is prepared by civil organizations, though Muslim legislation remains in force in the personal sphere and in matters of inheritance. There are civil tribunals everywhere, sometimes supplemented by religious tribunals, the competence of which is limited to certain areas. The *mufti* still has the official responsibility for giving juridical advice on the legality of particular decisions. The grand mufti and the heads of the chief religious establishments are always among the leading figures, but they do not stand alone.

Modern technology has been adopted, in principle, without any reticence. No one is surprised to see it at work in the construction of mosques and in their equipment, which includes loudspeakers installed everywhere to broadcast sermons or ceremonies. Offset machines are used to print religious books. All the study and propaganda organizations know how to use radio, television, tape recordings, etc.

Studies themselves have also been developed. To begin with, the first reaction was to seek to modernize existing higher education or to make specialists of some of those who emerged from it. The very dense network of quite elementary Qur'anic schools was in fact supplemented in each region by secondary schools and some great centres went even further: these include Cairo, with the al-Azhar, Tunis with the Zaytuna, Fez with the Qarawin, and so on. But this kind of modernization proved so difficult and so slow that it had to be speeded up. After an attempt at creating institutes of higher education like Dar al-Ulum (the house of the sciences) in Cairo, which came into being after many vicissitudes, as a faculty of Cairo University, it has been decided to establish a network of modern universities. Specialists in the Muslim sciences may, however, just as well belong to traditional mosques as to these universities.

Similarly, the needs of teaching, like those arising from the spread of Islam, have led to the creation of journals, periodicals and a whole literature of pamphlets and studies, and radio and television have been used at certain times to broadcast religious programmes. At present, in Cairo (The Voice of the Qur'an, a strengthening of which has been called for by successive congresses of its *ulama*) and in Saudi Arabia, stations have been set up entirely dedicated to the broadcasting of the Qur'an and religious programmes.

Study and propaganda organizations have been started either as 'research institutes' (one in Egypt dependent of al-Azhar, one in Pakistan at Islamabad, and so on) or as more committed organizations.

In Cairo, since 1960 there has been a 'Supreme Council of Muslim Affairs' which has produced a large number of publications. These are both scholarly editions of classical Islamic texts and well-produced popular pamphlets by the million. This organization has also produced a series of records of recitations of the Qur'an and records explaining how to offer ritual prayer, with words in Arabic for the liturgical texts and in various languages, including African languages, for the commentaries. As this organization clearly reflects Egyptian politics, Saudi Arabi decided in 1962 to establish a Muslim World League: this has offices in the most important cities in the Muslim world. Moreover, congresses bring together delegates from all Muslim countries at regular intervals. Finally, there are private missionary organizations, while others are sponsored either by a state like Libya or by the Muslim World League.

This adoption of modern technology in the service of propaganda must not lead us to forget the role that this same technology plays in other sectors of both private and public life. Here we can see complex *de facto* changes of all kinds. However, at a theoretical level, development is still at a relatively backward stage. Dominique Sourdel wrote in a brochure on Islam:

> Recent developments seem to confirm on the one hand both the failure or the uselessness of attempts at the reformation of theological thought and on the other the possibility of political and social transformations, the theoretical justifications for which are rarely lacking.

How have Muslim thinkers justified this modern development?

In the nineteenth century, thinkers first had to confront a group of very conservative figures who were disturbed by these changes and looked on all these novelties with a very bad grace. They had to expend a considerable amount of energy in an effort to convince this latter group, but gradually reform measures were passed and the main opponents grew old and then died. At the time of this confrontation and subsequently, a two-fold attitude emerged, to which perhaps a third attitude should be added, one which was adopted by a very small minority.

Some, the members of a first group, while wanting to be as Muslim as the rest, acted without being too bothered about what people would say. For them, to contribute towards the creation of Muslim states which were strong in every respect was to work for the power of Islam; it was therefore to do one's duty towards God and the community. Within this group practice varied, but many of them were concerned to observe the demands of the law: ritual prayer, fasting and service to the community.

The second group, who are sometimes called reformists, also worked, but adopted an apologetic attitude to justify this evolution. It is from among them that the members of the fundamentalist Muslim associations recruited their members. In a country like Egypt this latter group perhaps amounted to more than half the population affected by the current developments, and the first group remained numerically below half.

A very tiny minority which has been Westernized or is in process of being Westernized would amount to no more than three or four per cent in the most advanced cases, and much less than that in traditionalist countries. These are the people who have been principally involved in the brain-drain. In fact the members of the first group were the most effective at modernizing Muslim countries. They, above all, achieved the creation of modern states with their public services, the establishment of a press and publishing houses, created hospitals, universities and banks, published classical texts, and so on.

The reformist movement

Is this a movement? Or is it only a general attitude which appeared almost simultaneously in numerous points of the Muslim world? It seems that the great names of this movement adopted a set of apologetic views more rapidly than others and were the first to put them into clear formulae. Would this phenomenon have come about without their intervention? Probably, but their presence acted as a catalyst for forces which only wanted to be allowed to exist. Today these ideas have penetrated everywhere and they would seem in fact to have hardened since the 1970s.

In India, in the eighteenth century, this tendency already appears in a thinker like Shah Wali Ullah. In Arab countries and to a lesser degree in Iran and Turkey, the presence of a man with a strong personality, Jamal al-Din al-Afghani (1839–1897), gave impetus to the movement. It then spread to other Arab countries without being accepted by all of them, though it did influence important areas.

Similar positions were held in Turkey with Erbakan, in Pakistan with Abu'l-Ala Maududi (born around 1900, died in 1979) or in Indonesia, not to mention the Wahhabis of Arabia or the stricter Muslims of West Africa who also call themselves Wahhabis.

The ideas of these reformists are widespread at the present time. Even if many people do not adopt them, preferring to devote their energies to a more productive course of action, and even if the intellectuals do not follow them, finding them not open enough, it remains the case that around 1985, ninety-five per cent of what was preached and published within the realm of religious thought bore the mark of reformist apologetic. Of those who think otherwise, only a small minority dares talk openly. In 1973, in Nigeria, the religious pages of Muslim newspapers were still developing themes relevant to this apologetic. And I was told that in Tunis, where a group of open Muslim thinkers was living, visiting teachers from the Near East were still presenting the themes of this apologetic over recent years to audiences which would have liked something different.

The main themes developed by the reformists

From the beginning, the three major basic principles have been:
● A return to the Qur'an and to the authentic traditions of the original Muslims, those who have always been called the *salaf*: hence the name *salafiyya* which has been given to this movement in Arab countries. This return was a liberation from the works, texts, glosses and superglosses by mediaeval authors which people spent months studying instead of getting to essentials;
● the fight for the liberation of territories occupied by colonial powers:

• the fight against the Muslim rulers who rejected reforms, did not accept modernization or entered into pacts with the occupying powers.

Moreover a whole apologetic, intended to give confidence to Muslims, presented Islam as the religion of science and reason. The brilliant past of Muslim civilization was recalled and Qur'anic texts on knowledge restored to a prominent place. This apologetic justified the idea of scientific law by the idea that it is the custom of God to act in such and such a fashion. So these laws were the 'customs of God', which in no way contradict his omnipotence; moreover the terms 'custom of God' (*sunnat Allah*) occurs in the Qur'an. This apologetic combated fatalism, citing verses from the Qur'an which were a spur to action and presupposed human freedom.

This apologetic presented Islam as having worked for the suppression of slavery by progressive measures, like the liberation of women. It was opposed to polygamy for the reasons that I explained earlier, and a reformer like Muhammad Abduh was not afraid to stress the divisions and the conflicts which polygamy caused in many families. This apologetic stressed that Islam had created international law and that Islam had civilized Europe. The situation over lending at interest and the economy was more embarrassing. If the condemnation of loans at interest and of exploiting people whom need forced to borrow was absolute, a Reformist like Sayyid Rashid Rida (who died in 1935) thought that a general congress of prominent figures should meet one day to examine the problem that bank loans posed to Muslim law.

The majority of the arguments in this apologetic already appeared in a commentary on the Qur'an published in Egypt at the beginning of this century, in which the authors sought to justify a whole attitude to the modern world by the Qur'an.

In short, it was a matter of keeping a balance between the positions and characteristic contributions of the Muslim world and establishing the legitimacy from a Qur'anic point of view of all that was thought indispensable for the renaissance of Muslim countries.

An example of a reformer: Jamal al-Din al-Afghani (1839–1897)

A glance at the life and personality of Jamal alDin al-Afghani will show us what kind of figure a reformist could be and above all at what point he was involved in action and struggle.

His contemporaries long thought that he was Afghan in origin, as he claimed to be. However, after the publication of documents which he left and which were rediscovered after his death, it is now clear that he was Iranian and that he concealed this fact in order to be better received by the Sunnites. He was born in Iran in a place not far from the city of Hamadan (mentioned in the book of Tobit under the name Ecbatana) in 1839. He had the chance to go to India to study and it is probable that he was present at the 1857 mutiny against the English and its quelling. If he was not there at that particular time, he certainly was there in the months either immediately before or immediately after the mutiny. Hence the ferocious hatred which he had for the English all his life.

Around 1866 he was in Afghanistan, watched by the English intelligence service, who (according to British archives) thought that he was a Russian agent. He told his own life story, but more than one of his statements is open to question. It is certain that he was in Afghanistan at the time of the civil war between two rulers, one supported by Russia and one by England. When his candidate (the anti-English one) was ousted, he went to India and from then on began the life of a 'traveller without luggage', as a radio broadcast about him put it. He does not seem to have been married, though his personal papers include some correspondence with a woman in Paris with whom he had a relationship. He was to spend the rest of his life travelling, furthering the cause, training men, encouraging them to read, educating himself, engaging in journalism and preparing one day to be a statesman.

He left India for Istanbul (some have argued that he was a Turkish agent, but provide no proof of this), spending forty days in Egypt on the way. He worked and made contacts in Istanbul, but had to leave after a year because of the opposition which he provoked. Words spoken in an account of prophetism in which he stressed the social role of the prophets were severely censured by traditionalist theologians. Between 1871 and 1879 he was in Egypt, in Cairo. This was the time when foreign seizures began to be painful. Journals were founded. Jamal al-Din was surrounded by a circle of disciples, including future Muslim nationalist leaders, and a Jew and a Christian. He taught them to read the classics of Arab thought while launching them into political journalism. He became a freemason and worked actively, criticizing the government to such an extent that he was finally expelled, perhaps at the demand of a foreign consul.

He then went to India (1879–1882), where the English kept watch on him. The movement of ideas which he had launched in Egypt led to the revolution of 'Urabi Pasha against the Khedive (the ruler of Egypt) and the caste of Circassian (i.e. foreign) officers. For the English this revolt was the occasion for occupying Egypt on the pretext of coming to the Khedive's aid.

From India, Jamal al-Din went via the Suez Canal to Paris, where he rejoined one of his Egyptian disciples, Muhammad Abduh. Abduh had been exiled at the beginning of 1883 for having participated in the 'Urabi movement. The two of them edited a review in Arabic of which eighteen issues appeared; it already contains all the principles that the reformist tendency promoted ceaselessly. Thwarted by the English, who banned its entry into Egypt and India, the review had to cease publication. The secret society of the same name, of which it was the expression,

'The Strongest Link' (Al-'Urwa al-Wuthqa) developed. Muhammad Abduh made a journey to Tunis to extend it (1886), and then separated from Jamal al-Din, adopting a programme more centred on the reform of teaching.

Jamal al-Din continued his own line of action, both political and cultural. First he went to Iran, where he felt very much under surveillance, and then on to Russia where he remained until 1889, pleading, as he himself said, the cause of the Russian Muslims. After a journey to Paris he returned to Iran; this time he was permanently banished for his activities as an agitator in the name of Islam.

In 1892 he was in England, publishing articles in a journal in Persian in which he violently attacked the Shah, whom he could not forgive either for his despotism, or for ordering the banishment. Some years later the Shah was assassinated by a disciple of Jamal al-Din; however, the latter always affirmed that he had not been the instigator of this murder.

The Ottoman sultan, who was caliph at the same time, summoned Jamal al-Din to Istanbul. Up to that point Jamal al-Din had fought for the unity of the Muslim world (federal unity) under the aegis of the caliph; did the sultan now want to use him in order to implement reforms or just to have him near so that it was easier to keep an eye on him? The second hypothesis seems more probable. Jamal al-Din died in 1897.

He did not write much. His main work is a book called *Refutation of the Materialists* in which he extols the social role of Islam and the importance of religion for the flourishing of peoples in the face of those prone to atheistic materialism or evolutionism. He had in mind certain Muslims who, in their desire for modernization, came too close to the ideas fashionable in Europe. He was not a religious man, but above all a politician. What was his religious faith? That is still a mystery. But Islam is both politics and a religion.

Reformism in the Arab world: a brief survey

The disciples of Jamal al-Din included Muhammad Abduh (1849–1905), an Egyptian who later tried to reform the centre of higher education at al-Azhar and to promote more modern teaching there. Sayyid Rashid Rida, who was also active in Cairo, followed Muhammad Abduh's line, but he was much more involved in politics. He published a commentary on the Qur'an (called the Manar Commentary) in which he explained how he saw the Qur'an responding to the challenges of the modern world. The name *Manar* was that of a review which was very influential throughout the Arab world, and which appeared from 1898 up to his death.

Reformist thought is inseparable from the political and economic situation prevalent at that time. It was primarily an emergence from a lack of scholarly and university resources in order to confront Europe, whose success went with ideals which were often scientistic and atheistic.

The next stage came with the revival of nationalism and the first struggles for independence. The Indian Mutiny in 1857 and the Mahdi's revolt in the Sudan got nowhere. On the other hand, the outbreak of the 1914–1918 war and the solemn proclamation by President Wilson of the United States (on the principle of peoples' right to self-determination), along with the creation of the League of Nations (the forerunner of the United Nations Organization), revived hopes, and the struggle for independence began in several countries.

In Syria, where the Arab nationalists (Christians and Muslims) had long fought against the Turks and for independence, the 1914–1918 war ended with bitter deceit. Instead of the independence they had hoped for and been promised by certain European statesmen, they saw the creation of a French protectorate in Syria and Lebanon, and an English one in Palestine and Jordan which moreover implemented a policy of

The world dimensions of Islam

God has promised those of you who believe and do good works
to make them masters in the land,
as He has made their ancestors before them,
to strengthen the faith He chose for them,
and to change their fears to safety.
Let them worship Me and serve no other gods beside Me (Qur'an 2, 55).

This verse of the Qur'an has been taken up by the Reformers to give hope to Muslims in countries which were occupied at the time, and Muhammad Abduh commented on it like this:

'The Most High God has not yet succeeded in fulfilling his promise for us, but he has realized only part of it. It is destined that he will fulfil it by giving Islam mastery (*siyada*) over the whole world, including Europe which is hostile to it.'

Manar Commentary I, 170.

Zionist immigration that was to culminate in the creation of the state of Israel in 1948.

In Tunisia, the first attempts at reform saw the light of day very early, in the 1860s, with Prime Minister Khayr ad-Din (1822–1890), filtering through with the movements from Turkey before arriving later with the Manar.

However, it was between the two wars that strongly structured parties appeared, some with essentially political programmes of a secular kind, and others with a political and religious programme which was to end up in the present activist tendencies. Moreover the reality, like all reality, was very varied. In Morocco, a rebellion was led by Abd al-Krim in the mountains separating the two zones of occupation, French and

Spanish (1921–1926). The Independence Party (al-Istiqlal) led by Allal al-Fasi took a line which was more in sympathy with Jamal al-Din alAfghani than with Muhammad Abduh. In Algeria the Ulama movement, creating schools to prevent Arabic from disappearing under the pressure of the teaching of French, was inspired by Sheikh Ben Badis. He broadly took the *Manar* line, but there were political parties alongside him. The Algerian war of independence (1954–1962) was still far on the horizon.

The 'Muslim Brotherhood'

A new stage was reached when, in addition to the *Manar* reformists a political movement was founded in Egypt in 1929 with a firm structure and orientated on action: this was the Muslim Brotherhood (al-Ikhwan al-Muslimun). Its founder was Sheikh Hasan al Banna, regarded by his followers as a martyr since he was assassinated in 1949 for reasons of state. He surrounded himself with popular preachers, organized a party, and trained convinced and committed young Muslims. The movement managed to reach almost two million supporters or sympathizers in Egypt by 1950 and gradually spread into other Arab countries. Along with missionary activity went parliamentary action, first in Palestine and then in Egypt itself; hence the difficulties which ensued.

The great event in the Near East which is the origin of the present dramatic situation was the creation of the state of Israel in 1948. The mass immigration of Jews and the sense of rejection which followed led to a chain of upheavals which are far from being over, for all the years they have lasted.

The period between 1945 and 1960 saw the majority of colonized or 'protected' Muslim countries gaining their political independence. In Egypt there was a coup of free officers, following which Colonel Gamal Abd al-Nasser governed for eighteen years, trying first Arab and then socialist policies (1952–1970). Inde-

pendence met so deep a desire in the countries concerned that it unleashed a great wave of hope. Despite the deceits that might have been foreseen, the step was irreversible. In Pakistan (founded in 1947 with the partition of India), the Islamic associations of Abu'l-Ala Maududi played a role analogous to that of the Muslim Brotherhood, focussed on a return to an Islam which was both political and religious. The modern struggle for the Qur'an to be recognized as the constitution of the world was entering its active phase.

The struggle for the application of the Muslim law

Recent decades, above all those between 1967 and 1987, have been marked by a feeling of disappointment after the immense hopes of independence. Hence the appeal of Islam as the only means of getting out of the position. Though it took a long time for those involved to become aware of the depth of the problem, once it was realized the first crises broke out very quickly. They occurred in Egypt, where the Muslim Brotherhood was officially suppressed at the end of 1954 by Gamal Abd al-Nasser, after a short period of strained relations between it and the free officers. This was in fact a struggle for power. Two attempts to assassinate President Nasser in 1954 and 1965 (whether real or arranged) were the pretext: hence the executions and deportations which scattered the Brothers all over the Near East and gave them the aura of persecution. The repressive measures made a permanent gulf between Abd al-Nasser and the Brotherhood. In Syria, where the movement had been flourishing, the Ba'ath government had to use an even firmer hand some years later to repress its activities.

With the defeat of Egypt in the Six Day War (June 1967) and the impotence of the other Arab countries, which prevented them from coming to its aid, a new stage in contemporary history was about to begin. Several factors worked in the same direction: disillusionment over the Arab socialist politics of Abd al-Nasser and his alliance with the Communist countries; the claim that the Muslims had been defeated because they had not put the Qur'an into practice; the government authorization given to public demonstrations by the brotherhoods which had been forbidden since 1952; and a desire to forget everyday reality. Meanwhile the great international Muslim organizations with their periodic meetings had been founded: numerous of their conferences and the journals which supported the Muslim Brotherhood called for an immediate application of Muslim law and the revision of various constitutions which they felt to be too inspired by Western codes.

It is impossible to follow this fundamentalist reaction to the disappointments in detail. The Palestine affair and the refugee problem, still in suspense around 1970, were its two essential elements. The Arab countries would accept Palestinian refugees on condition that they were subject to a minimum of discipline in the host countries and did not form a state within the state. Circumstances meant that only Lebanon was obliged by its very weakness to receive these refugees without being able to obtain the basic guarantees from them. This specific point and a certain number of others lay at the origin of the tragic Lebanon war (which began in April 1975); in it a series of political, religious, confessional and international antagonisms played a role.

In 1969, the seizure of power in Libya by Colonel Qadhafi had reinforced the camp of those Muslims who were struggling for the establishment of the Muslim law. Even if the Colonel's theories were not universally accepted (in particular his position on the limited importance of traditions in theology and the obligation to take the Qur'an as a virtually exclusive basis), the political and financial help which he provided both for the fight to re-establish the Muslim law and for the missionary expansion of Islam, was considerable.

The emblem of the Muslim brotherhoods. The Qur'an, two swords and the first word of Qur'an 8, 60, giving the order to take up arms.

In Egypt, after the sudden death of Gamal Abd al-Nasser in September 1970, the Egyptian politics of Anwar Sadat again relied on the Islamic conservatives for greater liberation from Soviet tutelage. This was a risk that had to be run. On the one hand, old Muslim Brothers whom age had made calmer held many official posts, not to mention those who were preachers or teachers. On the other hand, the journals of the Muslim Brotherhood received authorization to reappear without the movement itself being authorized. 'Islamic Associations' (al-jama'at al-islamiyya) with names which evoked their Pakistani counterparts were marked by the influence of Arabic translations of the works of Abu'l Ala Maududi and by the doctrines of the great theoretician of these movements, the Egyptian Sayyid Qutb, whose hanging by Abd al-Nasser in 1966 had made him a martyr. They called for the immediate application of Muslim legislation. These movements were very influential in the Egyptian universities, above all in the faculties of science.

Some of their groups went further, like that which called for the physical elimination of rulers who were unfaithful to their Muslim duties and 'executed' Anwar Sadat on 6 October 1981.

Moreover, the policy practised after the October 1973 war between Egypt and Israel, which enriched the traditional oil-producing countries (notably Saudi Arabia and Libya), was not alien to this development since many of those actively involved in it received financial help from the oil producers.

The decision by Anwar Sadat to work for peace between the Arabs and Israel was to result in the Camp David agreement. Unfortunately the intransigence of Israel and its attitude during the first steps taken by the Egyptian president in 1977 finally put off all the hesitant Muslims, who refused to join in. And the peace-process had to continue come what may, after Sadat's assassination as before.

Finally, the seizure of power in Iran by Ayatollah Khomeni (1978–1979) and the Shah's departure profoundly modified the map of the Middle East. A modern Islamic state had just been born and the eyes of all those who had set their hope on a re-establishment of Qur'anic law turned towards it. In contrast to the West, whose corruption was widely stressed (cf. 'the great American Satan'), would there at last be a strong state, committed to securing happiness for people here and in the other world? The war between Iran and Iraq and then the complications of the war in Lebanon hardly contributed towards clarifying the situation, and the Persian Gulf, Israel and Lebanon are still hot-spots in the globe which are never far from exploding. The presence of Soviet divisions in Afghanistan after 1979 and the terrible repression of the Afghan nationalist uprisings did not help matters.

What will come of all this? God alone knows. For there is no really trustworthy analysis of the situation either from the West or among the Muslim countries. The Muslims ruthlessly reject any solution which has no place for God's rights,

Jihad

This is a notion which Westerners often misunderstand. The word means 'struggle', 'fight', with the connotation of effort, making an effort for.

This struggle can be an inward one against the passions: according to a tradition which contemporary Sufis want to restore, this is the 'great' *jihad*.

In fact the 'lesser' *jihad* or legal war (rather than holy war) has played a major role in the history of Islam. At first defensive and later offensive, often because the Muslims felt themselves to be threatened, it was inevitable in a world of struggle and war.

However, this warlike sense is not the only one. Bourguiba compared the struggle against under-development to a *jihad*. And efforts at propaganda, diffusion or cultural resistance, or as a counter to mendacious campaigns, are also forms of *jihad*.

and the most sensitive Westerners know that neither liberalisms nor atheistic socialisms are acceptable to men and women who are aware of their spiritual dimension. Their real aspirations need to be understood, and many people have the impression that that has not yet happened. So it is not surprising that the Muslims take refuge in a kind of miracle solution. Since no other valid solution is proposed to them, this risks continuing to be an ongoing temptation.

These 'fundamentalists despite everything' are not the only trend, even if they exist throughout the Muslim world: in Pakistan, to a lesser degree in Indonesia and even less in West Africa. Other Muslims affirm that the interpretation of the Muslim law has to evolve: in speeches and writings they make public statements to this effect and protest against a literal return to former interpretations. A mass of other people who dare not stand up and be counted support them in silence.

Here and there, some attempts at secularization

We leave aside the case of the newly independent countries of West Africa. The natural African tolerance has made them adopt a clause in their first constitutions that the state is secular, for example in Senegal. However, an increasing number of traditional Muslim countries (including some of their oil-producing sponsors) are inciting them to join the camp of those who declare Islam to be the state religion.

Formerly the only experience of secularization known in a Muslim country had been that of Turkey after the 1914–1918 war. The case of the Soviet Muslims cannot be considered an experience of this kind: theirs was a situation imposed by an militant atheist government, succeeding that of the Tsars who had colonized the country. In Turkey, the separation of Islam and the state was proclaimed after the 1922 revolution. Attempts were even made to replace Arabic in certain liturgical formulae (the call to prayer, etc.), but that proved impossible to maintain. For a long time the law has continued to apply certain principles different from those of the Muslim law (a Muslim converted to another religion, if he is a Turk, inherited from his family; elsewhere the convert was deprived of any right to inherit). But generally speaking the attempt ended in failure, and the religious tendency which had never ceased to exist at a popular level regained its vigour, especially after 1960. Experience elsewhere in Turkey has been orientated in a very particular direction by virtue of the fact that Islam was replaced among the dominant middle class by an extremely strong Turkish nationalism which was also very closed in on itself.

In Tunisia, President Bourguiba took some measures which went against the traditional conception of Islam, like banning polygamy or, around 1960 in connection with the fast of Ramadan, asking the Tunisians to give work priority over fasting if they were not capable of doing both at the same time. He saw work as part of a *jihad* against under-development and justified dispensations in this way, comparing them with the classic dispensations of the holy war. But the attempt was far from conclusive.

Finally, some works which caused quite a stir in their time favoured a secularization of society. But in fact, if incipient secularization has begun to affect customs (for example, the theoretical recognition of the principle of the equality of all citizens in civil rights and duties), and everyday life has developed a whole sector of secular activities, this development has not yet worked its way right through. With the revival of the fundamentalist movement (see above), the trend towards secularization has come up against very serious opposition. More profoundly, it seems that while open-minded Muslims no longer accept a mediaeval form of sacral society, they will never think it right to accept radical secularization. So where can they go? That is the question.

A pluralist society, Indonesia

This is a very special case. Indonesia is the country with the largest number of Muslims (officially 130 million in 1980, a figure which some contest on the grounds that in that area the name 'Muslim' also covers people with a very idiosyncratic faith). Moreover, since independence, Christians in Indonesia have so far enjoyed the utmost equality and freedom. However, the situation varies, depending on the region.

In 1945, on the eve of independence, the nationalist Indonesians agreed on five governing principles for a pluralist society in which Muslims, Hindus, Buddhists, Protestants and Catholics would all be recognized as full citizens, with the same rights and the same duties. The first of these five principles was belief in God: so one cannot call them secular.

Active Muslims would have liked to introduce some supplementary words into the constitution, so that the Muslim Law (the *shari'ah*) was recognized and became the civil and religious law of Muslims. The other tendencies refused, and the proposition was not passed. In 1949 these activists created a state in West Java which was later put down by the army; moreover, between 1952 and 1965 Islamic rebels held the south of Sulawese. An Islamic state was founded at Aceh in 1953, but that too finally disappeared. The Pandjasila, the term which denotes the 'five principles', still remains the foundation of the constitution.

If the few words which the fundamentalist Muslims would like to restore to the constitution were adopted, this real equality and freedom would risk becoming inconsistent with them. What will happen? Only the future can tell.

The socialist model

The impact of modern Western socialism has also contributed to a change in the social and political face of Muslim countries in recent years. Muslim society had retained many social customs, sometimes even patterns of collective, tribal or communal property in areas where animals were pastured. Similarly, there was a whole system of social support, legalized by the institution of the *zakat*. I shall not be discussing that here, since in fact in the nineteenth century the majority of Muslim countries which were still free were governed by authoritarian and personal régimes.

The model of capitalist development was first imposed by the force of events, because of the world economic order, but very soon it emerged that the developing countries were inferior partners in these systems. After 1920 the Soviet socialist model of development was also presented, with rapid industrialization in certain sectors of the economy (though at a very high price) when the country was far from being modern. The monarchical Muslim states were very wary of this model and the ideas which it embodied.

On the other hand, many national liberation movements in Muslim countries received Soviet support, and economic ties were created. The high dam on the Nile at Aswan in Egypt, a major enterprise, which was important not only as a symbol of national power but also for its economic effects, was financed by Russian loans and built by Russian engineers and contractors after the American refusal to support it (1956–1962). However, Muslims rarely accept pure Marxist socialism; countries like Mali, at the beginning of its adherence to Marxism, had an attitude which Marxist countries of the old brand would have found unthinkable.

Socialism generally appeared in a so-called Islamic form: nationalizations, free education, agrarian reform, the reduction of the private sector (to the advantage of the public sector controlled by the state) and social security went with support for and development of Islamic values. Between 1960 and 1965 several studies were published, demonstrating that Islam was basically socialist. Here, too, life preceded theory, and there was no lack of *a priori* justifications.

Since then, the Soviet advance in Asia and Africa has brought several Muslim countries under Marxist regimes, especially Afghanistan (after 1973 and above all after December 1979) and Aden (South Yemen), but here again the setbacks to socialism have been evident. It seems that if Muslim countries will not hesitate to ally themselves with the devil (to use a saying of Churchill's often repeated by some Muslim leaders) to get aid, they do so very reluctantly, apart from a small minority adapted to the principles of Marxism. Religious values are too deeply rooted among the Muslims for them to feel at ease under an atheistic dictatorship, whether that of a party or the proletarist. On the one hand countries like Egypt after Nasser and Somalia have been freed from all Soviet influence after having massive Soviet aid. On the other, it is impossible to tell how the Muslims in the Soviet republics of Central Asia, who form a substantial minority, actually feel. It seems that atheistic propaganda has not been able to put an end to the faith, as its propagandists had hoped. Recent studies even stress the role played in the maintaining of faith by an Islam parallel to official Islam, that of the brotherhoods.

Taking up the challenge of development

The most usual way for many Muslim intellectuals to see the challenge posed by the modern world to Muslims is to distinguish between Western technology (which is accepted) and Western culture (which is rejected). Such a view of the question is still a superficial one, since technology presupposes a particular mind-set in the person who puts it to work. Technology and culture cannot be separated purely and simply.

However, there are some more profound analyses of the situation. One of the most illuminating is that by Mamadou Dia, a Senegalese Muslim who was the first President of the Council of his country at the time of independence. He also sponsored development studies. His book appeared in Dakar in 1975, in French, with the title *Islam, African Societies and Industrial Culture*. It is interesting for us to note how an open and intelligent Muslim reacts to such a difficulty; moreover, here is an African stressing that all technology postulates roots in a culture.

The problem is this. Why has Muslim civilization, which knew times of brilliance in the Middle Ages, and counts among its ranks the best scholars of this period, succumbed to sclerosis? What are the causes of this state? How can it be remedied?

No Muslim doubts the possibility of emerging from it. 'Islam has the best resources for surviving the present crisis', writes Mamadou Dia.

How does he see the decline of Muslim civilization? He is familiar with the reflections of the principal Western specialists on the question and reports the essential features of their views, but keeps his freedom of judgment. He does not accept that Muslim culture is in a state of inferiority simply because it has refused to align itself with Greek thought, as some Westerners say. While warning Muslims against an exacer-

---

The great problem of years to come

Unbelievers are those who do not judge in accordance with God's revelations (Qur'an 5, 44).

Pronounce judgment among them in accordance with God's revelations (Qur'an 5, 49).

For a Muslim, legislation can only be based on revelation, i.e. primarily on the Qur'an. That is evident. But an important point needs to be clarified: in that case what are the principles of interpretation?

If the tendency to go back to the interpretation of past centuries gets the upper hand, we are moving towards years in which it will be difficult to live together.

If the tendency that wants the gates of 'research' to remain open, i.e. that does not rule out a degree of evolution *a priori*, comes out on top, a pluralist society remains possible.

So the great question is: Which will win – the tendency which allows a degree of evolution in interpretation, or fundamentalism?

We need to follow it very closely.

---

bated and sterile apologetic attitude (though he himself could not cease to have an apologetic attitude), he puts his fingers on the essential feature of development: the need to have a new mentality for which a fact is a fact and a thing is a thing; one which can plan, forecast and organize.

The problem is not just one of accumulating techniques, but of being open to a culture which postulates both idealism and realism in a harmonious synthesis. And if the West has to rethink its concepts in order to give a more human significance to science, technology and production, Muslim societies must deepen their effort at reconversion in the other direction if they are finally to avoid archaism and become progressive societies. They must accept, without a sense of going back, the logic of the industrial culture that they want to appropriate, and agree to question psychological notions which have nothing to do with dogma and which belong to cultural totalities which are obsolete. There is a need for certain realities which are the signs of an economic culture orientated on the future, like 'working hours' (which do not do away with social time), forecasting, economic calculations, in short all that gives specific form to a will to 'take possession of the future and implies new forms of conduct', to cease to be just superstructures and for planners, business leaders and financiers to enter into the customs of new societies. There is a need to create social infrastructures, i.e. new and economically effective motivations among the masses; in particular the two basic propensities of all modern economy, the propensity to work and the propensity to innovate. All this presupposes an effort at psychological transformation; here the options of the rationalization and decolonization of the élite are no guarantee of success unless the development is extended deep into the roots of the people (Mamadou Dia, *Islam*, Nouvelles Editions Africaines, Dakar 1975, p.153).

At the end of this quotation it is clear that Mamadou Dia is speaking of what is demanded by complete entry into an industrial civilization: work, honesty to facts and things, the spirit of invention, the abstract sense which discovers scientific laws, a creative imagination which makes it possible to see the consequences of abstract laws and plans, and a modesty which subjects ideas to the control of reality. This is a new mentality, that of the world of quantity and systematic measurement, whereas until recent centuries Muslim scholars were still concerned with qualitative observations and fragmentary measures. This is not a religious question, and Islam itself has kept aloof from it.

The one thing to be said is that so far too many Muslim intellectuals have been the victims of a state of mind which paralyses them. Some of them want to find everything in the Qur'an, even things that a religious book has no mission to say, as if nothing existed outside it. No reality has any value in their eyes unless they can apply a phrase from the Qur'an to it. This turn of mind has led too many men of religion to devote all their attention to discovering things in the Qur'an which are not there, including the announcements of the most recent inventions of modern science. Instead of looking at the facts, trying to discover the laws which govern them, checking their ideas constantly by comparing them with reality, they have lived in a world of imagination. This has proved infectious, so that too many others, without resorting to the Qur'an, have taken the easy way out and developed the habit of not looking reality in the face.

Mamadou Dia's book is interesting because it reminds his fellow Muslims of the conditions for participating in the industrial society of the future while rejecting its materialist aspect, whether this is an economy centred on profit, interested only in clients who can pay or help, and which is bound to be capitalist, or an atheistic dictatorship which obliterates humanity with surveillance, police and informers.

What Islam has to offer for the construction of a new world is its sense of God and its sense of human beings, and this can give a new society that religious dimension without which human beings are not human. As Mamadou Dia notes, Islam rejects a Promethean society in which human beings set themselves up against heaven or regard themselves as the unconditional masters of nature instead of taking their place in it. On the subject of Islam, Mamadou Dia adds:

At least it retains the honour of having been one of the rare movements which have maintained the message of spirituality on this earth which has been conquered by materialism (p.61).

In practice, and in a more immediate way, one meets in Muslim societies a certain number of positions some of which, while not related to dogma, raise problems for evolution. They result from an attachment to real values, have withstood testing and have marked society. Perhaps this attachment is the sign of a gut refusal to see them sacrificed in a new world. That must be taken into account if they are to have a real place, even if it is not such a prominent one. Mention should be made of:

• attachment to a form of education centred above all on memory. All oral civilizations called for the development of memory, and in return this memorization gave texts known by heart an authority, a hold on the senses, which they would not have had in any other type of civilization. Today, an abnormal stress on memory risks pushing people towards an exclusive cult of the past instead of prompting them to observe, discover and invent;

• the unconditional solidarity between the members of a family or a clan. This solidarity has so far lain at the basis of social life in numerous societies: it has contributed towards their solidity and growth. But the establishment of powerful public organizations – factories, transport, businesses – calls for a sense of the common good which differs from that of the economic needs of the family. The spirit of solidarity must now take account of the imperatives of production so as not to harm the development of the country. The world dimensions of co-operation are also in line with the influence of numerous international factors: commercial competition, a difference in salary scales depending on the area of production, the monopolies of major companies, the financial support provided by certain states, etc. The important thing is to reconcile these two types of solidarity;

• a last example: in the past, the activity of Muslims who wanted to serve Islam was orientated on a small number of precise aims like participation in martial efforts to extend the rule of Islam, the diffusion of Arabic as a language, and so on. Today, social life calls for new forms

of commitment and dedication. Here again adaptation is necessary; there is no reason why it should not happen.

Muslims in Britain

The earliest significant arrival of Muslims into Britain came about with the expansion of the British empire in the Indian subcontinent. Seafarers recruited along the maritime routes of the empire began to settle in British ports. They came from West Africa and India and, after the opening of the Suez Canal in 1869, increasingly from Yemen. During the early half of the twentieth century, these early settlers were followed by students and, in larger numbers, by demobbed military personnel. However, it was during the 1950s that Muslim immigration began to be more widely noticeable, both from the Indian subcontinent and from the Turkish part of Cyprus. In the early 1960s the major settlement of Pakistanis started, followed a decade later by Asians from East Africa and in the 1970s by the growth in Bangladeshi settlement. At this time also, growing instability in the Middle East brought Arabs and Iranians.

There are no reliable official religious statistics, and one occasionally sees figures as high as 2.5 million Muslims quoted. The most reasoned estimates indicate that a total of one million is more likely to be sound. About two-thirds of these have their origins in the Indian subcontinent, and over half of them from Pakistan. There are only a few thousand British converts to Islam.

Muslims are to be found in all larger cities and in many smaller ones too. Those from the areas around the Mediterranean are concentrated in London and the South East, while the greatest concentrations of people of Pakistani origin are to be found in the areas of Birmingham, Bradford and Manchester.

Most Muslims are British citizens, half of them because they were born in Britain. It is a very young community, since it was mainly young people who migrated and set up families here. Their children are now increasingly graduating from the education system, finding careers, and themselves beginning families.

Most of the immigrant generation of Muslims came from rural areas and fitted into British industry as semi-skilled or unskilled workers. So they have been particularly hard hit by the unemployment of the 1980s. There is, though, also a significant group of professionally trained people, accountants, lawyers, doctors etc., and many young Muslims are also entering the professions.

The first mosques were opened in the last century, during the 1880s in Liverpool and at Woking near London, the latter still standing today. The early Yemeni settlers had their small community centres, where they taught their children Arabic and the Qur'an. An Islamic Cultural Centre was established in London between the two World Wars, and during the 1940s it was given a plot of land in Regent's Park by the king in exchange for a plot in Cairo for an Anglican cathedral there. The mosque which can be seen today was opened in the mid-1970s. By then numbers of mosques had appeared all over the country, as Muslims had settled and established their family life here. Today there are over 400 mosques, mostly situated in converted dwellings, factories or warehouses. About twenty mosques have been purpose-built.

The mosque is the centre of Muslim community life, and it is through mosques that Muslim movements and organizations usually function. A number of such movements have come with the Muslims from their countries of origin. Among the Yemenis, their Alawi Sufi order was an early strong influence. Other Sufi orders and traditions have come with later immigrants, especially the Naqshabandi and Chisti orders from India and Pakistan. Equally important are probably the various 'revivalist' movements which appeared in the Muslim world during the last century and a half in the search for a Muslim response to Western predominance. From the

Indian subcontinent have come the intellectual Deobandi movement of religious scholarship as well as its rival, the more popular and Sufi-oriented Barelvi movement. Related to the Deobandi tradition is the pietistic 'internal mission' movement Tabligh-i-Jamaat, which has found a strong following also among North Africans in other parts of Europe. The small but highly effectively organized Jamaat-i-Islami, founded by Abu'l Ala Maududi, has established several organizations in Britain, including the Islamic Foundation and the UK Islamic Mission. The Muslim Brotherhood, of Egyptian origin, has been instrumental in organizing Muslim students, mostly foreign but increasingly also those from the Muslim communities in Britain.

It has been more difficult for Muslims to find a common form of organization across Britain. An early attempt was the Union of Muslim Organizations (UMO). More recently the Council of Imams and Mosques can make some claim to success. Another attempt is the Council of Mosques of the UK and Eire. The diversity is a reflection not only of the diversity of ethnic and linguistic backgrounds of Muslims as well as the varieties of religious thought related to the various movements. It also results from the tendency of Muslim groups to look to different parts of the Muslim world for moral and material support. In this context it should be stressed that the success of certain wealthy Muslim states to translate their financial support for Muslim efforts in Britain into political support has been, at the best, mixed.

It is worth noting that these internal differences are overwhelmingly within the majority Sunni group. There are not many Shi'ites in Britain, and these are mostly of Indian origin via East Africa. They have little sympathy with Iranian trends, especially the many who are Ismailis, following the lead of the Aga Khan. Ahmadis are a totally separate group with their own organization. Muslims in Britain overwhelmingly agree with their condemnation as non-Muslims.

Muslims in the United States

The first substantial Muslim presence in the United States coincides chronologically with that in Britain. The links were, however, not imperial. Rather, Muslim immigration came from the Middle East, in particular geographical Syria as part of a general migration from the Mediterranean region to North America in the decades before the First World War. While most, thus, were Arabs there were also numbers of people from India, in particular the Punjab region. The process of Muslim community building only really began seriously during the 1920s and 30s, primarily at the local level in the industrial towns where Lebanese and Syrian Muslims concentrated.

As this process was taking place a completely separate phenomenon was the appearance of the so-called Black Muslim movement. This arose out of the preaching of a man named W. D. Fard among the black population of Detroit. Claiming roots in Mecca, Islam, and the Qur'an he gave many black Americans pride in themselves. When Fard disappeared, the leadership was taken over by Elijah Muhammad (d. 1975) who proclaimed himself the caliph of Fard, the prophet. Of course, this was not a recognizable form of Islam, and the conflict came when Malcolm X, having been on pilgrimage to Mecca, took up the call to a correct Islam. The result was a split among Black Muslims with a large proportion aligning themselves with main-stream Islam. This process was assisted by the development of strong connections with Muslim organizations in the Arab world and with the organizations of students, academics and professionals which are much stronger in the United States than in Britain.

A number of Muslim organizations exists, by far the largest of which is the Bilalians, named after Bilal who was the first person appointed by Muhammad to call to prayer. These are the section of 'Black Muslims' which have joined main-stream Islam. According to one source, they accounted for over half of the around 270 mosques in the United States listed in Muslim sources in 1980. Given the fact that, of well over two million Muslims in the United States, between a quarter and a third are students and academics, the student organizations and professional associations are of particular significance. Another particular aspect is the historical link with the Arab world, but it is only in recent years that Arab organizations have begun to make themselves influential in a public lobbying context where the Israeli lobby has been extremely powerful. As this Arab-American lobby has gained in standing it has clearly had consequences also in a more positive presentation of Islam on the political scene.

10

Muslim-Christian Relations

Even if Muslim-Christian relations must finally be considered on the religious level, it is worth while beginning by surveying the ground and looking at the motivations behind them. Many political, sociological, economic and psychological factors have intervened and continue to intervene over the course of the centuries: to think of them will help to give each cause its due, to Caesar that which is Caesar's and to God that which is God's.

Given the multiplicity of factors at work, the type of relations will vary greatly from one place to another.

Multiplicity of situations

Relations can simply concern individuals within the same country (in an environment with either a Muslim or a Christian majority; in a land governed by Muslim or Christian authorities, or even governed by administrations accepting the neutrality of a lay state). Alternatively, they can be international relations between Muslim countries and countries with Christian inhabitants.

Even in individual relations within the same country, there are many variations. There are countries in which a once-flourishing Christianity has been entirely supplanted by Islam: that is the case in North Africa, from which almost all indigenous Christianity has disappeared, Christians now being almost all aliens living there for a limited period. Elsewhere there is no local Christianity and practically no foreign Christians: that is the case in Afghanistan.

By contrast, in the south of India, in Ethiopia and in the Middle East (leaving aside Turkey, which is a special case), important Christian minorities descended from ancestors who have always lived in the country have persisted over the centuries. In Lebanon (and in Ethiopia), Christians represent almost half the population, while in Iraq they amount to less than 3.5%.

In Asia, where Islam was established relatively early (for example in Pakistan), one comes across small Christian minorities made up of converts from religions other than Islam. In Marxist countries, like Russian Turkestan or Western China, the type of relations will be different again.

In Africa south of the Sahara, alongside areas which Islam penetrated seven or eight centuries ago, there are others in which both Christians and Muslims are recent converts. The racial question is then superimposed on the religious question.

Major emigrations in our time (by students, workers, middle and upper classes, diplomats, etc.) have created Muslim minorities in the West, and there is also a Christian presence in Arabia, where again the situation varies from one state to another.

To end with, one can add the differences between the past and the present, between cities and the countryside, between cultivated milieux open to new values and those which are primarily concerned to preserve the traditions. This first glance will show the complexity of the situation and explain why Christians in a particular area often accuse specialists of presenting Islam too theoretically; in their great designs they scarcely recognize the reality that they experience every day. When Christians in a particular area say what they feel about Muslim-Christian relations in a particular year, it does not follow that their opinion is the only one, or that it holds for other countries and other situations.

A two-fold demand

That having been said, a two-fold demand emerges. First of all we need to know whether in this varied set of cases there are not some constants which are worth identifying in order to have a better understanding of the situation as a whole.

Secondly, even while taking account of the tensions which have arisen in the past, is it possible to arrive at more peaceful kinds of relations? The Church wants this, and in the Vatican II Declaration on Relations with Non-Christian Religions calls for it explicitly (see the box).

This new orientation demands patience and clarity, and it will come up against a good deal of opposition. The questions of mission on either side and on the situation of Muslims in a country in which they are a minority (and vice versa) are the most obvious. Despite everything, a survey of the situation shows that the partisans of dialogue have several important trump cards in their hand.

The positive values in the faith of Muslims and Christians

The first thing to note, then, is that the daily problem of relations between Christians and Muslims is on a contemporary existential level, regardless of what may have been the historical events in the sphere of which the two religions were once a part. Muslim-Christian relations were first established on the human level, in social life. So for centuries Christians and Muslims have worked together in the cities in which they lived. This point is so evident that I shall not stress it. An identical concern for social justice, civic life and help for the underprivileged can be the cement of common activity.

The religious level is more tricky, since here there are two very different sets of themes. One set allows *entente* and harmony; the other is more particular.

Things in common on the religious level

First of all, both Muslims and Christians are aware that they are the creatures of one omnipotent God. They believe in him, and wish to serve him and do his will, even if they do not agree on all that God demands. Take this verse which commends abandonment to God:

> Submit yourselves therefore to God. Resist the devil and he will flee from you. Draw near to God and he will draw near to you (James 4.7).

Does not the word Islam specifically mean submission? On both sides there is this same decision to submit to God, of one's own free will, actively, without any of those feelings of constraint that the word submission sometimes evokes.

The personal relationship between human beings and their Creator is a mystery to which Christians and Muslims bow and which is the basis of a reciprocal esteem. And this relationship between human beings and their Creator is open to a perspective of grace and salvation. Even if each side professes that there is only one official way of salvation (Islam for the one, Christianity for the other), Christians and Muslims will often go on to recognize that many people, without fault on their part, do not succeed in discovering this way and that God can save them in other ways. The divine salvation can extend to men of good will who do not find themselves on the official main road. Christians say this when they teach that the grace of God is not bound in a limiting way to the sacraments. Muslims like al-Ghazali in the Middle Ages, or more recently Muhammad Abduh, also accept this possibility of salvation; and if one often comes up against more obdurate positions, there are nevertheless many faithful who think like al-Ghazali and Muhammad Abduh.

So far, attempts at dialogue, to my knowledge, have always begun from these two points: collaboration in civil or cultural work and a recognition of the essential religious elements common to any monotheistic faith and extending as far as some sharing of experiences. When a Christian nurse speaks of a good and merciful God to a sick Muslim, who is abandoning himself to the will of God as he dies, there is real and profound communion. When a Muslim reminds a Christian friend of one or other invocation addressed to a God who is present and very good, there is also communion.

And Vatican II, in the Declaration on Non-Christian Religions, lists the features which the Church esteems highly in Islam (see the box).

Or to put things another way, among the common features on the religious level we need to note the God who is alive, one, the infinitely good creator and master; his gifts, his forgiveness, and so on. This gives rise to a whole series of common attitudes: worship, thanksgiving, abandonment, asking for forgiveness, help, etc. Sometimes, as in Egypt, the same religious formulae are used by both Christians and Muslims: God be praised! Thank God! If God wills!

Similarly, the commandments of the Decalogue, a certain number of principles in civil organization, human advancement, development bring Muslims and Christians together. The idea that the future does not belong wholly to us, that everything on earth takes place under the face of God, the praise of God for the splendours of creation, and so on, are common to both Christians and Muslims.

We do not need so much to discuss these points as to live them out. A remark made in an article by a group of Little Sisters of Jesus, published in *Cahiers Marials*, gives a frank account of everyday relations.

> Contact with our Muslim friends has also taught us over the years that we must never discuss together, even the issues which bring us closest together, for we each have a different way of conceiving the same realities, and what unites us in the simplicity of everyday life can divide us in intellectual discussion.

These few pointers, which bring out the ideal of our brothers, will help us to be attentive and above all not to champ at current frustrations, forgetting the latent possibilities that are there. Inspired by Goethe, Fr Jean Abd el-Jalil (who died in 1979) used to say this:

> If we take people as they are we confirm them in their bad features; but if we take them as they should be, we help them to be what they can be.

And Fr Jean went on to add:

> I hope that I shall be forgiven for saying that I also find that in the gospel. Just take the parable of the murderers in the vineyard. 'They will respect my Son,' says God. God was well aware what was going to happen and Christ had no illusions as to

what there is in humankind; but to the last breath one has to appeal to the God in humankind, however minimal this may be, however rebellious humankind may be at letting good triumph over evil.

The problem of mission

Even if mutual respect is possible, at certain points relations between Christians and Muslims nevertheless remain very delicate. The main area of friction has been, and is, rivalry in expansion. A colloquy in Switzerland in 1976 held at the invitation of the World Council of Churches was the occasion for exchanges between several Muslim and Christian leaders on the subject of mission. The atmosphere was sometimes stormy and the tension great. That was understandable, since on both sides memories and actions had piled up and each side had a very specific view of the situation.

Christians know that thousands of their fellow-believers have gradually gone over to Islam and continue to do so. They have the impression that this begins when faith in Christ among them is weak or weakened, giving place to a general deism. At this point, an interest, a marriage or just the desire to stop being a second-class citizen and to play a full part in the life of the city is enough to lead to adherence to Islam. Sometimes this will be in order to be more united with those whose life they share. Only in rare cases has it been that former unbelievers discover faith in God in Islam. Christians have noted that usually those who have taken this step have been so captivated by the new community that they could no longer consider that they might be mistaken and be brought back. Was this by influence exerted on ways of thinking and feeling? Was it by a social pressure which went too far? Regardless of any explanations that may be given, the fact is there.

Conversely, the guardians of Muslim values do not look favourably on the action of Christian

---

What Vatican II has said about Muslims

The Church also has a high regard for the Muslims. They worship God, who is one, living and subsistent, merciful and almighty, the Creator of heaven and earth, who has also spoken to men. They strive to submit themselves without reserve to the hidden decrees of God, just as Abraham submitted himself to God's plan, to whose faith Muslims eagerly link their own. Although not acknowledging him as God, they venerate Jesus as a prophet, his virgin Mother they also honour, and even at times devoutly invoke. Further, they await the day of judgment and the reward of God following the resurrection of the dead. For this reason they highly esteem an upright life and worship God, especially by way of prayer, alms-deeds and fasting.

Over the centuries many quarrels and dissensions have arisen between Christians and Muslims. The sacred Council now pleads with all to forget the past, and urges that a sincere effort be made to achieve mutual understanding; for the benefit of all men, let them together preserve and promote peace, liberty, social justice and moral values.

(Declaration *Nostra Aetate* on relations between the Church and non-Christian religions, ch.3)

---

missions in Islamic countries, and they attribute the very rare conversions which result from them to self-interest, and material and cultural pressures. They are convinced of the superiority of Islam and its world-wide mission. More often, in Islamic countries, they ostentatiously celebrate the conversions of Christians to Islam, publicity which Christians find difficult to take.

This rivalry in the sphere of expansion has made some topics very tricky, particularly that of the role of war in the propagation of the two religions. If Christianity did not use force during the first three centuries of its history, the question is far from being so clear after Constantine. We shall need objective and honest historical studies on both sides to disentangle the explosive aspects of these problems and to help us to see how, on this earth where the material and the spiritual are constantly mixed, the expansion of religious and temporal values has taken place. Until this work has been done, the danger of vain apologetic discussions is in no way illusory.

Anyone who goes back to principles will also see that the duty of propagation is as pressing on one side as on the other. The texts which prescribe it are extremely clear – like this verse on the universal mission of Islam which is repeated identically three times in the Qur'an:

> It is He who has sent forth His Messenger with guidance and the true faith to make it triumphant over all religions, however much the idolaters may dislike it (Qur'an 9, 33).

All Muslims are agreed without any hesitation that this verse is about Muhammad, the Qur'an and Islam.

Christians recall this command of Jesus in the Gospel:

> Go therefore and make disciples of all nations, baptizing them in the name of the Father and of the Son and of the Holy Spirit, teaching them to observe all that I have commanded you (Matthew 28.19).

Furthermore, the whole practice of both Muslim and Christian communities shows the degree to which these texts have been an inspiration. Mission has taken various forms, with a lighter and more flexible organization in Islam; a more structured and more specialized one in Christianity. Basically, is it not a deeply human reaction to want to share with others that which gives one's own existence all its meaning and appears

---

What Vatican II has said about Muslims

Finally, those who have not yet received the Gospel are related to the people of God in various ways . . . The plan of salvation also includes those who acknowledge the Creator, in the first place among whom are the Muslims: these profess to hold the faith of Abraham and together with us they adore the one, merciful God, mankind's judge on the last day.

(Dogmatic Constitution *Lumen Gentium* on the Church, ch.16. The whole of this chapter is indirectly concerned with Islam)

---

as the height of what human beings can have in this world: faith in the God who loves them and whom they love?

The problem of mission is further complicated by the presence of marginal Protestants who are very aggressive in their propaganda, and post-Christian sects like the Moonies and the Jehovah's Witnesses. An intensive and indiscreet propaganda makes Muslims furious, and moderate Christians suffer the backlash.

In the face of this difficulty, it seems that the first step to take should be to seek a tacit agreement on human rights and honesty in choice of means. So far the United Nations Charter of Human Rights is still the best expression of respect for others in these spheres. It allows each individual the right to choose his or her religion and to be converted. It still needs to be universally accepted.

At a more modest level, the first aspect of honesty would be totally to reject false arguments and presentations. To purge the atmosphere it is necessary first of all to struggle against prejudices, to recognize the good as good, the great as great on all sides, even among

133

those who are not of one's own group. Even if rivalry in expansion is a fact, it is always possible to make an effort at honesty to discover and esteem the true values by which our friends live and respect what ought to be respected.

The problems of psychological attitudes

The question of Muslim-Christian relations does not arise only in the sphere of ideas or even in that of interests: its emotional and psychological connotations are evident at every moment. Islam has just as considerable a hold on the sensibility of its followers as it has on their intellect, if not more so. Or more precisely, the intellectual respect is accompanied by such a bundle of emotional features that it is correct to describe Islam, as the orientalist Hamilton Gibb did, as a 'romanticism of reason'.

Conversely, we should not forget the emotional dimension of Christianity. There are many real values by which Muslim peoples live which Christians risk failing to see. Like any religion, Islam signifies not only a type of relationship between human beings and God but also a whole collection of human attitudes which are preserved and protected by Muslim society. And as long as Muslims do not encounter real sympathy for their authentic values among Christians, they will feel an instinctive repulsion from those who do not understand them. The word of a wise man of Mali, Hampate Ba, still holds: if your brother does not understand you, it is because you do not understand him. When you have understood him, he will understand you.

By virtue of the simplicity of its presentation, its apologetic, the repetition of the same affirmations which have been understood since infancy and the atmosphere which it creates, Islam surrounds its faithful with a protective hedge. The sense of the sacred, the worship of the one God, the shoulder-to-shoulder solidarity, the basic values of the family and group support, the glories of past civilization – all this is enough for

those who experience it; why should they feel the need to look for anything else? Furthermore, the community watches over them and leaves them free, as long as they serve it, by closing its eyes to cases in which they allow themselves certain liberties with belief. However, the community would become capable of implacable rigidity if its members dared to stop pronouncing the *shahada* or put in question the very foundations of Islam.

The Qur'an contains many finely-chiselled phrases, engraved for centuries on the memory and in the emotions of the faithful. Some are truisms which, by recalling the fragility of life and human knowledge, send a shiver through those who hear them:

And no one knows in what land he will die (Qur'an 31, 44)

Others express in a very simple way the basic truths which underlie all monotheistic religion, showing that it is about the oneness of God, his greatness, his knowledge and his power. This kind of certitude also reflects, like a halo of light, on other affirmations which are less evident. But as these are expressed in a popular form, with the air of captivating stories, when they are told well everything gets through.

Christians who read the Qur'an are struck by the presence of a large number of stories which are known in rabbinic literature or the apocryphal gospels, like the death of Solomon whose body remains in equilibrium, standing, supported by the stick on which he was leaning, while the jinns continue to work for him, before him, without having any doubts (Qur'an 34, 14). The Muslim criticism which is now pursuing the *israiliyyat*, i.e. the Jewish legends which have found their way into Muslim religious literature, commentaries, etc., to put the faithful on guard against what is thought valueless, does not recognize any authority in similar stories when they are found in the Qur'an. What is in the Qur'an is above any criticism; this standpoint is justified by a reasoning which we shall consider later, one by which the Muslim seeks to prove the divine origin of the Qur'an. For him the psychological certitude of all its propositions is absolute.

Christianity in the form presented by the mainstream church (i.e. Catholics and Orthodox plus those Protestants who believe in the mysteries of the Trinity, the Incarnation and redemption) is *a priori* rejected for not being in conformity with reason as the Qur'an commends it, or with the role which the Qur'an gives to the teaching of Jesus.

This psychological attitude, which is legitimated in connection with the Qur'an by belief in the divine origin of the text, can also be found among many men of religion in connection with stories which have nothing to do with the Qur'an. Everything that seems to give the Qur'an more authority is accepted blindly: thus many apologists affirm that the Qur'an contains an announcement of all the most modern sciences and discoveries, like inter-planetary travel or the atom bomb. Even if a substantial number of genuine scholars do not believe in this kind of apologetic and have the courage to say so, others keep silent for fear of the community or pay the price of making such an affirmation. That will certainly change with time, as did the same apologetic attitude of concordism among Christians which flourished at the end of the nineteenth century.

This emotional attitude again comes into play in connection with the so-called Gospel of Barnabas, which I shall be mentioning again later. All serious critics regard it as a forged manifesto, but since 1908, when the Arabic translation was put on the market, masses of Muslims, including even the most eminent figures, obstinately rely on it, seeing it as the true Gospel, for the sole reason that it agrees with the Qur'an on many points. They do not see that the central thesis of the book is contrary to the Qur'an. Jesus affirms in this Gospel that he is not the Messiah and he announces that Muhammad will be the awaited Messiah, whereas Muhammad is never given

this title in the Qur'an and Jesus is called Messiah all through the surahs from Medina.

This predominance of emotional values in matters related to the Qur'an does not block the route to dialogue, but it does markedly reduce the range of subjects that can be touched on. A very educated Muslim, once involved in the struggle for the revival of Islam, put things clearly in a meeting between Muslims and Christians. 'We know that our two dogmas differ on specific points: let us accept being different. But there are other essential points on which we are in agreement. We can agree on those.'

The difference between Christianity and Islam

Many people are often tempted to say that Islam and Christianity are basically very similar. To claim such a similarity without qualification is tantamount to accepting the standpoint of Islam, for whom Jesus and Muhammad preached two very close forms of the one eternal religion.

The Christian position is quite different. While recalling that we have a number of essential points in common, it does not hesitate to identify the differences which exist between Islam and Christianity. If these do not always come to light, it is because some Christians and Muslims are still at the beginning of their life of faith. It is often difficult to distinguish between plants when they are very young, having hardly come up from the earth; they are strangely similar. But that does not prevent each plant from becoming itself when it has grown. So Christians and Muslims can have analogous reactions in everyday life; the difference will become greater, the more they live out their ideals. They were latent as openings, possibilities, appeals. Life brings them out.

It can equally be that the resemblance emerges not so much because the Muslim or Christian is at the beginning of the life of faith, but on the contrary as the result of a long experience of the presence of God and his grace which acts and transforms by making use of all too human theories.

I shall approach this issue at the level of principles which the two respective religions teach, and compare the directives which are given on either side.

At one point the Gospel describes the discontinuity between the Old and New Testaments, when Jesus proclaims in the Sermon on the Mount: 'You have heard that it was said to those of old time . . . But I say to you' (cf. Matthew 6). Now what was said to men of old time, not to kill, to respect certain norms in repudiating one's wife, or to limit vengeance to an equivalent, can also be found in the Muslim heritage.

Like the Old Testament, Islam is already on an elevated level. However, Jesus adds, 'But I say to you . . .' and then goes on to give some of the new commandments of Christianity. Jesus calls on his disciples to go further, to show a new spirit in comparison with the level on which the most scrupulous observers of the Law place themselves: 'Unless your righteousness exceeds that of the scribes and Pharisees, you certainly will not enter into the kingdom of heaven' (Matt. 5.20).

What Jesus requires is known in Islam, but is only suggested there as an option. By contrast, the Sermon on the Mount presents these demands as obligations. Forgiveness is contemplated and even praised in the Qur'an on certain occasions, but it is not the subject of a general and absolute law, as it is in the New Testament.

In short, this demand to go further under the impact of a new spirit is characteristic of the Christian programme. The question is no longer one of modifying the law on a particular point but, as the Gospel puts it, of following Jesus. That is what was said to the rich young man who had observed all the commandments of the law from his childhood. Christianity demands more, Islam demands less. Another of the most obvious differences is that Muslims are capable of accomplishing all that their law requires of them: they can then be satisfied. But even if Christians are saints, they will never accomplish all that is required of them; they will always have to set their sights higher. In the sphere of a law which demands love, who can say in all truth that he or she has really loved? True Christians can never say that they have accomplished all that God required of them.

Two examples, out of many others, will show this difference. A Muslim friend once said to me in connection with a quarrel in which he was involved: 'You're a Christian, you have a duty to forgive.' A Muslim is not bound by this duty. In fact, what the Muslim said was not quite correct, since there are calls to forgiveness in the Qur'an, whether to brothers in the community or even, sometimes, for general forgiveness. For example, there is an exhortation from the time at Medina, asking Muslim benefactors to continue to help the poor in the community which had offended them. But after having ordained forgiveness, the text adds:

Do you not want God to forgive you? (Qur'an 24, 22).

And it has become a custom to remind Muslims on the days of great festivals that they have to reconcile themselves with their brothers with whom they may have had quarrels. The Qur'an itself provides that an individual can renounce the reparations due under the *lex talionis*, and this remission of debt is regarded as alms. This is a possibility which the believer is free to make use of or not, as he wishes.

In fact Christianity asks us to go further. It formally ordains that the *lex talionis* should be exceeded and that forgiveness is extended to all men and women, both within the community and outside, and it connects the forgiveness which God gives men and women with that which they share among themselves:

Forgive us our trespasses
as we forgive those who trespass against us.

Islam does not know about 'turning the other cheek', and one can sometimes hear such an attitude being called unreal or impracticable, or destructive of society and favouring evil. Islam is the religion of power which struggles for what it believes to be law and justice, and does not lower the flag unless it is forced to. That is a very prevalent attitude on this earth; indeed, it is how Peter, the leader of the Twelve, reacted when Jesus announced his future passion for the first time. Peter could not accept that his master was abandoning the struggle and letting things take their course; he felt that he should resist and call for help. We all know with what clarity and energy Jesus opposed Peter on this point, going so far as to tell him that his thoughts were 'not those of God but those of men' (Matthew 16.23). The rejection of the crucifixion of Jesus, which is so characteristic of Islam, should be seen in this connection.

The second example which we should consider here is that of the woman taken in adultery. It so happens that Jesus and Muhammad were on occasion confronted with the same problem, as we are told by the Gospel according to St John (ch.8) and a tradition related in the commentaries on the Qur'an (on Qur'an 5, 42).

In the Gospel, a woman caught in the act of adultery is taken one morning to the temple where Jesus is teaching. To embarrass Jesus, the defenders of morality ask him what they should do. It is a trap. The Law is formal: it calls for stoning. Jesus does not contradict the Law: he is simply scornful of the accusers, who are so hard on this woman and so lacking in shame for themselves. 'Let him who is without sin cast the first stone!', says Jesus, and everyone leaves in silence, one after another. Jesus is far from approving the act of which the woman is accused. He calls sin sin and evil evil when he tells the woman: 'Go and sin no more'.

But his authority, his goodness and his firmness are striking: he acts as a teacher of the Law and his forgiveness far exceeds that of other men.

In the Muslim tradition there is a similar incident when Muhammad is in the oasis of Khaybar. Some Jews bring before him a woman

> *If you reckoned up God's blessings, you could not count them.*
> *He is forgiving and merciful.*
>
> Qur'an 16, 189

caught in the act of adultery: she is one of their people. They ask him what they should do. Muhammad calls for a copy of the Torah. Since it is formally stated there that the adulteress should be stoned, he orders her to be stoned. Obedience to the Law comes before everything.

In one case Jesus decides. In the other the decision belongs to the Law. Here we find two basically different attitudes to life, to human beings and to God, corresponding to the different demands of the two respective dogmas. The comparison could be taken further by considering the two personalities of Jesus and Muhammad as they are described in the earliest sources: the Gospels and the *Sira* of Ibn Hisham (the latter is in Arabic, but there is an English translation).

When it comes to Muslim and Christian views of human nature, it seems that on the Muslim side the present state of humankind is regarded as normal. Men and women must choose between good and evil, but there are no constraints in the tendency to evil, and men and women can overcome it with God's help.

'God has not made evil more attractive and likeable than good, despite what certain moralists claim', said Muhammad Abduh; he also said: 'A bias towards the good has been put into human nature'. It is enough to purify the will by healthy belief and to reinforce it by appropriate exercises.

On the Christian side, a more realistic consideration of human nature, its greatness and its wretchedness, illuminated by long experience and the teachings of the Old Testament, shows that men and women are subject to a congenital weakness. St Paul sums up the situation in words which are a good explanation of the human predicament:

I do not understand my own actions. For I do not do what I want, but I do the very thing I hate (Romans 7.15).

For the Christian, the present state of humankind is abnormal, marked by decay and sin (original and personal). We know that we are called to greater things, provided that we are saved by the forgiveness of God in Christ and collaborate actively in response to this gift.

'Without me you can do nothing', Jesus said to his disciples (John 15.5).

Both sides, Christians and Muslims, know that we are threatened by a violent egocentrism. Moreover, is not all education concerned to discipline this egocentric force to help children, future adults, to integrate themselves into society? This integration is strongly stressed in Islam, which emphasizes self-control and the service of the community. Moreover, the self-control is helped by the impact of society on the sensibility of its members. Obedience to the law is the great way of fighting against this egocentrism. The Muslim thus seeks to escape his inclinations to evil in order to be saved from aberration and to be guided on the right way.

In the Gospel Jesus went further. He brought out clearly the danger of another type of egotism, collective egotism, based on self-interested *quid pro quos* at the heart of society, or even ending up by distinguishing between those who are brothers and sisters and those who are not. Jesus called on his followers to regard all men and women as their brothers and sisters, and he said

specifically that it was impossible to love God without loving one's neighbour and vice versa. It is good to teach love of neighbour, but it is also necessary to specify who is one's neighbour. This question is clearly raised by the parable of the Good Samaritan. Jesus asks his followers to die to their selfishness in order to be reborn to a new life in the power of the Spirit. That is the direction he sought to follow for us, dying on the cross for us and rising for us. In Christianity there is a mystery of salvation which is bound up with a mystery of obedience, but the obedience finally enters the sphere of the love of God.

Consequently, on the one hand men and women will sometimes fight to establish justice, as Islam does when it finds itself up against opposition. On the other hand, they know that though recourse to force is sometimes necessary, it cannot be enough to resolve all problems. They are aware that at certain moments the Christian ideal calls for sacrifice and self-giving in the steps of the crucified Christ: like the grain of wheat put into the ground, one has to die to allow the birth of a new life.

In practice this two-fold human attitude is essentially bound up with a two-fold way of imagining God. For the Muslim, God is the one Master, infinitely good and all-powerful, whose mystery is beyond human understanding. Like a servant waiting at the gate of the master whom he loves to serve without entering his house, the Muslim is God's servant at the heart of the community which the Qur'an also calls God's people or party.

For Christians, God is revealed in stages. They believe that after emphasizing his unity for centuries in the face of the threat of idolatry, God then shed light on the mystery which is at the very heart of this unity: the mystery of one God substituting in three distinct persons and the relationship between these three persons. He called men and women to imitate him, to participate in his own life; a new scale of values, that of the Beatitudes given in the Sermon on the Mount, replaced the old one. The mystery of this inner life of God, one in essence, subsisting in three persons, is bound up with the revelation of the God who is love. Humankind is saved and salvation is adoption into this new life.

The Word was the true light that enlightens every man, coming into the world. He was in the world, and the world was made through him, yet the world knew him not.

He came to his own home, and his own people received him not. But to all who received him he gave power to become children of God . . . (John 1.9–12).

Two conceptions of revelation go with these two representations of the same God. On the one hand God speaks through books which he gives to humankind, the main ones being the Torah, the Gospel and the Qur'an. On the other hand, having spoken by the prophets within a particular people chosen by him, God then does so by his Word (cf. Hebrews 1.1). For the Muslim, the supreme gift of God is the Qur'an, the word of God made into a book. For the Christian, the supreme gift of God is the Christ, the eternal Word of God made flesh. On the one hand we have the revelation of a book; on the other, that of a person.

For anyone who adopts the perspective of Jesus, who tells the woman of Samaria, 'If you knew the gift of God and who it is who is saying to you . . .' (John 4.10), the whole difference lies in the way in which one envisages the gift of God and the personality of Jesus.

11

The Problem of Muhammad

One last question deserves a chapter to itself. Even if it is not always raised explicitly, it remains in the sub-conscious of those with whom we talk, prompting many of their reactions. It came up in the first official encounters in dialogue between Christians and Muslims after Vatican II. We are also likely to find it hard to take a new step on the way to dialogue unless we have seriously reflected on it. The question is this: Who is Muhammad for Christians?

The issue can come up in two ways:

Muslims may say clearly to Christians: we recognize Jesus as a prophet. Why do you not recognize Muhammad as a prophet?

Or they may recall what the mediaeval West said about Muhammad, making bitter and unjust attacks and slandering his name.

It is not worth spending long on the mediaeval statements. We need only recognize that they are unacceptable today. Such legends show at what point ignorance of the other was total. As for the falsity of the affirmations, the hurtful character of many assertions, they can be explained against the background of a time when education was weak and there was lively resentment of Muslims in the wake of their military invasions of the West. Today there is no question

of Christians repeating the slanders, and on the Muslim side we must hope that the page will be turned. At one meeting between Muslims and Christians, when a Muslim began to list all these charges all over again, one of his fellow-Muslims in effect said to him: 'Are we going to keep turning over the past, as the pre-Islamic Arab tribes used to do in their literary jousts and rivalries of honour?' That made good sense.

The first argument is more specious. The parallel between the respect Muslims have for Jesus and the attitude of Christians to Muhammad seems so clear that more than one person has been disturbed by it. It runs counter to what would be unjust depreciation of the personality of Muhammad. But to push it to a conclusion would be to go far beyond its premises, for in fact the parallel between the two attitudes conceals a very different *de facto* situation.

While Muslims may seem welcoming in their regard for Jesus as a prophet, this approach does not completely modify their basic attitude, since in Islam Jesus speaks like the Qur'an and lives like the Qur'an. To recognize Jesus as a prophet does not put Muslims under any further obligation. It does not cost them anything, but it is useful to them, since one of the roles of Jesus in

Islam is to support Muhammad. The Jesus of Islam is at the service both of the Muhammad whom he announces and of the Qur'an. Muslims, too, have every interest in proclaiming him a prophet so as to give more weight to his support.

By contrast, if Christians were to accept the prophecy of Muhammad in the strict sense, they would have to go against everything they are told by the weightiest religious documents in their possession. The situation is certainly not the same in the two cases.

What precisely do our friends want?

The mass of Muslim believers are convinced that Islam is the true religion, and the impression that its truth is evident prompts many Muslims to seek the conversion of Christians. This involves an explicit and total recognition of the prophetic character of Muhammad.

For most Muslims, a prophet is a man who brings a message from God and who must be obeyed unreservedly. So there was an immediate effect when a Christian bishop, full of good intentions but not realizing the effect of his words, proclaimed to the Islamic-Christian Congress in Tripoli (Libya) that dialogue would be impossible as long as Christians did not accept a certain number of positions – and in particular that they should recognize the prophetic character of Muhammad. He himself affirmed that he accepted that God was one and that Muhammad was his Messenger. The next day the local papers announced in bold headlines that the bishop had been converted to Islam, which was hardly the intention.

But what of those other Muslims who are well aware that we are Christians and have serious reasons for wanting to remain so?

During a meeting between Muslims and Christians at al-Azhar, in Cairo, in April 1978, the grand imam Sheikh al-Azhar, one of the leading figures in Islam, told the partners in dialogue representing the Vatican of his deepest reactions. In essence, he said that no dialogue would be possible as long as Christians did not

---

The Qur'an recalls God's goodness to Muhammad as a child

Did He not find you an orphan and give you
*   shelter?*
Did He not find you in error and guide you?
Did He not find you poor and enrich you?
Therefore do not wrong the orphan,
nor chide away the beggar.
But proclaim the goodness of your Lord.

Qur'an 93, 6–11

---

modify their attitude on a number of points. In particular he mentioned respect for the person of Muhammad. I no longer recall whether he spoke of recognizing him as a prophet.

When we were relaxing after this first working session, I was talking with one of the Muslims in the official delegation from al-Azhar and told him that the grand imam had asked Christians to respect Muhammad. I put it to him that everyone is agreed on rejecting the manner of speaking which was current in the Middle Ages and which is now inadmissible. We know that Muhammad was a religious figure, an exceptional politician, a brilliant man. But if Christians respected Muhammad as Muslims do, they would become Muslims. 'How do you want us to respect him,' I asked, 'while remaining Christians?'

In essence, the sheikh replied that he personally was not a Hindu, but that he had a great respect for Gandhi and admired his person and actions.

This was talk in parables, and every story which adopts this literary genre has to be interpreted. Moreover, his was a personal opinion. What are we to conclude from it? A first very useful step would be for Christians to be aware of the historical person and role of the founder of Islam. It is all too easy to explain away the great events of history which do not take the direction we would like by irrelevant arguments. Here again, to recognize in all honesty what is the case will allow us to protest more firmly where our own actions are attributed by our conversation-partners to non-existent motives or it is claimed that we are convinced of the truth of Islam but refuse to proclaim it out of envy or bad faith. On both sides, the banishment of caricatures is an indispensable preliminary to any mutual understanding.

The question of the person of Muhammad and of his place in the divine plan of salvation began to be posed in a new way by some Christian theologians in the 1930s. Since then, several standpoints have been adopted: I shall try to describe the main ones.

The first is pragmatic. It consists of drawing conclusions from a certain number of observations. First, it is a fact that millions of human beings have heard God spoken of through Islam, that they have learned to pray in a Muslim setting, and that they have received a set of moral rules from Islam. Their experience of God lies within Islam, even if they often appeal to basic human religious attitudes. Christians have to respect this relationship between Muslims and God and the role which Muhammad played in achieving this openness to God. In short, Christians should recognize the action of the Holy Spirit in the world and accept that he was equally at work within the Muslim community and even, to some degree, in its founder.

Christians who adopt this first position will not forget that in many other areas Christians and Muslims are in confrontation and that we cannot recognize other basic affirmations of our brothers and sisters as coming from the Holy Spirit. In the end, Christians remain silent before the mystery of the action of God on this earth and the way in which human action works with or against that of God. Those who hold this first position feel an invicible antipathy to what was once called indiscreet theology, i.e. theology which did not accept that there are areas in which we are ignorant, and wanted to have its say on everything, even when what had been revealed was too tenuous to allow us to say anything. Moreover, these same people will note that no matter what theories are developed about Muhammad as a prophet and what form the refusal to give him this status may take, in practice the attitude of open Christians will always be the same with Muslims. So what is the point of embarking on nebulous theories?

Then there is the position which is sometimes called minimalist. Noting how Christianity collapsed in the face of the Islamic advance and the rivalry of the two religions, those who hold this position give the least possible credit to the founder of this community, which they think was a scourge of God. For them there is no question of speaking of Muhammad having been a prophet, or at least a true prophet. Since Jesus has told us that a prophet can be recognized by his works, just as a tree can be recognized by its fruits, they stress above all the negative aspects of Muslim influence. Here too there is no possibility for dialogue. There can only be struggles, interspersed by times of peaceful coexistence. This perspective is too well known for us to need to dwell on it.

Over against this attitude there is another which could be called maximalist. It sees no problem in saying that Muhammad is a prophet sent by God. However, there are many different nuances within this tendency. There are those who seek to associate Islam with the blessing of Ismail in Genesis. Abraham is thus said to have had two religious lines of descendants, that of Isaac and that of Ismail, and a parallel is drawn between the work that Jesus accomplished in the descendants of Isaac and that which Muhammad accomplished among the descendants of Ismail. Given the very scanty biblical basis on which this theory rests, and that it goes against the whole of Christian tradition, which sees the descendants on whom the great promise of God to Abraham rests as one great history, this theory, which is put forward within small groups, has not yet received much support. Besides, it goes against all that the Muslims have so far believed.

In another direction, in the new perspectives of Catholic theology since 1950 many Christians have sought to discover principles on which it becomes possible to call Muhammad a prophet. They stress above all the psychological and experiential aspects of prophecy. The revelation of God to his prophet was through the prophet's experience, and there is no reason, they say, to refuse the title of prophet to Muhammad, given his real and profound religious experience which marks the beginning of the powerful movement of Islam. In this perspective the word prophet has taken on a new significance; however, it is hard to see whether those who use it are calling for obedience to the prophet or whether they are leaving each individual to choose what he or she likes in Muhammad's message and leave aside the rest.

How the problem that a prophet's message may contain errors is tackled depends on the particular group. There are those who affirm that the Qur'an contains nothing which contradicts the Christian message and that its condemnations relate only to distortions of Christianity that we too would reject. Others do not feel disturbed that a prophetic message could contain dogmatically doubtful expressions. Besides, for some theologians today, what is a dogmatic formulation anyway?

The future will tell whether this attitude favours dialogue. So far it is clear that Muslims react when the word prophet is devalued, even if only slightly. At the second colloquy in Cordoba in 1977, a Christian theologian surveyed the different meanings of the word prophet. He explained that nowadays the word sometimes has the very broad sense of a man with insight and intuition, who is sensitive to situations and makes a mark on the course of history. One might, he said, call Karl Marx a prophet. He added that in this sense he had no objection to Muhammad being called prophet. But the major-ity of Muslims present did not like this parallel; it made them feel uneasy.

Would it be preferable to talk of a kind of prophecy akin, with some qualifications, to that of the Old Testament? It is not clear whether our friends would accept that. Many of them, usually very open thinkers, have argued that if a Christian says that Muhammad is a prophet and does not become a Muslim, either he does not know his religion or he is a hypocrite.

Could not respect manifest itself in another way?

It is not easy to say, because any approach risks hurting very sensitive feelings. Even the omission of certain formulae of respect which are not customarily used in European languages can be misunderstood.

If we look at the most reliable ancient documents which have come down to us, the strong personality with which Muhammad was endowed stands out. He had a profound religious sense and he felt called to proclaim ceaselessly the primordial truth which is at the heart of Islam and which Fr Abd el-Jalil described like this:

The claim that God has the sole right to Lordship (*rububiya*) and worship (to the service of human-kind: *ubudiya*) underlies all the other affirmations of the Qur'an. In the soul of every Muslim who has grown up in an Islamic milieu, however uneducated and insignificant, even if he or she engages in popular devotions which are not very Islamic, this claim of the exclusive right of God to worship, to the service of his creatures, is more or less alive. It militates against all 'associationism' (*shirk*) and therefore against all idolatry: to worship only God, to serve only Allah, to expect all from Allah and nothing from his creatures, however powerful and effective they may seem to be. That is the heart of Islam.

Endowed with a strong personality, Muhammad exercised an indubitable ascendancy over his companions. A leader of men, he was capable of demanding much at certain times and leaving people free at others. He had a considerable influence over them, and it is through his teaching that many people have learned to pray and to worship God.

He himself was a very simple man, contenting himself for most of the time with a minimum of physical necessities. At his death he possessed just a few pieces of land, plunder taken from the Jews, in an oasis in northern Arabia. He worked alongside everyone else when that was necessary, for example in the building of the mosque of Medina or in the digging of the famous ditch which protected the city from the attack of the confederates in 627. A brave man, he faced the enemy in battle, and at the time of the defeat of Uhud in 625 his tenacity succeeded in redressing the situation and avoiding disaster.

A skilful politician, he could make concessions when they were needed, for example at the truce of Hudaybiya, and give pardon after victory. A number of declarations which lighten the obligations imposed by Islam are attributed to him. He knew his compatriots and acted in such a way that they were finally converted to Islam. The plunder which he promised them served to rally them; but at the same time he was very firm with those who, like the nomads, thought only of plunder. He wanted both this world and the next, and claimed that he could lead people to happiness in both. He preached a religion of mutual support and force; he was not a monk, and the great effort demanded was that of obedience and will. This solidarity and the holy war were both in the Arab tradition.

The beginnings of Islam were hard and formative. The influx of riches and plunder came only after his death and provoked a terrible crisis in the divided community. Before that, for almost twenty years, Muhammad was accused by his enemies of ruining Arab values, of opposing the patrimony of the fathers. In reality, the message which he preached grafted simplified biblical or para-biblical ideas on to an Arab stem and today, for the vast mass of Muslims, he has become the very symbol of Arab authenticity.

To complete the picture, however, we would have to note that he was harsh at certain moments of his life: he approved the violation of a sacred month so as not to miss attacking a caravan, took vengeance on a number of his enemies, and arranged the political assassination of Jews. He could not bear poets to write verses against him. A well-known *hadith* says that he loved 'prayer, perfume and women'. And certain traditions praise his virility. Here he behaved like a chief of his time, susceptible to feminine beauty but also concerned by his marriages to consolidate alliances with those clans or families from whom he took a wife; and he was far more moderate than many others.

In short, he was a great politician and a religious genius. His life marks a decisive moment in the history of humankind.

Two delicate points

However, thinking Christians have always been preoccupied with two specific points, and any complete survey needs to examine them. First, there is the question of Muhammad's sincerity, and secondly, the assertion that Islam is the crown of earlier religions, summing them all up and proclaiming that nothing essential on the level of religion and human conduct has been omitted from the Qur'an.

The problem of Muhammad's sincerity has often been discussed among Christians: it goes without saying that for Muslims it does not arise. And Muslim manuals go into great detail to prove that Muhammad was, all in all, the most faithful of men. On the Christian side, even if the excesses of mediaeval polemic have now been abandoned, difficulties nevertheless remain. The Qur'an asserts that Muhammad did not know any of the ancient stories, whether in the Bible or not, and therefore that their presence in the surahs is miraculous. Now on the one hand the Qur'an does no more than allude to this past and does so in a very simplified way; it is not that it knows the Bible so much as that it takes up scattered elements from a Qur'anic perspective, often in a very tendentious way. Because the Qur'an has such an allusive character, it evokes the past only in a number of rapid surveys. Basically, only Moses has any personality in the Qur'an – and perhaps also Abraham and Jesus – the other figures perform roles rather than having any individual features.

Furthermore, some documents claim that there were people at Mecca, including members of Muhammad's own family, who knew these stories. Opponents, too, as the Qur'an recalls quite clearly, accused Muhammad of having all these stories told to him and then affirming that they had been revealed by God.

A text in the surah called 'The Bee' records this charge that Muhammad used information provided by others, i.e. had informants.

> We know that they (the opponents) say: 'A mortal taught him'. But the man to whom they allude speaks a foreign tongue, while this is eloquent Arabic speech (Qur'an 16, 103).

This text is a reply: Muhammad is accused of having received the text of the Qur'an from others. So in all probability this accusation once again presupposes that there were people at Mecca who knew these stories.

The reply is a denial. But the argument is about the style and not about the content of the ideas. It is certain that if this informant was a foreigner, he could not have been the author of the remarkable style of the Qur'an. Someone who stumbles through Arabic cannot produce a masterpiece in that language. So if the passage is accepted in its literal sense, and there is no reason not to do so, its point is the need to recognize the impossibility of the text having been composed at Mecca by a stranger and then dictated to Muhammad.

At this point the commentators on the Qur'an give the names of several slaves or freemen whose workshops or homes Muhammad visited; they are described as having known earlier stories or even books. So it is difficult to avoid the conclusion that a large number of accounts which figure in the Qur'an were known at Mecca and came to the ears of people who had not themselves engaged in any course of systematic study in this sphere.

In that case what does it mean to say that Muhammad was sincere? For those who want to explain everything by purely human causes, there is such a thing as subjective sincerity. Given the intensity of feeling which can drive a person to speak, those of former times could easily think that they had been given superhuman or even divine inspiration when in fact the drive came from the sub-conscious, which had stored this knowledge and then forgotten that it had acquired it. This position, which is that of rationalists, is also adopted by the 'minimalist' Christians whom I mentioned earlier.

However, it remains the case that in itself divine action is in no way incompatible with the role of the human sub-conscious. Christian theology thinks that God often acts by using human beings, their psychology and their knowledge as his instrument. So far, Muslim theology has never accepted this in the case of the Qur'an. However, when Christians see in the Qur'an stories which were well known at this time and which bear the mark of a characteristic environment, they do not feel that it tells against subjective sincerity, nor does it in any way rule out the possibility of a divine action which could be identified more specifically. The question remains open.

The second delicate point is that of the complete, finished character of the message of the Qur'an. We saw earlier that some Christian orientalists were of the opinion that the Qur'an did not contain anything which went against the Christian message of the mainstream church: the criticisms of the Qur'an would bear only on heresies that we too reject. Others, by contrast, think that the Qur'an contains a condemnation of several essential features of the Christian message of the mainstream church.

Without going into the details of the debate, it is possible to make one comment. Regardless of the position of the Qur'an itself, it is clear that from the beginning of Islam almost all Muslims have interpreted it in a sense which is the opposite of the position of the mainstream church; from the beginning the exegesis of several key passages has almost always been anti-Christian.

Another factor must be taken into consideration by anyone who is trying to get a rounded view of the question: even if the Qur'an passed over the main Christian dogmas in silence and did not attack them, its silence would nevertheless be a condemnation, since the Qur'an is presented as being complete and its message as finished, valid until the end of the world – and any substantial addition would be tantamount to a distortion. In the final analysis, any silence is more than silence: it signifies that God does not want, and would never want, to say more. No revelation may follow that of the Qur'an.

If we take the situation as it is, the Qur'an truly is a new message of good news, i.e. a new gospel, different from that which the church claims to have received. And even if an angel came down from heaven to bring a different gospel from that which has been entrusted to it, the church would not feel it right to accept it (cf. Galatians 1.8).

Nevertheless, anyone who leaves this aspect of completeness out of account will note that Islam contains great intuitions which are profoundly true, the importance of which Christians are beginning to forget. There is, for instance, the belief that God himself has supreme Lordship by right.

To this should be added the Islamic protest against divisions among Christians, whose churches, which have become nationalist, are opposed to one another under the cover of different theological positions. One might also add the protest against the pretensions which end up by excluding the Arabs from their religious world, not to mention the other criticisms of the all-too-human conduct of certain monks and rabbis.

In short, at that time what Christians needed was a reform or a revival of the Spirit of Jesus. From this perspective, the remark by Arnold Toynbee which I cited above becomes fully valid.

> Islam, like Communism, succeeded to the degree that it claimed to be reforming the abuses which had crept into the Christianity of the time. And the success of Islam from the beginning shows the power that a heresy can have when it claims to be reforming an orthodoxy which does not seem inclined to reform itself (*The World and the West*).

The role of Muhammad in the religious history of the world must be seen in the light of these observations.

A charisma for reformist leaders?

The word reform will take us in an even more precise direction. The term prophet is in fact the cause of many misunderstandings. The period in which the only alternative was that of true and false prophets gave place to times during which the notion of prophet became singularly flexible, was stretched and transformed. Nowadays the only points which seem clear are these:

1. If the word prophet is given an absolute sense, and denotes someone all of whose words pronounced in the name of God are vested with divine authority so that all then have to obey them, Christians cannot concede this title to the founder of Islam. They cannot obey him without reserve, for that would be to become Muslims. To accept Muhammad as a prophet in the strict sense, which includes showing faith and obedience, is impossible for Christians. Christians will always use the word prophet with qualifications; in other words they will not accept all that a

'prophet' says, but accept some things and reject others. Here the criteria of acceptance is no longer faith but personal judgment.

2. Within the religious history of the world, Christians recognize that the prophets who prepared for the coming of Christ have a unique character. Even minor prophets like Zephaniah share in this unique character; minor prophets in a major line, read in the communion of the church, they are followed in the faith.

In the steps of a teacher who has been called to God and whom I do not want to name, so that he is not identified with all that this book says (since perhaps he would not have agreed with it), I personally think that in the present instance we have to avoid the word prophet. To use it would entail giving it a limited sense which Muslim faith would not accept. It is better to express ourselves in another way: to recognize the truths that the Muslim message contains, to respect the spiritual journey of sincere Muslims, and to see Muhammad as a religious and political genius. Or alternatively, we should recognize that within Islam numerous believers are in a relationship with God that grace has brought about in them.

3. Finally, set in the context of the religious history of the world, Islam appears as an attempt at reforming Judaism and Christianity (by replacing them). And a comparison between this attempt and others which took place in the course of the history of the church could be illuminating.

Every time that the Christian message has been too influenced by the society in which it has been presented instead of remaining universal, and each time its messengers have forgotten the meaning of one or other of the basic intuitions of Christians, the need for reform has emerged. And when Christians have delayed or gone adrift in their attempts at internal reform, the situation has blown up in their faces and the reform has been made in groups which have separated from the church or have become opposed to it. This is very clear in the case of the Protestant Reformation: a reform was needed; it had been required for two centuries, but nothing had happened. The basic intuitions of the Reformation were specific ones, and Catholics recognized them, particularly the insight that we are justified by faith in the grace of God. But the church of the time could not manage to revive these values within itself, and the situation exploded, to the detriment of both sides.

Similarly, the birth of Marxism went with a lack of Christian involvement at the time of the formation of the working class and the inadequacy of the efforts or the intelligence of those who had grasped the problem. And what could and should have been a new humane development within this emergent class, which was being shamefully exploited at the time, has become the ideological and ultimately totalitarian movement that we know. Is it also worth recalling movements which wanted to retain a number of African practices in the face of Europeanized Christianization, and ended up in the birth of separate African churches?

Islam, too, was born in the face of a Christianity which was divided, complicated, a prisoner of nationalisms – in an abnormal situation. Like the reformers I have just mentioned, it too founded a separate movement.

At the present time it seems necessary to invent a new theological category to denote those who are profoundly religious but are in radical opposition to existing official frameworks, and who are rebelling against forms of Christianity which have either become fossilized or are caught up in cultural or national questions. If the Christian message is presented with too many purely human elements, it will have difficulty in getting through. A saint could achieve genuine reform without betraying the essentials of the message. Rebels who are not saints re-read the message of the Bible in their own way, in their own cultural context. This new form may illuminate particular points (in Islam, for example, the Lordship of God), but reject other essential ones. It is a kind of devaluation which for the moment lets part of the message get through. Might Islam not have been born in this way, in accordance with the will of God, given the circumstances and the situation of the time? God only knows.

In his *Summa Theologica* St Thomas once recognized that God could send an angel to reveal or teach specific truths to men who would speak without delegation on his part. In this way he would guarantee the knowledge of several absolutely necessary truths to those who could not acquire them otherwise. Would it be permissible to suppose that reformers (and their followers) who opposed a fossilized church were strengthened by grace from God which confirmed their true intuitions, and that God's inspiration will have helped them to express certain true and essential aspects of their message? Their very existence might then have stimulated the church to emulate them and drive Christians to reform themselves without abandoning the other truths which the explosion of the reform had failed to recognize. In this way they would rediscover the aspects of their ideal that they had neglected.

12

Muslim Apologetic

Official Muslim apologetic is presented in a variety of publications. Since it is the same in all the great Muslim centres of the world – a few nuances aside – and is almost the only communication from the Muslim side at present, it deserves special consideration. In fact it reveals a very characteristic aspect of Islam: the claim to be the religion of both revelation and reason. What part does the particular temperament of each of the Muslim peoples play in this fact? How much goes back to the doctrine of Islam itself? The subject really calls for a long objective study. Here I simply want to draw attention to a certain number of points which dominate the rest.

First of all, in many respects the Qur'an itself is a book of apologetic. It often discusses or reports discussions, exhorts, threatens, accuses opponents of not understanding anything, of being deaf and blind, or of having no intelligence. Some verses can be cited as they are in the guise of arguments. Here human salvation is presented in a simple framework: God creates, God nurtures, God ordains, God forgives, etc. Faith itself is not directed towards a mystery of new birth, adoption or supernatural life with God. Human beings relate directly to God the creator and to what God has created, willed and done. Hence the clarity of Islam.

A minimum of essential propositions is affirmed relentlessly and presented in varied imagery. The arrival of men and women at the last judgment is the occasion for saying once again why they have been condemned and why they have been saved. The stories of the prophets take up these same basic affirmations in another form.

The Qur'an also provides a whole series of vivid arguments which engrave themselves on the memory and thus are that much weightier. First of all it reminds men and women that they do not know many things: the sex of the infant whose birth is awaited by its parents, the place where one will die, or the number of years one will be in the tomb between death and resurrection. Then it asserts that God is one, as is shown by the world order, which would be inconceivable if it were the work of a multiplicity of deities in rivalry with one another.

Furthermore, the whole Qur'an is suffused with an atmosphere of prayer. After the text has spent some time expounding legislation or theoretical principles, very soon an elevation or an ejaculatory prayer brings respite from the reasoning and directs the believer towards God.

The Qur'an echoes polemic directed against Islam at the beginning of its history which ended when it was accepted by the pagans who had been subjugated by the victories of the believers. Thus two sources give Muslims their absolute certainty: reason and the Qur'an.

Here again, reason is reason as Muslim theology has conceived it, i.e. as the capacity to affirm that a particular position is necessary, impossible or possible. This tripartite division dominates all Muslim apologetic. For example, Qur'anic exegesis regards expressions which do not respect the absolute transcendence of God as impossible. At one point the Qur'an speaks of the 'hands' of God: the most widespread official exegesis rejects the literal, 'impossible' sense of the word and interprets the expression by seeing in it the gifts, the generosity of God. Similarly, Muslims reject distinctively Christian dogmas because they find 'impossibilities' in them.

In practice, this logical instrument – the distinction between necessary, impossible and possible – is applied only to major principles. In the sphere of contingency in which the majority of beings and things are merely possible and could just as well have not been, this instrument of intellectual analysis is no longer used. If the Qur'an then speaks on the subject, or if Muslims think that it does, then as far as they are concerned the question is settled. Only the Qur'an counts.

Take the case of whether or not Christ was crucified. All modern critics in the West, even atheists, accept that the most certain historical fact about the life of Jesus is his crucifixion. Without this ignominious death there would not have been a church, since from the beginning, as all the earliest traditions show us, the apostles preached Jesus crucified and risen. The account of the substitution of a double who takes the place of Jesus is absolutely unknown in the ancient texts; moreover it would presuppose that God had allowed all the disciples to be grossly deceived about this fact for a century and more. It is after the generation of the apostles that the story of the substitution of the double appears, and it does so in the very limited sphere of the docetists; later it spread among the Manichaeans. Both movements were dominated by manifestly *a priori* ideologies: for all these Gnostics, matter was evil, and Jesus could not have had a real material body. His body was just something that looked like a body; moreover the docetists derive their name from a Greek word meaning 'have the appearance of', 'resemble'.

So healthy logic would require anyone who denied the crucifixion to advance some proof. In practice, the only proof that Muslims produce is the Qur'an. Any affirmation which falls within the logical category of the 'possible' and which seems to go against an affirmation of the Qur'an is rejected. If it is a historical fact, arguments will always be found to minimize the ancient witnesses, relativize knowledge based on the senses and argue, as sceptics used to, that human beings are subject to all sorts of illusions. The same approach will be taken to the ancient sacred history. While the biblical documents show clearly at how late a stage belief in the resurrection of the body appeared, and how both revelation and dogma are progressive, Muslims only accept the Qur'anic view of the religious history of the biblical world before Islam.

Such an attitude has as its first principle that only the Qur'an is a source of absolutely certain knowledge on this earth. Its truth is absolute, since for the Muslim it has been revealed by God and has then been protected against all alteration. In that case reality will be seen through the grid formed by the affirmations of the Qur'an.

The principle of the divine authenticity of the Qur'an

It is here that Muslims and non-Muslims differ. For the Muslim, the authenticity of the Qur'an is proved in the way that the Qur'an itself has indicated. After Muhammad had undergone the

Titles borne by Muslim men of religion

1. **Imam**, president (of prayer, the mosque, etc.).
2. **Katib**, preacher.
3. **Muezzin**, the man who 'calls' to prayer.
4. **Shaykh** (Sheikh), man of religion, head of a brotherhood, etc. (literally the elder, the presbyter).
   Malem, man of religion in Africa south of the Sahara.
   Mullah, man of religion (Turkish, Persian, etc.).
5. **Talib**, student (one who 'asks for' religious knowledge).
   Fqih (Faqih), literally jurist; often denotes the master of a Qur'anic school.
   Qadi, religious judge.
   Mufti, Grand Mufti, officer consulted over the law.
6. **Khalifa**, formerly caliph, temporal head of the Muslim community; still used today in the brotherhoods for a regional leader.
   Muqaddam, certain leaders of local brotherhoods.

mockery and criticism of opponents who asked him for proof of the authenticity of his mission and who reminded him that the earlier prophets had done miracles, he proclaimed the Qur'anic oracles according to which the Qur'an itself was presented as a miracle; there are also several verses in which opponents are challenged to imitate the Qur'an. Can they produce a few surahs – indeed, just one – comparable with those of the Qur'an? It was clearly understood that this challenge implied that Muhammad's opponents wanted to prove that human beings were capable of producing a text like that of the Qur'an. And if they were unable to do this, it was because such composition was beyond human capability and the Qur'an came from God.

If you doubt what We have revealed to Our servant, produce one chapter comparable to this book. Call upon your idols to assist you, if what you say is true (Qur'an 2, 23).

This challenge (*tahaddi*) was repeated several times. In fact no one took it up, and the only examples of imitations cited in Muslim history are worthless pastiches. It follows from this that the divine origin of the Qur'an is rationally proved in the eyes of all Muslims.

Muslims also add that since Muhammad never studied, and had not read the ancient scriptures, he could not have produced such a masterpiece as the Qur'an from his own resources and it was impossible for him to have been the author.

Here we come to the heart of Muslim certainty. Its basis in a literary miracle is to my knowledge unique in the religious history of the human race. Its consequences are immense. Since in the Muslim perspective the whole Qur'an comes from God, it is the source of all certainty; it can provide a perspective on events, and all the faithful who see reality from its point of view feel both personally confirmed and totally secure in their approach. Everything else becomes relative. Hence the role of Qur'anic schools and, as a result, the teaching of Arabic in Muslim proselytism. The student learns to see everything here through the perspective of the Qur'an.

It is over this challenge that non-Muslims part company with Muslims. The argument underlying it does not prove anything to anyone who is not a Muslim; for the Christian, Islam is an argument without proofs. Here we probably have the heart of the confrontation between Christians and Muslims. And even if Christians keep quiet on this subject out of tact (or a feeling that it is useless to say anything since it will serve no purpose), Muslims cannot understand that they are not convinced by the evidence, and some even go so far as to suspect them of bad faith.

Christians have always seen the religious history of the world as God allowing human beings their own experience: that is the specific theme of the book of Job, who does not understand that on this earth the righteous are not automatically recompensed. If God has intervened in a specific number of cases, it does not follow that we have the right to generalize and to see everything in the light of these particular instances. A literary text is always inimitable because it is singular and reveals the sensibility, the experience, the natural gifts of its particular author. No two geniuses are alike and imitation will never produce more than a pastiche 'after the style of'. That is the law of the genre.

Besides, since the Qur'an has been read solemnly and religiously for centuries, and has always been presented as the norm of all literary success, as the height of eloquence, Muslim sensibility has been impregnated with it. Muslims find it difficult to enjoy other forms of literary beauty, and for them the Qur'an becomes the inimitable masterpiece.

It is difficult to see how to get out of this impasse. Neither side is on the same ground and encounter is impossible. For the Muslim, anyone who does not accept the argument of the challenge (the *tahaddi*) is like some kind of troglodyte

who does not want to see the light of the sun; on the other hand, admiration for the literary beauty of the Qur'an does not utterly suppress Christian critical faculties, and the fact that the Qur'an has never been imitated does not prove what our conversation-partners would like it to prove. In practice, in encounters between Muslims and Christians this subject is taboo unless the number involved is very small, the participants in the group already know one another very well and are agreed in thinking that the risk can be run with some chance of success. At all events, the one thing to be wished in this area is that Christian theologians should understand as well as possible why the challenge and the arguments behind it are decisive for a Muslim and that vice versa Muslims should see the serious reasons why Christians think differently from them.

Is it advisable for Christians to use Muslim texts as a basis when speaking of Jesus?

This question is often raised by Christians living in Muslim countries. If Muslims only trust the Qur'an and if neither our scriptures nor the historical facts themselves are of any importance once the Qur'an has spoken, some Christians ask whether Muslims might not rediscover Christian dogma through the Qur'an.

In some cases, the way in which these Christians proceed seems more like sleight of hand than objective study. For example, at the beginning of the century a Christian orientalist sought to rediscover the affirmation of the divinity of Christ in a verse of the Qur'an by changing an accusative into a genitive through the modification of a vowel, but without any textual tradition and contrary to the explicit teaching of the rest of the Qur'an. This is hardly a serious proposition, and no Muslim would accept that such a manipulation could have passed unnoticed.

All true understanding of the person of Jesus between Muslims and Christians will remain difficult as long as Jesus is known only as he is in the Qur'an. Christian faith is based on experience of the person of Jesus, his conduct, his goodness and what he has revealed in his actions and his life as well as in his words; or more precisely, revelation is expressed by the indissoluble combination of his life and his words. Without this experience, a theologian is condemned to the mere manipulation of theoretical concepts.

Is Muhammad foretold in the Old and New Testaments?

Similarly, only a serious and dispassionate examination of the texts can show whether or not Muhammad was predicted in the Old and New Testaments. This point was one of the first to be touched on in polemic between Muslims and Christians. The Qur'an in fact asserts that the Torah, the Gospel and Jesus announced the coming of Muhammad: here, too, there are two standpoints on the Muslim side. Either Muslims say that this announcement does not appear in the texts of the Bible or the Gospel as they now exist and conclude that these texts have been forged. Or they seek at any price to find predictions in the Bible and the Gospels which can be applied to the coming of Muhammad. Both these standpoints can be encountered among Muslim intellectuals concerned with this question.

The *Sirah* of Ibn Hisham (who died in 834), which is the earliest life of the prophet to have a systematic collection of documents, talks of this prediction. And it seeks to find the prophecy about Muhammad in the announcement of the coming of the Paraclete. The Paraclete is identified with Muhammad by virtue of the resemblance of the two words in Syriac. Others have tried to connect them via the Greek, identifying *Parakletos* with *Periclytos* (when read aloud the two words sound similar), which means 'illustrious, praised': as Muhammad means 'praised' in Arabic, the play on words is an easy one.

In fact, Christians believe that the whole Christian tradition based on the Gospels and

Acts tells of the expectation and the coming of the Holy Spirit, whom Jesus called the Paraclete. This coming took place fifty days after the resurrection of Christ, on the day of Pentecost, in the year 30 or at the latest in 33. After that Christians awaited only the parousia, i.e. the return of Jesus at the end of time – nothing else. We would need to be more familiar with the history of the marginal sects to know whether one of them awaited a prophet. It seems that the Elkesaites did, but these sects, as St Irenaeus remarked (and he knew them well), did not rely on any tradition going back to the apostles.

The Old Testament has been the object of similar investigations. Several Muslim apologists have already collected the passages traditionally associated with the Messiah (or the majority of them), from the prophet foretold by Moses in Deuteronomy to the beloved in the Song of Songs, and have applied them in turn to Muhammad. Everything depends on the principle by which one justifies such an operation, since it is easy to apply it to virtually any text about future expectation. The important thing is to know what the principle is.

It seems difficult to come to any agreement on this topic as long as there has not been a quiet reading of the sacred texts, without *a priori* apologetic. In the case of the Paraclete the situation is clear; in that of the ancient prophets, the very vagueness of the material encourages a variety of applications.

The problem of Jesus

The problem of Jesus plays a major role in Muslim apologetic. In fact the Qur'an gives a number of titles to Jesus which it does not give to anyone else: Messiah, Word of God, Spirit of God. Moreover, there is never any mention of either sin or forgiveness in connection with him. Although his person is alluded to in a very evocative way, it appears in a distinctive framework marked by his miracles and his very great goodness. These features, which could suggest an echo of Christian dogmas, have always been interpreted in a qualified way in Islamic countries, in line with the general teaching of the Qur'an. Jesus, the apologists say, is called Word of God because he has been created by a word of God, directly, without having a father, as was already the case with Adam. In spite of everything, some Muslims have been struck by these titles, which have made them think, though the vast majority sees here only what the Muslim tradition sees. In stressing the titles, Christians are simply drawing the attention of Muslims to a possible opening.

On the question of Jesus as Christians see him, the most illuminating parallel seems still to be that of the Qur'an. The problem of the Jesus of Christians is that of the presence of the divine and the human in a single person. Stressing that Jesus cannot have divine status, the Qur'an argues that if he walks, if he goes into the souks, if he eats, it is simply because he is leading a human life. Now when the Muslims were discussing the problem of whether or not the Qur'an had been created (in the eighth and ninth centuries of our era), Christians had already drawn parallels between the case of Jesus and that of the Qur'an. On both sides, believers saw the word of God as being divine and incarnate in creation. If Jesus walked, was hungry, etc., the Qur'an for its part was made of paper, ink, etc. The question is how to show that this union of the created and the uncreated is not a blasphemous invention of disciples who were unfaithful to Jesus but that it is already there in nucleus in all scripture given by God to humankind. On the one hand the Word was made flesh, and on the other the Word was made book.

Christians have tried to show Muslims that the mystery of the divine oneness is not a monolithic unity, like mathematical oneness. On the contrary, this oneness is compatible with a degree of multiplicity, that of the divine attributes. The unity of the divine essence allowed a multiplicity of attributes. It is along these lines, in the awareness that in Arabic the terms for nature and substance have connotations which are shocking when applied to God and therefore should be avoided, that analogies have been sought to facilitate the exposition of Christian doctrine: for the divine essence is one, while the three consubstantial persons are only subsistent relations.

Towards a more open training for teachers of theology

Muslim-Christian conversation also presupposes a solid theological training, however little doctrine may be involved. Those who work in this dialogue have to have reflected on the problem of the divine unity, that of the three persons, and on many other matters. Why do not clergy and laity who have had theological training come across these questions in their studies? Ordinary professors of dogma and exegesis in theological faculties or in seminaries should be capable of discussing them with their students. Instead of spending so much time in detailed study of the positions of Paul of Samosata, Arius and others, might not teachers pass over them more quickly to save time for examining at leisure what Muslim dogma says on these essential points? We Christians have been so unprepared for these questions that we often have to resort to very risky, last-minute improvisations in these tricky areas.

At the level of exegetical principles, there are subjects which would be very useful for clergy and laity in countries where Christians and Muslims live side by side to know. These include the Muslim theory of revelation, the explanation of verses always used by those who deny the divinity of Christ, the solidity of the manuscript tradition of the Gospels, and so on, not to mention the universality of the mission of Jesus and the exact meaning of the verse: 'I was sent only to the lost sheep of the house of Israel.'

154

It seems that a movement is beginning to develop which wants the authorities responsible for planning theological education to be open in this direction. Effective measures are called for.

What does the Qur'an teach about the corruption of the Torah and the Gospels?

So far we have touched on the problem of apologetic, keeping as far as possible from the Bible and the Gospels, the evidence of which Muslims do not accept. It remains for us to see why they do not.

The attitude of Muslims derives from the categorical distinction that they make between the Torah and the Gospel (in the singular) in the past, which Moses and Jesus are said to have received directly from heaven, and the scriptures as they now exist, which they claim have been altered. There is therefore a complete contrast between the theoretical books, which have been forgotten and become almost mythical, and those with which we are familiar. Moreover the respect that Muslims profess for the theoretical books remains purely on a Platonic level, since they do not believe they can trust the books which do exist.

It would be interesting to know the precise views of Muhammad on this point. We have no more than the Qur'an, and the fragmentary, allusive character of the passages which relate to the alteration of the earlier scriptures does not make our task any easier.

In the Qur'an, several accusations are levelled against the people of the book, first the Jews but also the Christians. They are accused of having manipulated and distorted their scriptures, of having 'forgotten' certain points, and of twisting their language when they recite certain passages. The Arabic words are different in each instance and it is not easy to say precisely what they mean.

Does the accusation only have certain specific groups in mind, or is it addressed to all Jews and all Christians? Sometimes it clearly refers only to one group which is distorting the text (cf. Qur'an 3, 78). Elsewhere, all Christians are thought to have 'forgotten' a part of their revelation (cf. Qur'an 5, 14). Does this accusation refer to the falsification of the text itself or to a biassed exegesis of an authentic text? To enter into the details of this problem would take us too far afield; it is enough to know that the problem exists. Perhaps one should also stress two characteristic features of the Qur'an: that it is very concise and that its explanations are very allusive. And the features which contribute to the beauty and charm of many of its pages is not much help when it comes to interpretation.

The vast majority of Muslims (indeed, perhaps all of them) think that the very text of our scriptures has been infected with corruption. But among the more brilliant minds, many people like Fakhr al-Din al Razi, the mediaeval physician and theologian and commentator on the Qur'an (who died in 1210); Ibn Khaldun, the sociologist and historian (who died in 1406) and recently Muhammad Abduh, argue that our texts are authentic and that it is only the exegesis which is in fact distorted.

Muhammad Abduh based his opinion on the following argument: if someone falsified the texts to suppress the announcement of Muhammad or to oppose Islam, that could only have happened at the time of Muhammad and in Arabia. But not all the other copies of scripture which have circulated all over the world and have been translated into different languages can have been falsified. So there are still original texts here and there.

In fact the real reason why the majority of Muslims reject the authenticity of the text of our scriptures is that some passages cannot be reconciled with the teaching of the Qur'an (in respect of their view of the religious history of the world, the history of salvation, and so on). Now as the Qur'an is the very criterion of the truth, the other books must have been falsified.

When we look at the Qur'anic texts more closely, it seems that the accusation of falsification is levelled only at specific groups, and when the accusation is general it speaks of false interpretation rather than falsification of the text. Published studies by Christians stress that in the Qur'an the Jews of Medina really seem to believe that they have an authentic text in their hands. When Muhammad is confronted with the case of the woman taken in adultery, he asks the Jews to bring the Torah. In the Qur'an itself, two passages are striking. One is about Jews going to consult Muhammad and taking him as an arbiter; the Qur'an stresses that this was abnormal because 'they already have the Torah which enshrines God's own judgments' (Qur'an 5, 43).

In another passage, the Qur'an challenges the Jews to argue against what it teaches and summons them to go and look at the Torah to see that this is evident: 'Bring the Torah and read it, if what you say be true' (Qur'an 3, 93). In both cases the whole force of the argument is lost if the Jews only have a falsified text.

The problem of the authenticity of our scriptures is a difficult one, but it is one of the most important points on which light needs to be shed. No serious discussion with Muslims is possible as long as we do not agree on the authenticity of the text of the Bible and the Gospels. At a meeting between Muslims and Christians in Tripoli, Libya, in 1976, Fr Landry of the White Fathers solemnly made two requests in the course of a masterly conference. First of all, in the name of Christians, he asked forgiveness for all our unjust treatment of Muslims in the past; he then asked firmly for Muslims to take the text of our scriptures seriously. The first request prompted indescribable emotion and much embracing; the second met with total indifference and fell on deaf ears. However, one can hope that it will be acknowledged in due course.

The Pseudo-Gospel of Barnabas, or the wrong solution to a real problem

This is a very curious story, which it might have been better not to mention because of the state of mind which it reveals. Unfortunately, as it is about a text which is the basis of much polemic, it must be told. The work in question is called the Gospel according to Barnabas, and a large number of Muslim scholars have believed it to be the authentic Gospel which once existed. The Gospel was published for the first time in an Arabic translation in 1908. It then circulated in numerous Muslim countries. It is now mentioned in both Indonesia and Pakistan, in Arab countries, and in both East Africa and Africa south of the Sahara.

The story begins around 1700. At this time a humanist in Holland came across a manuscript written in Italian, containing a text which claimed to be the Gospel written on the orders of Jesus by one of the Twelve, the apostle Barnabas. It then became known in a Spanish version, which was recently rediscovered in Sydney. The humanist wondered whether this might not be a text which existed in Arabia at the time of Muhammad, and whether Muhammad had known it, and so became interested in the Gospel. Then it returned to oblivion.

In 1907 a Protestant pastor and his wife published the Italian text (which meanwhile had been acquired by the National Library in Vienna, where it still is) with an English translation and an introduction. The introduction indisputably established the age of the manuscript (which was written on a kind of paper with a distinctive grain that began to be made in 1575). The age of the text itself could only be fixed by internal criticism: it could not be earlier than 1300 and probably dated from the sixteenth century. It had been written in the Western Mediterranean by an author who was clearly ignorant of the geography of Palestine.

The Gospel was a forgery to the glory of Islam, but its central theme ran contrary to the Qur'an, since Jesus asserts in it that he is not the Messiah and declares that Muhammad will be the Messiah. By contrast, in the Qur'an Jesus is officially called Messiah:

> Mary, God bids you rejoice in a Word from Him. His name is the Messiah, Jesus the Son of Mary (Qur'an 3.45).

The name Messiah is never given to Muhammad in the Qur'an. However, as the Gospel has many passages which accord with Islam, it was welcomed with enthusiasm. It presented alleged prophecies containing the name of Muhammad from the time of Adam. The portrait of Jesus above all was in conformity with the Qur'an, the messianic question apart. He was only a prophet, and vigorously denied being the Son of God, which the Roman soldiers supposed he was. Condemned to death by the Jews, he was taken up into heaven by the angels, and Judas, suddenly transformed into his master's double, was crucified in his place by mistake. Very many details were taken from the four canonical Gospels, modified, distorted and amplified, and the whole work was provided with explanations of a spirituality which was utterly mediaeval, with one anachronism piled on another. Since then, critics have noted that the Gospels are quoted from a version of Tatian's Diatessaron, a harmony which was well known in the West at that time. The title was not new and figured on a list of works that were condemned in the sixth century, denoting a work the content of which was quite unknown. Did the forger simply take over the title and then compose his forgery? That seems the most probable explanation. Or perhaps he rediscovered this ancient text and completely reworked it. A thesis published in France in 1977 sought to prove this, but it was not accepted by the majority of critics. At all events, the Italian text, whether composed from scratch or as the complete revision of an earlier work, was certainly not that of a Gospel going back to the time of Christ.

The Arabic translation made in 1908 by a Syrian Christian received a warm welcome in Muslim publications, and since then it has been mentioned every now and then. Some serious studies of it were made in Europe. It seems that the Gospel must be associated with the forgeries known to have been made in Spain by victims of the Inquisition as a way of avenging themselves on those to whom they had to submit. The fact that Jesus is refused the title Messiah suggests, rather, a Jew by origin, while knowledge of the commonplaces of mediaeval Christian spirituality would point towards a Christian religious environment. The most attractive hypothesis so far is that the author was a Jew converted in Spain at a time of persecution who then went to Italy, as did so many others, and entered a religious community. He would then have left it again to become a Muslim. Research continues. Others ask whether the Gospel should not be associated with the conversions which spread in the Crimea during the sixteenth century among the Italians settled there. However, regardless of the identification of the author, there are no problems over a late date of the work and the orientation of its author suggested above.

There is no point in mentioning the Pseudo-Gospel where no one has heard of it. But if a Muslim mentions it first, here is what should be said.

If the Muslim is sensitive to historical-critical arguments, a recapitulation of the contents of the preface of the 1907 English edition will be useful (unfortunately none of the Arabic translations has translated this preface).

And in any case the following points can be made:

1. The central theme of this Pseudo-Gospel goes against the Qur'an. It refuses Jesus the title Messiah, though this title is given him in the Qur'an. That is so evident that the Arabic translator took fright, and instead of translating the word Messiah, which is absolutely clear in the Italian, by its Arabic equivalent, he simply transliterated the Italian word in Arabic characters. This means that it passes by the reader

unobserved.

2. The text was unknown in dialogue before 1908, so it is not indispensable.

3. The figure of Barnabas is *a priori* congenial to Muslims who know that he clashed with St Paul and left him. It is only one step from there to thinking that he rejected Paul's teaching for doctrinal reasons. In fact he agreed with St Mark, whose ideas we do know, and who thought as Paul did. So the quarrel was not over any basic doctrinal disagreement, and the Barnabas of Acts never spoke in the tones of the Gospel which bears his name.

This problem can be broached with educated Muslims. If they see the point, that in itself will clear the atmosphere.

Names given to Muslim men

Muhammad, in memory of the Prophet of Islam.
Ahmed
Mahmud } other names of the Prophet.
Mustapha (the elect).
Abu Bakr, first caliph (632–634).
'Umar, second caliph (634–644).
'Uthman, third caliph (644–656).
Ali, son-in-law and cousin of Muhammad, fourth caliph (656–661).
Hassan, **Hussein**, grandson of Muhammad.

Biblical names: **Ibrahim** (Abraham), **Ismail**, **Yusuf**, **Musa** (Moses), **Dawud** (David), **Suleiman** (Solomon), **Yahya** (John the Baptist), **Issa** (Jesus), etc.

Other names are compounds with Abd (the Servant) and a divine name, e.g. Abd al-Qadir, the servant of the powerful God: Abd al-Nasser, the servant of the God who gives victory, etc.

Other names use the word din, religion:
thus Salah ad-Din (Saladin), integrity of religion;
Nur ad-Din, light of religion;
Jamal al-Din, beauty of religion, etc.

Honorific titles borne by Muslims

1. **Amir al-Mu'minin**, Commander of the Faithful (once reserved for the caliph).
2. **Alim** (plural **Ulama**), doctor of the law, specialist in the study of religion.
3. **Mawlana**, master (a religious leader);
   Ustaz, master (lay or religious);
   Daktor, **Doktor**, doctor (increasingly frequent in addresses to someone with a doctorate).
4. **Hajj** (feminine Hajja); in Africa south of the Sahara **Hajji**, **Elhajji**, pilgrim, one who has gone to Mecca.
5. **Ayatollah** (among the Shi'ites), miraculous sign of God.
6. **Shahid** (plural **Shuhada**), martyr, someone killed in the holy war, more generally one who has died in battle.

Conclusion

One last word needs to be said at the end of this study. I have tried to present various aspects of Islam, but the method I have followed has involved fragmentary analyses and some cutting. This first stage was necessary to attract the reader's attention. It must be supplemented by a second step, that of personal attention which seeks to understand the life of Muslims as it is actually lived.

The previous pages have concentrated on introducing those aspects of Muslim faith and practice which are encountered most often. In our evolving world the situation can change rapidly: what will things be like in fifty years' time? Today, a number of sporadic attempts are appearing either in Qur'anic exegesis or in legal theory. In 1966 a Pakistani author, Fazlul Rahman, even went so far as to make a statement which would transform the theology of revelation if it were accepted. In effect, he said that the Qur'an is entirely from God and yet in a sense entirely from Muhammad. An introductory study of the notion of literary genres was also attempted in Egypt between 1940 and 1947. But in both cases the experience was brought to a sudden stop by a powerful opposition. Other authors are writing in a similar vein. Will they have a large audience? At present we have no more than a few sparks, and we do not know whether they will go out in due course or whether they will kindle great blazes.

Modern Muslim literature is still largely apologetic. Is this because since Islam wants to regulate all human affairs, both religious and political, it has to maintain the ardour of its members, and pointing to the dangers which threaten the community is always a good way of mobilizing energy? Does Muslim apologetic direct the critical faculties at external objects because self-criticism is not allowed in the area of the major traditional options of Islam? Not that the answer to this question is very important.

For basically, future developments in the sphere of religious studies are inseparable from developments in life generally. The spread of education is still too recent to have been completely effective, but until the day when historical criticism and the humanities, which in the case of religious studies are still in their infancy, have gradually been accepted as legitimate, as elsewhere in the secular sphere, it will be important for religious investigations to note the mood of the time.

Islam still has a number of trump cards to play against the modern world. Confronted with developments in the West, it rejects all atheistic or Promethean adventures and contributes to the maintaining essential religious values. Confronted with the positive sciences (leaving aside the humanities), it recalls that since the cosmos is God's creation, anything that helps us to know its nature better, whether this be in physics, chemistry, astronomy, medicine or whatever, manifests the glory of God and the perfection of his work.

In the past Islam has been able to assimilate many cultures and it still retains its flexibility in the face of the modern world. What once happened with so many local customs can still happen today. The capacity of Islam to adapt is always there, provided that its requirement of monotheism incarnate in a simplified liturgy has been met.

At a deeper level, the vitality of Islam derives above all from that profound commitment of its members to their community and their ideal. This is a gut commitment: the child learns it in his or her family, in the Qur'anic school and at a later stage throughout his or her environment. Its rational aspects must never obscure its sentimental roots, which sometimes go deep into the emotions with pride in being Muslim: 'You are the noblest nation that has ever been raised up for mankind' (Qur'an 3, 110), says a famous verse of the Qur'an which is often quoted.

What is the summit of this ideal in the sphere of relations with God? Islam brings Muslims into the presence of God, makes them see the world as dependent on the Creator, and draws their attention to the magnificence of the creation and the goodness of its author; it calls on them to abandon themselves to it and to obey its law in the framework of the community. These are ideas by which a large number of people live, and which bring them peace and security. The practice of ritual prayer roots them in life; for in Islam dogma and prayer are closely related. The main values which Islam contains at the level of human relations with God (faith and religion) are those of a first stage common to all monotheisms. The religious level of Islam is comparable to that of the Old Testament, with some simplifications (the absence of priests, offerings and sacrifices).

However, Islam differs profoundly from the Old Testament in its rejection of divine imagery which may be anthropomorphic. It is developed outside the promise of God to Abraham, which is so essential in the Old Testament, and its view of history is quite different. For Islam, Abraham is the prophet who by his prayer gets God to send Muhammad to the Arabs, ordains the pilgrimage and obtains divine favours for the inhabitants of Mecca. Islam is an Old Testament, reread and simplified, and does not have any New Testament.

Islam is total self-surrender to God, but at the same time it is very human, and in the last resort, in many areas Muslims do as they please.

In Africa, time has been on the side of Islam, which has propagated itself slowly and has had leisure to set down its roots. The absence of foreign clergy and the fact that the Muslim missionaries were lay Africans made things easier. The religious sense of God and nature which is so widespread in Africa has been satisfied by Islam. Since its morality is on the level of the Old Testament, it is more acceptable in questions relating to women and war. The verses in the Qur'an about Moses, Solomon and magic covered many ancestral magical practices; amulets, talismans, and so on. Belief in jinns mentioned in the Qur'an allowed the adoption of the cult of the spirits in various forms. Today, in healing rites, the medium requires conversion to Islam in the name of the healing spirit, which is Muslim: Gilles Bibeau has studied practices centring on a spirit called *ruhani* in the east of Zaire.

Some aspects of African traditions are lacking in Islam, for example sacrifices, intermediaries, etc. In practice, in Africa as elsewhere, many Muslims often make private sacrifices in spite of the official teachings of Islam.

To recognize the force and religious values of Islam, along with other of its aspects, is in no way to devalue the Christian ideal. It is normal to take note of truth wherever it may be; and this attitude will allow us to speak all the more freely when it comes to Christianity. Once the first decades have passed in a region where Christianity is a newcomer, it will take on an African countenance. Is that not already true in Egypt and Ethiopia, where it was implanted well before Islam? The flexibility of its liturgy and the forms of its prayers, its expression in the languages of the countries concerned, its sense of offering and sacrifice and of the communion of the saints between this world and the beyond offer a whole series of possibilities.

If Christianity is accused of being alien because it requires that much more, we should remember that this same charge has been levelled against it all over the world. Christianity also offers something more, an opening on reality, respect for the vocations of men and women, and a sense of renunciation, all of which are the factors which allow it to do great things. It opens up new possibilities. It reveals – and has already revealed – to Africans the riches that they have within themselves, which can develop into a profound deep authenticity. The call of God to humankind which is revealed in many aspects of traditional life marks a first step along a way which ends up in the grace of adoption as children of God in Christ.

Bibliography

General books

Khurshid Ahmad (ed.), *Islam, its meaning and message*, The Islamic Foundation 1976.
  Articles by key figures in the modern tradition of Maududi, the Muslim Brotherhood, and the Wahhabis.

H. A. R. Gibb, *Islam: A historical survey*, OUP ²1980.
  A scholarly introduction by the leading British academic of his time.

B. Lewis (ed.), *The World of Islam*, Thames and Hudson 1976.
  Simple but sound articles with illustrations.

S. H. Nasr, *Ideals and Realities of Islam*, Allen and Unwin 1966.
  A thought provoking reflection by a leading Shi'ite academic.

F. Rahman, *Islam*, Weidenfeld and Nicolson 1966.
  An authoritative introduction by a Muslim 'modernist'.

F. Schuon, *Understanding Islam*, Allen and Unwin ²1981.
  A sympathetic and attractive account by a European convert to Islam.

R. Tames, *Approaches to Islam*, John Murray 1982.
  A very useful introduction to the subject and resources, designed for teachers.

Chapters 1–3

F. Gabrieli, *Muhammad and the Conquests of Islam*, Weidenfeld and Nicolson 1968.
  A straightforward chronological survey.

P. K. Hitti, *History of the Arabs*, Macmillan ²1970.
  Although the historical approach and judgments are generally criticized, this remains a useful and readable reference.

H. Kennedy, *The Prophet and the Age of the Caliphs*, Longmans 1986.
  A sound historical account which generally ignores the religious history.

M. Lings, *Muhammad: His life based on the earliest sources*, Allen and Unwin 1983.
  An honest retelling of the life of Muhammad from Muslim sources with a minimum of interpretation.

M. Rodinson, *Mohammed*, Penguin 1971.
  A serious attempt by a French thinker to understand the Prophet, although disapproved of by many Muslims.

W. M. Watt, *Muhammad: Prophet and Statesman*, OUP [2]1977.
A widely acclaimed and readable account.

Chapters 4–7

A. J. Arberry, *Sufism*, Allen and Unwin 1950.
A good basic introduction.

N. J. Coulson, *A History of Islamic Law*, Edinburgh University Press 1964.
An easily readable survey of the development of Shari'a from the time of Muhammad till the present.

M. F. Jamali, *Letters on Islam*, OUP 1965.
The letters of an Iraqi politician to his son written from prison.

M. Lings, *What is Sufism?*, Allen and Unwin 1975.
A simple introduction to basic concepts.

M. Momen, *An Introduction to Shi'i Islam*, Yale University Press 1985.
A solid survey of both history and theology.

M. Nawawi, *The Forty Hadith*, Holy Koran Publishing House 1977 (from most Muslim bookshops).
A beautiful translation of sayings of the Prophet in a traditional collection for pious reflection.

C. E. Padwick, *Muslim Devotions*, SPCK 1961.
An anthology of prayers and poetry of popular piety with a sensitive introduction and commentary.

J. Schacht, *An Introduction to Islamic Law*, OUP 1964.
A chronological survey by the leading scholar of European critical scholarship; the second part is a systematic outline of the content of the law.

Chapter 8

X. Jacob, 'Christianity as seen by the Turks', *Research Papers: Muslims in Europe*, no. 22, June 1984.
Modern Turkish textbooks illustrate traditional Muslim stereotypes of Christian teaching.

G. Parrinder, *Jesus in the Qur'an*, Faber 1965.
A sound and detailed study of the figure of Jesus in Islamic sources and belief.

A. M. H. Shboul, *Al-Mas'udi and his World: A Muslim humanist and his interest in non-Muslims*, Ithaca Press 1974.
A constructive classical Islamic approach.

Chapter 9

J. L. Esposito (ed.), *Voices of Resurgent Islam*, OUP 1983.
A representative collection of important modern Muslim thinkers.

A. Hourani, *Arabic Thought in the Liberal Age*, CUP [2]1983.
A now standard study of Arab intellectual reaction to the West in the nineteenth and early twentieth centuries.

G. Kepel, *The Prophet and Pharaoh: Muslim Extremism in Egypt*, Saqi Books 1985.
Focussing on the assassination of Sadat, the author provides an excellent account of
the tradition of the Muslim Brotherhood and its present-day heirs.

R. Levy, *The Social Structure of Islam*, CUP ²1965.
A valuable general introduction to the history, culture and organization of classical
Muslim society.

S. H. Nasr, *Islamic Science: An Illustrated Study*, World of Islam Publishing 1976.
An easily accessible account of an area in which Islamic civilization has made a
major contribution.

Piscatori, J. P. (ed.), *Islam in the Political Process*, CUP 1983.
Articles analysing the role of Islam in the politics of various parts of the Muslim
world.

J. Schacht and C. E. Bosworth (eds.), *The Legacy of Islam*, OUP 1974.
A collection of articles surveying the main aspects of belief and culture.

W. C. Smith, *Islam in Modern History*, Princeton University Press 1957.
Still one of the most thoughtful and considered analyses of the meeting between
Islam and the West.

D. Sourdel, *Mediaeval Islam*, Routledge and Kegan Paul 1983.
An introduction to the central characteristics of mediaeval Islamic society and state.

Chapters 10–12

Churches' Committee on Migrant Workers in Europe, *Christians and Muslims talking
Together*, British Council of Churches 1984.
A basic study of the differences and common ground of the two religions.

K. Cragg, *The Call of the Minaret*, Collins ²1986.
A classic study of Islam and its interaction with Christianity.

N. Daniel, *Islam and the West: The Making of an Image*, Edinburgh University Press 1960.
Analyses the history of mutual perceptions.

J. -M. Gaudeul, *Encounter and Clashes: Islam and Christianity in History*, 2 vols, Pontificio
Istituto di Studi Arabi e Islamici, Rome 1984.
A very useful collection of studies and source texts.

J. Jomier, *Bible and Qur'an*, Desclier, NY 1964.
A comparative study of the content and significance of the two scriptures.

The Qur'an

The two most widely used English translations of the Qur'an by Muslims are:
The Holy Qur'an by A. Yusuf Ali, The Islamic Foundation 1978, which includes
extensive notes and commentary; and *The Meaning of the Glorious Koran* by M. M.
Pickthall, Allen and Unwin 1976. A. J. Arberry's verse translation *The Koran
Interpreted*, OUP 1983, can also be recommended.

Both the first two have subject indices, but one can also use excerpted translations thematically arranged:

T. B. Irving, *The Qur'an: Basic Teachings*, The Islamic Foundation 1979; K. Cragg, *Readings in the Qur'an*, Collins 1988.

Essential for the history, organization and use of the Qur'anic text is W. M. Watt, *Bell's Introduction to the Qur'an*, Edinburgh University Press 1977.

Index